AN ARCHAEOLOGICAL GUIDE TO NORTHERN CENTRAL AMERICA

Belize, Guatemala, Honduras, and El Salvador

By Joyce Kelly
Photographs by Jerry Kelly and the Author
Drawings and Maps by the Author

University of Oklahoma Press : Norman and London

Also by Joyce Kelly

The Poetic Realism of Alan Flattmann (Jackson, Miss., 1980)
The Complete Visitor's Guide to Mesoamerican Ruins (Norman, 1982)
An Archaeological Guide to Mexico's Yucatán Peninsula (Norman, 1993)

**Library of Congress
Cataloging-in-Publication Data**

Kelly, Joyce, 1933–
  An archaeological guide to northern Central America : Belize, Guatemala, Honduras, and El Salvador / by Joyce Kelly ; photographs by Jerry Kelly and the author ; drawings and maps by the author.
      p.   cm.
  Includes bibliographical references and index.
  ISBN 0-8061-2858-5 (alk. paper)
  1. Mayas—Antiquities—Guidebooks. 2. Central America—Antiquities—Guidebooks. I. Title.
  F1435.K47   1996
  917.2804'53—dc20   96-21333
                                           CIP

Text design by Cathy Carney Imboden. Text typeface is Esprit Book.

1   2   3   4   5   6   7   8   9   10

This book is affectionately dedicated to the people of Belize, Guatemala, Honduras, and El Salvador, who have graciously shared with us the fruits of the labor of their ancient ancestors; and to the archaeologists, who by the sweat of their brows bring these spectacular structures and marvelous monuments to light.

CONTENTS

ILLUSTRATIONS

Maps

ALPHABETICAL LIST OF SITES AND MUSEUMS WITH SECTION NUMBERS AND MAP NUMBERS

(B) *Belize*
(G) *Guatemala*
(H) *Honduras*
(S) *El Salvador*

Abaj Takalik and Museum (G): (5) 5 and 5B
Aguateca (G): (4) 4 and 4D
Altun Ha (B): (1) 1 and 2
Belize Museum (B): (2) 2
Belmopan Vault (B): (2) 2
Bilbao (G): (5) 5, 5C, and 5C1
Cahal Pech (B): (2) 2, 2A, and 2A1
Caracol (B): (2) 2 and 2A
Cara Sucia (S): (7) 8
Cerén and Museum (S): (7) 7 and 7A
Cerros (B): (1) 1
Chichicastenango Museum (G): (5) 5 and 5A
Cihuatan (S): (7) 7
Comayagua Museum (H): (6) 6
Copán and Museum (H): (6) 5, 6, and 6A
Cuello (B): (1) 1 and 1C
Dos Pilas (G): (4) 4 and 4D

El Baúl (G): (5) 5, 5C, and 5C1
Finca El Baúl (G): (5) 5, 5C, and 5C1
Finca Las Ilusiones (G): (5) 5, 5C, and 5C1
Finca Pantaleón (G): (5) 5, 5C, and 5C1
Floral Park (B): (2) 2 and 2A
Guatemala City Museum (G): (5) 5
Iximché and Museum (G): (5) 5 and 5A
Kaminaljuyú (G): (5) 5
La Democracia Plaza and Museum (G): (5) 5 and 5A
La Entrada Museum (H): (6) 6
Lamanai and Museum (B): (1) 1
Lubaantun (B): (3) 3 and 3A
Mixco Viejo (G): (5) 5
Nakum (G): (4) 4 and 4A
Nim Li Punit (B): (3) 3 and 3A
Nohmul (B): (1) 1 and 1B

Pacbitun (B): (2) 2 and 2A
Popol Vuh Museum (G): (5) 5
Quelepa (S): (7) 9
Quiriguá (G): (5) 5
San Andrés and Museum (S): (7) 7 and 7A
San Salvador Museum (S): (7) 7
Santa Rita (B): (1) 1 and 1A
Seibal (G): (4) 4 and 4D
Tazumal and Museum (S): (7) 7 and 7B
Tegucigalpa Museum (H): (6) 6
Tikal, Museum, and Lithic Museum (G): (4) 4 and 4B
Topoxte (G): (4) 4 and 4A
Uaxactún (G): (4) 4 and 4C
Utatlán and Museum (G): (5) 5 and 5A
Uxbenka (B): (3) 3 and 3A
Xunantunich (B): (2) 2 and 2A
Yaxhá (G): (4) 4, 4A, and 4A1
Zaculeu and Museum (G): (5) 5

PREFACE

One of the great rewards of being a guidebook writer is learning that someone has benefited from your efforts. Perhaps they learned of an interesting site of which they were previously unaware or discovered how to reach a site they wanted but did not know how to visit. It is indeed gratifying to know that you have helped someone.

The frustrating side of the occupation is that as soon as the ink dries on the page—or a sheet of manuscript comes out of the laser printer—whatever you have just written will no longer be true. A good road deteriorates, a dirt road gets paved, a museum changes its visiting hours, or a cleared site becomes overgrown. This doesn't happen *all* the time, but it happens all too often. The writer can only warn the reader that changes are to be expected.

On balance, the rewards outweigh the frustrations—by far. Otherwise I would not continue along this chosen path or try to make improvements in my methods.

The changes incorporated in this book, which I hope will be regarded as improvements over my last one (*An Archaeological Guide to Mexico's Yucatán Peninsula*), are mainly in the maps and site plans. The maps (and the text) now include distances in kilometers as well as in miles, and driving times for each segment of a trip have been added. For aesthetic reasons—and because drawing on computer turned out to be such fun—I have included Emblem Glyphs on the site plans for sites where they are known. On the other site plans, I used a drawing of a monument or artifact from the site.

Following my usual procedure, I have included only sites and museums that I have visited personally. Three site museums of which the reader should be aware, however—Cahal Pech, Xunantunich, and Copán—were not yet open when I last visited those sites. No doubt all would be worth a visit when you are there. The locations of these museums are given in the text, and museum symbols for them are shown on the maps, but the museums are not rated or included in the alphabetical list of sites and museums. In the case of Copán, the museum in the town of Copán Ruinas is covered; it is separate from the new site museum.

In the Central America section of another of my earlier books, *The Complete Visitor's Guide to Mesoamerican Ruins*, twenty-two sites and thirteen museums were covered; this volume includes thirty-eight sites and twenty-five museums for the same area. Of the sites and museums in my original book, all but four sites were revisited in the preparation of this work. I believe you will find the added sites and museums interesting.

ACKNOWLEDGMENTS

During the preparation of this work, several people provided me with information, some of which would have been unavailable otherwise. To all of them I express my heartfelt thanks and sincere gratitude. My job was made easier because of their kindness. They are E. Wyllys Andrews V, Frederick Bove, Victoria Bricker, Nicholas Dunning, Diane and Arlen Chase, Molly Mignon, and Debra Walker.

I would also like to thank my husband, Jerry, for accompanying me to the sites, for taking and printing the black-and-white photographs used in this volume, and for offering constant and loving encouragement while this work was in progress.

PART ONE

• • • •

INTRODUCTION

THE ARCHAEOLOGY OF NORTHERN CENTRAL AMERICA
Belize, Guatemala, Honduras, and El Salvador

The story of the archaeology of northern Central America is part of the broader story of the archaeology of Mesoamerica—and of the entire Western Hemisphere. The generally accepted theory begins with the migrations of people from eastern Asia across the Bering Strait at a time of glacial advance, when a land bridge formed. These migrations started perhaps as early as 40,000 years ago (although the earliest widely accepted date is 15,000 years ago) and continued in several waves.

The early immigrants were hunters who followed game across the land bridge. Once across, they followed the ice-free routes in present-day Alaska and Canada, heading south and eventually spreading throughout the Americas. There is evidence that the southern tip of South America was occupied by at least 7000 B.C.

The early inhabitants of the New World were a mobile population. In addition to hunting, they gathered wild plants to supplement their food supply. In the coastal areas where some of the earliest settled villages formed (about 3000 to 1000 B.C.), the sea provided bountiful food resources, although people consumed agricultural products as well. Some of the wild plants that were originally gathered were later cultivated and domesticated, and as time went on, these agricultural products became an increasingly important part of the diet. This shift gradually resulted in some groups' becoming semisedentary and, later, in the formation of settled inland villages. These changes proceeded at an extremely slow pace that varied in different regions.

Plants domesticated by the ancient Mesoamericans included maize (corn), beans, squash, chili peppers, and amaranth. Maize was the most important of these foodstuffs and remains so today in the diet of the native peoples.

Some areas of northern Central America were occupied (albeit sparsely) by early hunters around 9000 B.C. Stone tools produced by these hunters have been recovered at Richmond Hill in northern Belize and at three sites in the Guatemala highlands. At San Rafael, just west of Guatemala City, a fluted projectile point of obsidian was found by a schoolboy; at Los Tapiales, somewhat to the west, an assemblage of stone tools was found; and at a site on the outskirts of Huehuetenango, mastodon bones bearing butchering marks were found together with four stone tools used in the butchering process.

By 1000 B.C., small populations of farmers were occupying the central Petén of northern Guatemala, although a pollen core recovered from the bed of Lake Petenxil suggests that a little maize was being grown near the lake a thousand years earlier.

The earliest ceramics known from northern Central America were produced by a culture called Barra, about 1800 B.C. This pottery was first discovered on the Pacific coast of Guatemala near the modern border of Mexico. In recent years, remains of the later Ocós phase have been found in the same area and as far east as western El Salvador. The Early Preclassic Ocós potters produced sophisticated vessels and figurines from about 1500 to 1300 B.C. The people lived a settled life in wattle-and-daub houses set atop platforms, and there is evidence of ranking in their society.

The area around Copán, Honduras, was settled in the Early Preclassic period, and a house that may date between 1200 and 900 B.C. was discovered there.

The Chalchuapa zone of western El Salvador was occupied between 1200 and 900 B.C.

Olmec-style monuments have been found in northern Central America at Abaj

Takalik on the Pacific slope of western Guatemala; they may date to the Early Preclassic period. During the Middle Preclassic period (900 to 400 B.C.), populations increased, and most parts of northern Central America were occupied to some extent, both highlands and lowlands. Ceramics were produced in the Petén for the first time during this period. Olmec-style ceramics have been found in very early Middle Preclassic contexts at Copán. At Las Victorias in the Chalchuapa zone of western El Salvador, a natural boulder was carved with Olmec-style figures that date to the Middle Preclassic.

In the Late Preclassic period (400 B.C. to A.D. 250), Maya civilization experienced its first florescence. There were major architectural undertakings in many areas: at sites such as Tikal, Uaxactún, Mirador, and Nakbé in the Petén; at Lamanai and Cerros in northern Belize; and at Kaminaljuyú in the Guatemala highlands. Architectural sculpture (some of enormous proportions) is found at some of these sites. To the east, a large Late Preclassic stone altar was found at Quelepa in eastern El Salvador.

Free-standing sculpture from this period is found in the highlands at Kaminaljuyú, on the Guatemala Pacific slope at Abaj Takalik and Monte Alto, and at other sites.

During the Early and Late Classic periods (A.D. 250 to 830), the Mayas reached their intellectual and artistic peak. There were large populations, a flourishing economy, and widespread trade. There were also bloody wars among polities and shifts in power among the elites. Some of the great architectural centers of the lowlands grew tremendously in area and volume of construction, and monumental sculpture was produced in staggering quantities.

On the Pacific coast of Guatemala and nearby parts of El Salvador, the Cotzumalhuapa culture developed during the Classic period. This culture, with an art style quite different from that of the Mayas, had its roots in Mexico, and Mexican deities, symbols, and calendrics are carved on its monuments.

In the Terminal Classic period (A.D. 830 to 1000), many of the lowland Maya centers in northern Central America were abandoned or nearly so, though remnant peasant populations remained at some sites for a time. The elite activities of great architectural construction and monument carving came to a virtual halt in this area.

In the Postclassic period (A.D. 1000 to 1540), there was some architectural activity near the lakes in the Petén, and the important centers of Topoxte and Tayasal were built during the late part of this period. Nevertheless, these and other Postclassic remains cannot compare to the great Classic cities in size or grandeur.

On the Pacific coast, which had been heavily populated during the Classic period, comparatively few remains of Postclassic date have been discovered.

Although little building was under way in the lowlands or on the Pacific slope during the Postclassic period, a good deal of construction was going on in the highlands of Guatemala and El Salvador. Many centers were built in defensible positions atop hills surrounded by ravines. There was warfare among groups in this area that continued until the Spanish conquest in the sixteenth century.

CHRONOLOGICAL CHART

The sites included in the chronological chart are large and important ones where significant excavations and ceramic studies have been undertaken. The thick lines in the chart indicate the major period (or periods) at the site, the thinner lines indicate the time the site was occupied, and a dashed line shows a period when a site was abandoned for a time.

The information used to compile this chart came from various sources and reflects the views of several authorities. Others use slightly different beginning and ending dates for some of the periods and for the

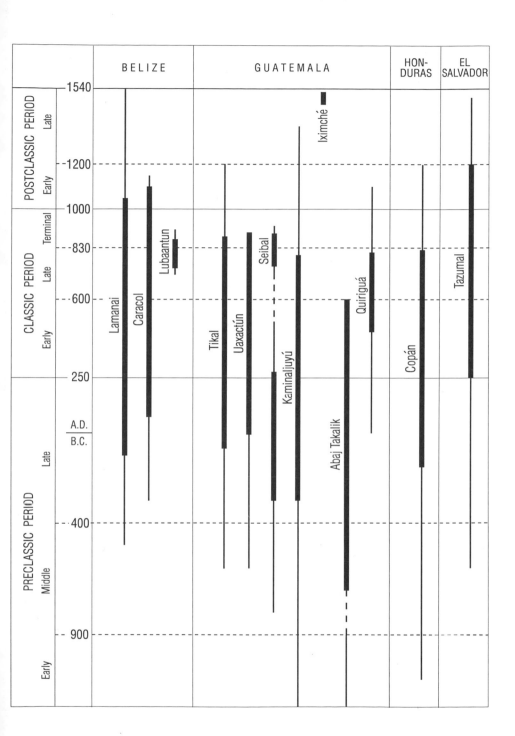

major period at some of the sites. Some archaeologists divide the chronology into more periods, especially for certain areas, but for simplicity's sake those periods have not been included in the chart shown here. These periods are the Terminal Preclassic, or Protoclassic, period (A.D. 50 or 75 to 250), the Middle Classic period (475 or 550 to 650 or 680), and the Middle Postclassic period (1200 to 1400). In any case, the chart should give the reader a fair idea of what was happening in northern Central America (at least at a few sites) during the times in question.

A Note on Dates Used in the Text

The hieroglyphic dates for inscribed Maya monuments given in the text have been converted to the Christian calendar using the Goodman-Martínez-Thompson (11.16.0.0.0) correlation.

GEOGRAPHIC DIVISIONS

Northern Central America, as the term is used here, includes all of Belize and Guatemala, western Honduras, and all of El Salvador. This book covers each of these countries in the foregoing order. For ease of presenting travel information, Belize is subdivided into three divisions (northern, central, and southern), and Guatemala is subdivided into two (northern and southern), giving a total of seven geographic divisions.

For each country there is a general information section that lists entry requirements, exchange rates between the local currency and United States dollars, demographic information, and so forth. For Belize and Guatemala there is also a separate general information section for each division. It includes the availability of accommodations and restaurants, how to reach the area, and any special points of interest. For each of Honduras and El Salvador (which are each a single division), there is only one general information section, and it contains both sets of information. I recommend reading the general information sections while your trip is in the planning stages.

Reference points for each of the seven geographic divisions are given in the general information for each section; these signify the exact point or points from which distances and driving times are tabulated.

A map of northern Central America is included, as is one for each of the countries; these do not bear numbers, only names. In addition, there are maps for each of the seven geographic divisions, numbered in coordination with the text for each section. For some areas, even more detailed maps are included. They bear the number of the section followed by a letter and sometimes by another number. For example, southern Guatemala is covered in Section 5, and the map covering all of that region is map 5. Map 5C is a detail of part of the area, and map 5C1 is a detail of 5C. The area covered by the detail maps is indicated on the sectional maps. The northern Central America map and the country maps give an overall idea of the location of the sites and museums; the sectional and detail maps show how to reach them.

To aid the reader in locating a particular site, an alphabetical list of sites (and museums) is given at the front of the book, after the list of illustrations. Following the site name is a letter (in parentheses) indicating in which country the site will be found; following that is a number (in parentheses) showing the section where the site is covered. This is followed by a number indicating on which sectional map the site will be found, and sometimes by additional notations. For example, the entry "Bilbao (G): (5) 5, 5C, and 5C1" indicates that Bilbao is in Guatemala, that the text for the site will be found in Section 5, and that the location of Bilbao is indicated on maps 5, 5C, and 5C1.

My sincere hope is that these features will help readers find the information they want easily and quickly.

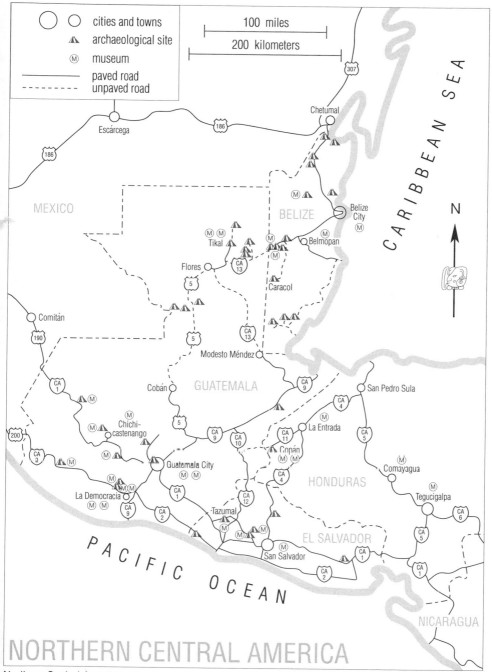

Northern Central America, showing archaeological sites and museums covered in the text.

GENERAL ADVICE AND MISCELLANEOUS NOTES

Driving or Flying: The Pros and Cons

The four Central American countries covered in this book can be reached by car from anywhere in North or Central America; you can also drive from one country to another. Having your own vehicle will save travel time once you get there and will give you more flexibility in making travel plans.

On the minus side, if you are starting from Canada or the United States, it is a rather long drive. (Since you would be driving through Mexico, you would need to check with the nearest Mexican consulate for *current* regulations for driving a vehicle *through* Mexico.) Most of the roads covered in this book are paved, as are the connecting roads through Mexico. There are some rather long unpaved sections, however, in the Petén of Guatemala, and a shorter unpaved section in southern Guatemala that goes to Copán, Honduras. Belize's Southern Highway is also unpaved. See the general information sections for more detailed road information.

It is more complicated and time consuming to enter any of the countries with a vehicle at a land border; it is easier to get through immigration and customs when you fly in. We have done it both ways, depending on our particular destination at the moment.

There are flights from several cities in the United States and from Mexico City to the capitals of all the countries included here, as well as flights from the capital of each country to the capitals of the others. This is, of course, the easiest way to get to and around the area. Each country requires payment of a departure tax when you leave. At land borders it is very little; when you fly out the tax ranges from about $10 to $20 in United States currency.

Flying in and renting a vehicle is the ideal way to get around the individual countries—if your budget permits. Car rentals are rather expensive in this part of the world. Places where you can rent a vehicle are covered in the general information for each section. In some cases you will need four-wheel drive, while standard vehicles (which cost less) are adequate for other areas. When a high-clearance vehicle or one with four-wheel drive is needed to reach a particular site, it is mentioned in the text for that site.

There are adequate numbers of gasoline stations in most of the areas covered; in areas where they are not plentiful, a gas pump symbol is used on the maps to indicate the stations that will be of use. In all areas, if you start looking for a station when your tank is half-full, you should have no problems. The cost of gasoline in all of the countries is higher than it is in the United States.

Buses travel all the main roads, in all the countries. Where buses can get you to, or almost to, a site, it is mentioned in the text. To reach some sites you must have a private vehicle, and this is likewise mentioned.

General Guidebooks

For your travels in Central America you will want to have one or more guidebooks that offer more detailed general information than it is possible to give here, such as full hotel and restaurant listings, bus schedules, and points of interest other than the archaeological sites. Some guidebooks cover a single country, some include two or three, while others encompass all of Central America. The following are recommended and can be found in large bookstores in Canada and the United States, and sometimes in the countries they cover.

They are *Belize Guide,* by Paul Glassman, published by Passport Press (1989); *Adventure Guide to Belize,* by Harry S. Pariser, published by Hunter Publishing (1992), which also contains some city and town maps; *Belize: A Natural Destination,* by Richard Mahler and Steele Wotkyns with color photographs by Kevin Schafer, published by John Muir Press (1991) and aimed at visitors interested in the natural wonders of Belize; and *The New Key to Belize*, by Stacy Ritz, which has a slant toward ecotourism and is published by Ulysses Press (1994).

The Real Guide: Guatemala and Belize, by Mark Whatmore and Peter Eltringham, is part of the *Real Guide* series published by Prentice Hall Press (1990). It has some city and area maps. *La Ruta Maya: Yucatán, Guatemala, and Belize*, by Tom Brosnahan, also includes the route from Guatemala to Copán, Honduras; it was published in 1991 and is one of a series of guides published by Lonely Planet Publications. It contains many good city and area maps.

Guatemala Guide, by Paul Glassman, is published by Passport Press (1990). This reliable guide is an updated version of the one first published in 1977; it has some city and area maps. *Guatemala Alive*, by Arnold Greenberg and Diana K. Wells, published by Alive Publications (1990), is a second edition of the original 1976 publication; it has some city and area maps.

Central America on a Shoestring, by Nancy Keller, Tom Brosnahan, and Rob Rachowiecki, is published by Lonely Planet Publications (1992). Like other Lonely Planet books, it has many clear city and town maps. As you can tell from the title, this guide is aimed at budget travelers. It lists only inexpensive hotels and restaurants, but it includes detailed bus information. *Central America*, by Natascha Norton and Mark Whatmore, is one in a series of Cadogan guides published by Cadogan Books (England) and Globe Pequot Press (Connecticut) (1993). It includes some clear city and area maps and lists hotels in all price ranges.

Maps and Site Plans

The road maps included in this volume are intended to help readers reach the archaeological sites and museums covered in the text. They do not show *all* the roads and towns in the area. For that, and for con-necting roads between countries, you will want to have one or more good road maps. The site plans are to help you get around the sites; buildings and monuments of interest are included, but not *all* buildings are shown.

The best and most detailed road maps of Central America that I have seen are those published by International Travel Maps. These maps are highly recommended; they can sometimes be found in map specialty stores in the United States, Canada, and England, or they can be ordered from the publisher at 345 West Broadway, Vancouver, British Columbia, V5Y 1P8, Canada. In the United States they are available from the Barbachano Foundation, 9500 South Dadeland Boulevard, Suite 710, Miami, FL 33156. There is one map for Belize (1:350,000 scale) and another for Guatemala and El Salvador (1:500,000 scale) that also includes the western part of Honduras (where Copán is located). These maps show virtually every road in the countries they cover, distances between points, archaeological sites, and, in some cases, gasoline stations. International Travel Maps also produces a map of all of Central America. At a scale of 1:1,800,000, it is less detailed than the others and it does not show distances.

In 1989, the National Geographic Society published "Land of the Maya: A Traveler's Map" at a scale of 1:1,609,000. It shows the major and some minor roads, along with archaeological sites and museums. It also includes useful archaeological information, but it does not show distances. It can be ordered from the National Geographic Society, Washington, D.C., 20036.

Tourist departments in the various countries generally have maps of those countries. Some gasoline stations also sell maps of the country they are in. Road maps and city maps are generally available from car rental agencies; the quality varies.

Getting Lost and Unlost

While you should have no problems getting around on the highways of the various countries, you may have problems getting to where you want to go within the cities, or getting out of the cities to the exit of your choice. This will be especially true when streets are blocked off for repair work (a frequent occurrence) and you have to change your preselected route. When this predicament arises—and it will—the solution is simple. Find a taxi. Tell the driver where you want to go and settle on a price. Pay the amount up front and ask the driver to lead the way. This can save a lot of time and a great deal of frustration. Drivers will not leave you stranded if you catch a red light and the taxi does not; they will wait for you to catch up. At one time or another we have done this in all of the countries covered here and in Mexico as well. Taxi drivers have always conscientiously led us to where we wanted to go.

Language

Belize is the only country in Central America where English is the official language, and even there Spanish is widely spoken. If you do not speak some Spanish, I recommend carrying a small Spanish-English phrase book and dictionary. Berlitz's is the best known.

A Note on "Connections"

The times listed for driving are *when the roads are in fair condition.* If a dirt road is very muddy, it will, of course, take longer. Road conditions (as far as it is possible to tell) are mentioned in the text for each site. But it should be noted that the condition of roads, especially unpaved roads, is subject to change.

Is It Dangerous?

One question we are often asked is, "Is it dangerous to travel alone in the remote areas?" I assume the questioner wants to know whether one is in any physical danger from the people. The answer is emphatically no. Maybe we have been inordinately lucky, but we have never felt the least bit threatened or even uncomfortable, and other frequent visitors report the same

thing. In fact, the more remote the area, the nicer the people.

If news reports indicate that there is political or social unrest in an area you wish to visit, you could check with the Department of State in the United States to see whether there is a travel advisory. Consulates of the country involved should also be able to provide current information on areas that should be avoided (if any). In some cases it may be that only certain parts of a country are affected, in which case you could check with local authorities. If you rent a car in one of the countries, your car rental agent will probably also have updated information.

Even when it is peaceful, however, you should take normal precautions. Do not leave luggage or camera gear visible, even in a locked car. Keep the items out of sight in the trunk, and keep the trunk locked, especially in the more touristed areas.

A second question we often hear is, "What about snakes?" Yes, there are snakes, but we have encountered few, and never in a threatening situation. You will find insects to be a bigger problem. Nevertheless, it is advisable to look where you are stepping when you are walking along jungle trails.

What to Take

FOOTGEAR: Comfortable footgear is a must. If your only goal is the larger, cleared sites, tennis shoes or the equivalent will suffice. If, however, you plan to visit some of the remote sites, you will need something more serious, like good hiking boots. When you are climbing rocky trails or walking muddy ones, boots are better than tennis shoes. I was once accused (jokingly, I hoped) of having a foot fetish. Maybe so, but my sense of adventure dwindles in direct proportion to the increase in discomfort of my feet. If boots are recommended for a particular site, it is mentioned in the text; otherwise, tennis shoes may be considered adequate.

CLOTHING: For visiting the ruins the most comfortable clothing is lightweight but fairly sturdy cotton. Denim jeans or khaki work pants are fine. For the major cleared sites, women will find split skirts (culottes) more comfortable than pants for climbing.

I recommend pants (or culottes) with belt loops whether or not you use a belt (see the section "Camera Gear" for why). Cotton or cotton-synthetic blends are best for shirts. Those that are 100-percent synthetic are hot as Hades and cling to you uncomfortably when you get wet, which is always. Long sleeves offer more protection from the sun, insects, and thorny bushes, while short sleeves are cooler. I use one or the other depending on the trip. For evenings in the highlands, you will want to have a sweater or light jacket.

You will find a few large handkerchiefs or bandanas useful to wipe the sweat from your brow. Facial tissue just won't do.

Other items you should have are sunglasses (preferably glare free) and a sun hat (lightweight and with good ventilation), especially for the larger cleared sites.

MISCELLANEOUS GEAR: If you are traveling by car (yours or a rented one), by all means take or buy an ice chest. It will repay you a thousandfold. Inexpensive plastic-foam chests are available in cities and larger towns. Ice, water, and cold drinks whenever you want them can extend your endurance considerably.

Take a couple of terry-cloth towels. When dipped in the cold water in your ice chest and applied to your face and the back of your neck, they can be incredibly refreshing, especially when you return to your car after climbing around ruins.

To get rid of the bugs on your windshield, take along a pot cleaner, the sponge kind with a plastic mesh covering. The sponge holds enough water to make the job easier, and the plastic mesh won't scratch the glass.

You will also want a plastic bottle for carrying drinking water with you in your vehicle. There are times when beer or refrescos (soft drinks) just won't do.

When you are walking to a site and will be away from your vehicle for more than an hour or so, you should have a canteen of water with you. When this is needed, it is mentioned in the text.

For long trips to remote sites, you should also have some food along. Canned tuna, deviled ham, and crackers are available almost everywhere (don't forget a can opener), or get something from your hotel restaurant before you leave.

You should have insect repellent with you for all the sites, since even the cleared ones can have insects. Repellent is crucial for sites that are somewhat overgrown.

CAMERA GEAR: Since all photographers will have their own favorite equipment (preferably well tested), only general recommendations are made here. You will have a normal lens, of course, and a telephoto will sometimes be useful. Absolutely essential, however, is a wide-angle lens (the wider the better, short of a fish-eye), especially for sites that are not well cleared. Often it is impossible to back off far enough from a structure to get an overall shot with a normal lens. A wide-angle zoom lens (24 mm to 35 or 50 mm) is about ideal.

There are two problems that photographers will encounter at some archaeological sites when taking pictures of bas-relief monuments. One arises when the monuments are lying on the ground, and the other when they are covered with thatch shelters—and sometimes both problems appear at the same time. In the first case you can improve your chances of getting a decent head-on photograph by doing the following. Attach your camera (with a wide-angle lens) to a telescoping monopod. Hold it over the monument and get someone to stand on the side to help you get the proper alignment. Use the camera's self-timer and the fastest speed you can to minimize camera shake, which will be considerable; fast film will be a help. You will have to prefocus the lens, but you should be able to estimate that accurately enough. You may have to try a couple of times to get this setup properly adjusted.

To photograph thatch-sheltered monuments, off-camera flash is your best bet (at sites where flash is permitted). Get the longest coiled PC cord (the cord that at-

Top to bottom: Camera; screw that fits into camera bottom with attached metal ring; snap clip attached to leather loop, to be connected to belt or belt loop. Unless otherwise noted, black-and-white photographs are by Jerry Kelly.

screws that fit into the bottom of the camera (the case may have to be removed). A machinist can make these for you. To our belt loops we attach a leather loop with a snap, to which is attached a spring-type clip. The clip can be hooked through the metal ring hanging from the camera. It is easy to engage and disengage (see illustrations). This arrangement is extremely helpful, especially if you are carrying more than one camera. Lens caps should be kept in place except while actually shooting.

Your gear will get dirty, and you should have lens-cleaning liquid, tissue, and a brush. Sunshades are a help, and a flash unit will be useful.

Bring your film from home. It is available in the cities and larger towns and at some sites, but it is more expensive, and often the selection is limited.

Photography for personal use is freely permitted at the archaeological sites and museums, but some sites and most museums prohibit the use of flash equipment

taches to the flash unit and plugs into the camera) you can—10 to 15 feet if possible. Position the camera for a head-on shot of the monument and have someone else hold the flash unit at a raking angle to it; the lower the relief, the greater the angle should be. On-camera flash is not a good way to photograph bas-relief monuments; the direct light tends to obscure the designs.

If you are visiting a site that requires a long hike and you have a lot of camera gear, carry it in a waterproof backpack. This is more comfortable than a shoulder-strap bag on long hauls.

While we are at a site, we wear the cameras around our necks and attach them to our belt loops, which leaves our hands free for climbing. This way we don't have to worry about banging an expensive new lens against a stone. We attach metal rings to

Camera, screw and metal ring, and snap clip and leather loop, as they should be assembled

Camera, screw and metal ring, and snap clip and leather loop, attached to belt. Shown as used. Photograph by author.

Where this is the case, it is mentioned in the text. If in doubt, ask before using your flash. Photography for commercial purposes requires special permits.

Auto Insurance

If you are driving your own car to Mexico and Central America, you must buy auto insurance; your United States or Canadian policy is not valid.

Sanborn's, one of the best-known agents, has several offices in the United States near the Mexican border. Sanborn's also sells a Central America package that includes all the countries covered in this book. Belize, however, also requires that you buy Belizean insurance *in* Belize. It is relatively inexpensive. There are agents near both of Belize's land border stations, and you will have to show your policy before you are allowed through customs and immigration. If you want your Sanborn's policy (or policies) ahead of time, write to Sanborn's Mexican Insurance Service, Post Office Box 310, McAllen, Texas 78502. They will also give you excellent road logs for your trip. Other agents can be found near the border as well. The American Automobile Association also sells insurance for Mexico and can provide you with a map and tour guide of that country.

If you fly to one of the countries and rent a car, you can get insurance through your rental agent.

You should drive carefully, of course, and avoid night driving on the highways. Hazards include people walking along the edge of the road and slow-moving vehicles without taillights.

Climate and Travel
in the Rainy Season

The tropical lowlands are warm to hot year-round; this includes most of Belize, the Petén and both coastal areas of Guatemala, and the coastal areas of Honduras and El Salvador. The highland areas are more moderate and can be chilly at night, especially in the winter months. The rainy season is roughly from late May to October, with some regional variation; in some areas there is a slackening of precipitation in July and August. Generally it rains hard, but for short periods, in the afternoon or evening, and usually the rain does not interfere with travel plans. If you plan to travel on unpaved roads, however, you should check locally about their condition. Extremely wet weather can render some unpaved roads impassable, even for vehicles *with* four-wheel drive—for example, the road to Caracol in Belize and the road to Nakum in Guatemala.

Archaeological Sites
and Artifacts

Fees are charged to enter some of the archaeological sites and museums, but they are reasonable and vary with the site or museum. Other places are free. Sites are generally open every day from around 8:00 or 9:00 A.M. to 5:00 P.M.; exceptions are noted in the text. Check locally if in doubt.

Laws prohibit the removal of pre-Columbian artifacts in all of the countries. These items are considered part of the national patrimony, and the United States Customs Service cooperates in preventing the entry of such items into the United States.

Looting of the ancient sites has reached alarming proportions, and the governments of all the countries are enforcing their regulations more stringently than ever to halt this illegal traffic. An incredible amount of information is lost to the world of archaeology because of this illicit digging and thievery.

Museum Names

In each museum section, the formal name of the museum is listed first, followed by the popular name. The popular name indicates the city or site of the museum.

The popular name is used in the table of contents in this book, in the list of sites and museums by ratings, in the photographic captions, and in the alphabetical list of sites and museums.

Glossary

Many specialized words, foreign words, acronyms, and names of deities are used in the text. Those that occur frequently are explained in the glossary at the end of the book. Those used infrequently are explained in the text.

THE RATING SYSTEM

The rating system was devised to help readers see at a glance how worthwhile a visit to a particular site would be. The rating does not necessarily indicate the relative importance of a site in ancient times but reflects a combination of factors, of which relative importance is one. Other considerations are the degree of preservation or restoration and ease of access compared with the visual rewards received. For instance, Nohmul is rated one star, even though it is a large site and was obviously

an important one in ancient times. Nohmul, however, is almost totally overgrown, so there is little to see there today. At one time it was cleared and some of the architecture was consolidated (stabilized to prevent further deterioration). If it should be cleared again, undoubtedly it would merit a higher rating. Another example is Nakum, which is rated two stars. Part of the site has been nicely cleared, and it has a fair amount of standing architecture. Unfortunately, access is rather diff cult. If Nakum were on a paved road, it would clearly deserve three stars.

Ratings

★★★★ A world-class site that should be seen by all visitors.

★★★ A site of major importance and a must for the enthusiast. Fairly to very interesting for others, depending on the site.

★★ Of some importance and moderately to very interesting for the enthusiast. Slightly to moderately interesting for others. (I recommend reading the text for these sites before deciding upon a visit. You will find some more appealing than others, primarily because of access.)

★ Of interest only to the enthusiast. Others may ignore these.

No Stars Of minor importance—only for the avid enthusiast.

LIST OF SITES AND MUSEUMS BY RATINGS

(B) Belize
(G) Guatemala
(H) Honduras
(S) El Salvador

Four Stars ★★★★
Copán (H)
Guatemala City Museum (G)
Popol Vuh Museum (G)
Tikal (G)

Three Stars ★★★
Abaj Takalik (G)
Altun Ha (B)
Caracol (B)
Chichicastenango Museum (G)
Copán Museum (H)
Finca El Baúl (G)
Iximché (G)
La Democracia Plaza (G)
Lamanai (B)
Lubaantun (B)
Mixco Viejo (G)
Quiriguá (G)
San Salvador Museum (S)
Seibal (G)
Tazumal (S)
Tazumal Museum (S)
Tegucigalpa Museum (H)
Tikal Museum (G)
Tikal Lithic Museum (G)
Uaxactún (G)
Xunantunich (B)

Yaxhá (G)
Zaculeu (G)

Two Stars ★★
Abaj Takalik Museum (G)
Belize Museum (B)
Belmopan Vault (B)
Bilbao (G)
Cahal Pech (B)
Cerén (S)
Cerén Museum (S)
Comayagua Museum (H)
El Baúl (G)
Finca Las Ilusiones (G)
Iximché Museum (G)
Kaminaljuyú (G)
La Democracia Museum (G)
La Entrada Museum (H)
Lamanai Museum (B)
Nakum (G)
Nim Li Punit (B)
San Andrés (S)
Santa Rita (B)
Topoxte (G)
Utatlán (G)
Uxbenka (B)
Zaculeu Museum (G)

One Star ★
Aguateca (G)
Cerros (B)
Cihuatan (S)
Cuello (B)

Dos Pilas (G)
Finca Pantaleón (G)
Nohmul (B)
Pacbitun (B)
Quelepa (S)
Utatlán Museum (G)

No Stars
Floral Park (B)
Cara Sucia (S)
San Andrés Museum (S)

PART TWO

• • • •

THE SITES AND MUSEUMS

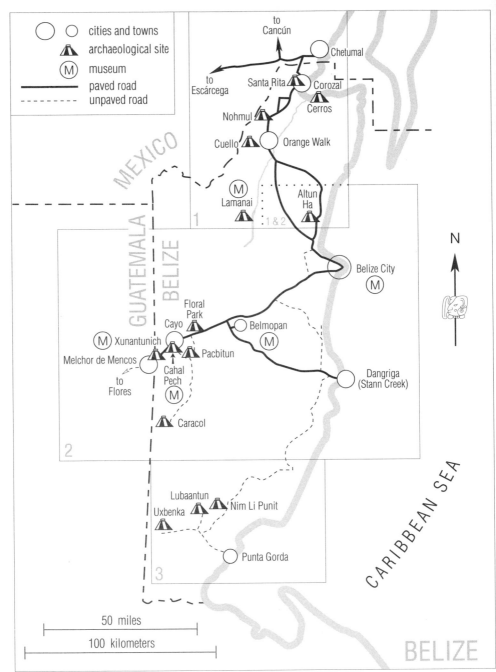

Belize, showing areas delimited by the sectional maps.

GENERAL INFORMATION FOR BELIZE

Belize—called British Honduras until 1981—is a small Central American country, covering 8,867 square miles [22,965 square kilometers]; it is sparsely populated, with about 200,000 inhabitants. It is bordered on the north by Mexico, on the west and south by Guatemala, and on the east by the Caribbean Sea. Belize City is the largest city in the country, with a population of around 46,000; it was the country's capital until the creation of Belmopan in 1971. The capital was moved inland after Hurricane Hattie damaged Belize City heavily in 1961.

Belize has a wealth of natural beauty, including tropical flora and fauna, a barrier reef, and innumerable cays, or cayes (pronounced *keys*), that are a paradise for divers. It also has a great many fascinating ancient Maya ruins.

For Central America, Belize is atypical. The polyglot population is composed of Creoles (African-European, the largest group), Garifunas (African-Indian), mestizos (Spanish-Indian), Mayas, Europeans, and some Near Easterners and Asians.

The official language in Belize is English, though Spanish is widely spoken; you will also hear Maya, Garifuna, and Creole. Most of the buildings in the country are made of wood and have a Caribbean rather than a Central American style.

All visitors to Belize need a valid passport. Citizens of certain countries also need visas, while others (such as citizens of Canada, the United States, Mexico, and some Central American countries) do not. Inquire at your nearest Belizean or British consulate for requirements, or write to the Belize Tourist Board, Post Office Box 325, Belize City, Belize, Central America. The tourist board will send you a current list showing countries requiring visas. They will also include the *Belize Information Guide*, which lists hotels, restaurants, points of interest, and other information, all free of charge.

The unit of currency in Belize is the Belizean dollar (BZ$ in front of the number). The exchange rate is two Belizean dollars to one dollar in United States currency; the rate is fixed. Throughout the country, United States currency and traveler's checks are also accepted, as are major credit cards at the better hotels and restaurants. It should be noted, however, that sometimes a service charge is added to the bill when you are paying with a credit card.

Maps of Belize are available in the country. One, called *Belize Facilities Map*, has plans for Belize City and the other important cities and towns in the country.

Car rentals are available at the international airport at Ladyville, at several agencies in Belize City, and at Punta Gorda in southern Belize. Most agencies have four-wheel-drive vehicles available.

There are gas stations throughout the country, although in some areas the stations are not as frequent as you might wish; for this reason a gas pump symbol is included on the area maps indicating the availability of gas. Driving in Belize, especially the Northern and Western Highways, can be a pleasant experience. There are, however, few highway signs or signs marking cutoffs or the names of villages (especially in some areas). In some cases you will have to rely on odometer readings to get where you want to go.

Buses travel all the major highways and some of the minor roads in Belize. There are connections to Mexico at the northern border of Belize and to the Petén of Guatemala on the western border.

Domestic flights and short international flights are covered in the general information for the individual sections.

SECTION 1

• • • •

NORTHERN BELIZE

Stone mask on the south side of the west facade of Structure N9-56, Lamanai. Early Classic period.

GENERAL INFORMATION FOR SECTION 1, NORTHERN BELIZE

There are three areas in which to overnight in northern Belize: one of the hotels in Corozal, at Consejo Shores (north of Corozal), or one of the hotels in Orange Walk. The best are Tony's in Corozal—an old-time favorite—and Adventure Inn at Consejo Shores. They are also, of course, the most expensive. The best hotel in Orange Walk is Barons—another old-time favorite. There are restaurants in all three places, some connected with hotels. In Orange Walk, Chinese restaurants are about the only kind to be found, though some offer other fare as well.

The Northern Highway runs from Belize City north to the Mexican border; it has been greatly improved over the years, and for the *most part* it is a good paved road. Part of its alignment was changed and a new stretch was introduced in the mid-1970s. This section begins 0.5 mile [0.8 kilometer] north of Sand Hill and reconnects with the Old Northern Highway 0.9 mile [1.4 kilometers] before the Tower Hill toll bridge. The new section is 10.8 miles [17.4 kilometers] shorter than the old section, and the driving time is 53 minutes less. The old section, which goes through Maskall, was once a narrow paved road; it is now in poor condition. Also in poor condition is a stretch of the Northern Highway between the junction with the road to the airport at Ladyville and the junction of the Old and New Northern Highways. This section runs 10.0 miles [16.1 kilometers].

At one time the main route of the Northern Highway bypassed Corozal (although you could get there via a couple of side roads). Now, the route through Corozal is the better choice since a section of the highway (between Louisville and Chan Chen) has deteriorated.

Distances and driving times to the sites in northern Belize are from the following reference points: (1) in Corozal, the Shell gasoline station on Santa Rita Road at the junction of 7th Avenue; (2) in Orange Walk, the junction of Queen Victoria Avenue (the Northern Highway) and Baker Street (on the east) and San Antonio Road (on the west). The Orange Walk fire station is on the northwest corner of this junction.

Note: Although the site of Altun Ha is in northern Belize (and is included in that section in this book), the best access is from Belize City. See "General Information for Section 2 (Central Belize)" for the reference point in Belize City.

In northern Belize there are tour operators in Consejo Shores, Corozal, and Orange Walk.

There are scheduled flights from Belize City to Corozal.

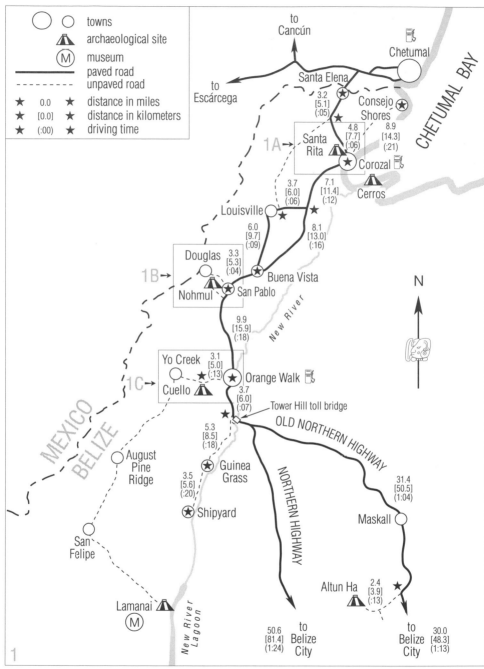

Northern Belize

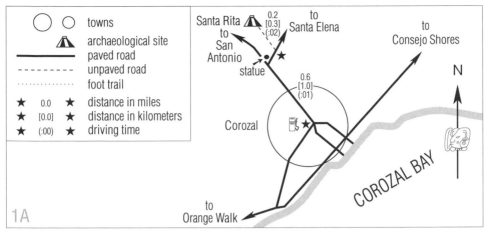

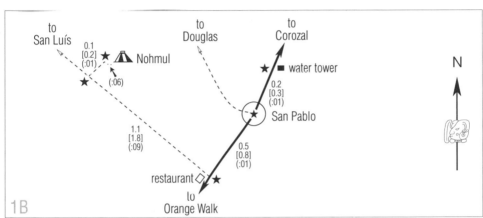

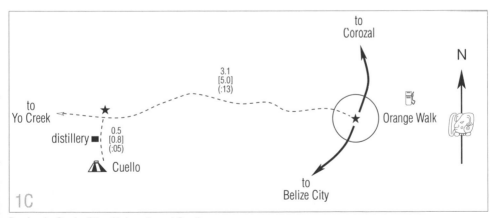

Routes to Santa Rita, Nohmul, and Cuello

★ ★
SANTA RITA
(SAHN-tah REE-tah)

Derivation:
Spanish for "Saint Rita."
Original Name:
Probably Chactemal (Chetumal).
Location:
Northern part of Corozal
District, Belize.
Maps: 1 (p. 24) and 1A (p. 25)

The Site

Much of the site of Santa Rita has been destroyed by the encroaching development of the town of Corozal, and many of the stones from the ancient site have found their way into modern buildings and streets. More than 200 structures have been recorded at Santa Rita and many more once existed. The site once extended from the modern town of Paraíso (north of Corozal) probably to El Ranchito (southwest of Corozal), a distance of about 2.5 miles [4.0 kilometers].

Santa Rita is best known for its Postclassic remains of ceramic censers, modeled and painted figurines, and vessels. Archaeological and ethnohistorical data indicate that Santa Rita was probably the protohistoric Maya province of Chactemal (Chetumal), in existence at the time of the Spanish conquest; it is believed to have been an important port of trade.

The site of Santa Rita, however, was occupied from much earlier times. The earliest radiocarbon date from the site is 1920 ± 120 B.C., presented in a table in a 1988 work by Diane Z. and Arlen F. Chase. Ceramics related to the Swasey phase were discovered at the site. This ceramic phase, first identified at Cuello, was originally believed to date to the Early Preclassic period, but reassessment now places it in the Middle Preclassic.

Although Structure 7 is the only one of interest for visitors today, it is well worth seeing. It is the tallest and most massive structure at Santa Rita; originally it was about 50 feet tall. Structure 7 faces south onto a plaza that is bordered on the east and west by other structures that are simply mounds today.

The approach to Structure 7 is from the south over a well-kept lawn with a scattering of tropical plants. Excavation has shown that the area was occupied in the Late Preclassic period and that Structure 7 itself was built and rebuilt during Protoclassic and Early Classic times.

The multiroomed building seen today (Structure 7-3rd) dates to the Early Classic period and was the only well preserved architecture discovered during excavation of the building. It has since been consolidated. It consists of three rooms in a row and one room on each side. Beneath the floor of the central room was found an Early Classic burial containing the remains of an elderly female and a variety of objects. A slightly later burial of an adult male was found in a tomb below the front room of the structure. Among its elaborate grave goods were the remains of a very eroded codex and a jadeite and shell mask. Scholars believe that the interred was probably an important ruler.

Later in the Early Classic period, the floors of Structure 7-3rd were burned and covered with smashed pottery, and incense burners were placed in a niche in the inner room. The structure was then filled and encased within the newer Structure 7-2nd. The final building, Structure 7-1st, covered 7-2nd and was probably constructed during the Late Classic period. Only a few remains of these last two structures were discovered during excavation.

Structure 7 continued to be used into the Early Postclassic period, and in the Late Postclassic an intrusive burial was made through the steps.

Another important building at Santa

The front (south side) of Structure 7-3rd, Santa Rita. Early Classic period.

Rita was Structure 1, which contained painted murals when it was investigated by Thomas Gann at the turn of the century. Gann copied most of the murals, but before he could complete his work the remaining portions were destroyed by local people. The murals dated to between A.D. 1350 and 1500 and were similar to murals found in Structure 16 at Tulum, Quintana Roo, Mexico. By 1979, Structure 1 had been bulldozed.

Recent History

In the late nineteenth and early twentieth centuries, Gann was the first to conduct investigations at Santa Rita. He was a medical doctor stationed at Corozal, and even at this time the site was being robbed of stone for building materials for the town. Gann made a rough map of Santa Rita and excavated many of the structures, most notably Structure 1.

During the early 1970s limited excavations were undertaken by Ernestene L. Green, Duncan C. Pring, and Raymond V. Sidrys. In 1979 the Corozal Postclassic Project began under the direction of Diane Z. and Arlen F. Chase of the University of Central Florida, and it continued through 1985. It was during this work that Structure 7 was excavated and consolidated. Major funding for the project came from the National Science Foundation.

Connections

1. Corozal to Santa Rita: 0.6 mile [1.0 kilometer] by paved road (:01), then 0.2 mile [0.3 kilometer] by good rock road (:02).

2. Orange Walk to Corozal (via Louisville): 30.0 miles [48.3 kilometers] by paved road (:49).

3. Belize City to Corozal: 84.3 miles [135.7 kilometers] by paved road (2:20).

Getting There

1. From Corozal, head northwest on the Santa Rita Road, which goes toward the Mexican border. After 0.5 mile [0.8 kilometer] you will come to a statue where the road curves to the right. Follow it and go 0.1 mile [0.2 kilometer] to the first cutoff on the left (just past Hennessy Restaurant). Turn left and go 0.2 mile [0.3 kilometer] to the entrance to Structure 7. You will pass a basketball court on the way, and from there you can see the structure off to the right. There is a two-story house on the left, directly opposite the entrance to Structure 7.

2. From Orange Walk, head north on the Northern Highway to Corozal, then follow the directions just given.

3. From Belize City, head north on the Northern Highway and then the New Northern Highway to Corozal. Then follow the directions just given.

You can get a taxi to Santa Rita from Corozal and a bus from Orange Walk or Belize City to Corozal.

The caretaker of Santa Rita is the friendly and informative Peter Ponce. He will happily tell you about the site and show you around. He will also point out the vegetation he has planted and which he lovingly cares for.

Santa Rita is open from 8:00 A.M. to 5:00 P.M. daily. There is no food, drink, or rest room at the site, but these are available in Corozal. Allow 30 minutes to visit Structure 7.

★
CERROS
(SEHR-rohs)

Derivation:
  Spanish for "Hills."
Other name:
  Cerro Maya. Spanish for "Maya Hill."
Location:
  Northern part of Corozal District, Belize.
Map: 1 (p. 24)

The Site

Cerros, a relatively small site by Maya standards, lies on a peninsula that juts into Corozal Bay. The site core covers an area of about 0.5 square mile [1.3 square kilometers], and it can be seen from Corozal, about 3 miles [4.8 kilometers] away, as a hill that stands out on the horizon above the surrounding vegetation.

The site is unusual in that all of its architecture dates to the Late Preclassic period, unencumbered by later Classic or Postclassic additions, although many artifacts from these later periods have been found there, the result of colonization during the Terminal Classic.

Initially Cerros was a fishing and trading hamlet, and it remained so from around 350 to 100 B.C. It boasted at least one pyramid and a small public precinct at this time. Even during this early period there is evidence that Cerros was trading as far north as the north coast of Yucatán, where there are salt deposits, and as far south as the highlands of Guatemala and El Salvador, where obsidian and jade are found. Cerros was probably involved in the export of chert tools manufactured to the south at Colha.

Starting around 50 B.C., large-scale ar-

The front (south side) of Structure 5C-2nd, Cerros. Late Preclassic period.

chitectural endeavors were undertaken at Cerros, and according to David Freidel, Robin Robertson, and Maynard B. Cliff, this "involved such an explosive transformation that it is fitting to speak of massive urban renewal." The site reached its apex from 50 B.C. to A.D. 100. During this time the original fishing village was almost entirely buried beneath a 2-meter-high plaza on which subsequent buildings were constructed.

In addition to the five major building groups, three ball courts, several large plazas, and public buildings that were constructed, a canal almost 4,000 feet long was dug, encircling the southern and eastern part of the principal ceremonial precinct. The canal was part of a system of raised fields, and within its perimeter, 103 buildings, both public and domestic, have been recorded. A sample of these has been excavated as well.

Several of the pyramids at Cerros were adorned with masks modeled in stucco and painted. The four masks on Structure 5C-2nd have been widely reproduced. These images were well preserved when they were discovered; they had been protected by Structure 5C-1st, which covered them. The masks represent the rising and setting sun on the lower level, and the planet Venus as morning and evening star above. This indicates the paired passage of these two astronomical bodies as they move through the heavens.

Structure 5C-2nd lies at the northernmost tip of the peninsula; you can get an especially good view of it from the top of the massive Structure 4, which lies to the south. Unhappily, you will not be able to see the masks on Structure 5C-2nd; they have been re-covered for protection.

Another reason to climb Structure 4, the main pyramid at Cerros, is to see the remains of the lower walls of the temple on top. A rocky path that follows the original stairway on the east gives access to the summit. Structure 4B, which sits atop the basal substructure, is under consolidation that began in 1994.

The site center has now been cleared by the ongoing research project.

Recent History

Cerros has been recognized as an archaeological site since about 1900, and Thomas Gann was among the first to do so, although people in the area had always referred to the site as "The Bluffs." Gann, who is probably responsible for the loot holes in the major pyramids, believed that the pyramids at Cerros might have been Late Postclassic lookout posts. On the basis of surface finds, others thought Cerros was probably a minor center of Late Classic or Postclassic date. In 1969, Peter Schmidt and Joseph O. Palacio visited the site and registered it with the Belize Department of Archaeology. Shortly after that a nonprofit organization was formed to excavate and reconstruct the site and build an on-site museum and tourist facilities. Although the organization went bankrupt and the development was never realized, some funding was provided for the early stages of excavation (the Cerro Maya Project). The company also donated the site to the government of Belize.

In 1973 and 1974, Ira R. Abrams and Freidel (both of Southern Methodist University) co-directed work at Cerros, and Freidel continued work at the site through 1981. This work was partly funded by the National Science Foundation, and during this time the site was surveyed, excavated, and partly consolidated. No further work at the site was undertaken until 1983, when Cathy Crane, also of Southern Methodist University, studied pollen and other organic remains in the ancient canal and its associated structures.

In 1991, at the request of the Belize Department of Archaeology, Debra Walker of Florida International University began a joint research and economic development project at Cerros (the Cerros Cooperative Development Project, or CCADP). Two excavation seasons were completed in 1993 and 1994.

Although small in scope, the new research has revealed a third small ball court (Structure 2C/D), located in the main plaza just east of Structure 3. The ball court dates to the Late Preclassic period; it is oriented north-south like the other two ball courts at Cerros.

Excavations in 1993 revealed a well-preserved building inside Structure 3, Structure 3A-2nd, which exhibited a broad stairway and plastered frontal facades. No modeled stucco was recovered; however, the building originally may have had masks similar to those on Structure 5C-2nd. Structure 3A-2nd was reburied during the same season.

During the 1994 season, consolidation began on Structure 4B-1st. A 2-meter-high wall was consolidated and partly restored. This marks the first in a series of small projects designed to make Cerros more appealing to visitors. The site center has also been completely cleared, making it much more attractive as a destination. There is now more to see at Cerros than at any time in the recent past.

The CCADP plans several more summer seasons. Late July (the mini–dry season) is the best time to visit if you want to see the archaeologists in action.

Connections

1. Corozal to Cerros: About 3 miles [4.8 kilometers] by boat from the dock at Tony's Motel in Corozal to the landing place (:10 to :15), then a short distance by foot trail to the site (:10).

2. Orange Walk to Corozal: 30.0 miles [48.3 kilometers] by paved road (:49).

3. Belize City to Corozal: 84.3 miles [135.7 kilometers] by paved road (2:20).

Getting There

1. Tony's Motel is the best place in Corozal to charter a boat. The boat will get you to the landing place for Cerros, where a care-

taker and his family live. (They speak only Spanish.) One of the family members will then lead you to the site. Depend on your boat captain for tour information.

2 and 3. From Orange Walk or Belize City take the Northern Highway heading north to Corozal and proceed as just described.

There are no facilities, food, or drink at Cerros. Carry cold water and other drinks in your boat. Allow 30 minutes to visit the site once you reach it. Long-sleeved shirts are recommended.

NOHMUL
(noh-MOOL)

Derivation:
  Yucatec Maya for "Great Mound."
Earlier name:
  Douglas.
Location:
  Northern part of Orange Walk District, Belize.
Maps: 1 (p. 24) and 1B (p. 25)

The Site

On the plus side, Nohmul is an important Maya regional center with twin ceremonial groups and a settlement area of more than 7 square miles [18.1 square kilometers]. It has an abundance of architecture, some of which has been consolidated; Structure 2 at the site is the tallest building in northern Belize. Nohmul had an extensive population in the Late Preclassic period and trade connections with central Mexico at that time. Many burials and caches containing jade jewelry, polychrome vessels, human effigy figures, and other artifacts have been found at the site. It has been long known and well studied. This is enough to give it a one-star rating.

On the minus side, the site is totally overgrown, so there is little for visitors to see today. At one time it was hoped that Nohmul would be developed for tourism (as

other sites in Belize have been), but so far this has not occurred.

When you visit Nohmul you walk a short distance from the parking area (at ground level), then make a rather steep climb up the ridge on which the site lies, and then even farther up to the summit of Structure 2. At the top you will see a projecting stair of six steps, covered with stucco, that dates to the Early Classic period, and nearby the entrance to an inner room. From the top of Structure 2 there are lovely views of the countryside and the village of San Pablo below. We were disappointed when our guide said there was nothing more to see at Nohmul itself.

Structure 2 is part of an acropolis in the East Group of Nohmul, connected by a *saché*, or causeway (of Preclassic date), to the smaller West Group. It is believed that the West Group was constructed at the end of the Late Preclassic period and the beginning of the Early Classic, with minimal later construction. The East Group has structures dating to this time, and after a hiatus of several centuries, construction began again during the Tecep phase (A.D. 800 to 1000), when Nohmul was once again densely populated. It is unusual to find this amount of activity during a time when other sites in the southern lowlands were being abandoned. The style of construction of these late structures suggests that they were elite residences for people with a Yucatecan cultural affiliation.

Excavations and surface collections at

Nohmul have established a ceramic sequence dating from the Middle Preclassic through the Late Postclassic period.

In addition to trade with central Mexico during the early history of the site, trade with highland Guatemala has been documented for Nohmul's late period. The site was included in trade networks and was a distribution center for goods.

Recent History

In 1897 Thomas Gann was the first to record the site (under the name Douglas). He later named it Nohmul—the local name for the main mound group. Gann worked at the site in 1908 and 1909; he dug burial mounds and discovered human effigy figures and polychrome vessels. He made surface collections in 1911 and 1912, and with his wife, excavated in the main group in 1935 and 1936. Most of his finds were taken to the British Museum.

In 1940, during construction of a road from San Pablo to Douglas, one of Nohmul's structures was partly demolished for road fill. This uncovered three rich burial chambers, and 24 ceramic vessels were salvaged by A. H. Anderson and H. J. Cook. These were only a small part of the contents of the burials.

As part of her location analysis of sites in northern Belize, Ernestene L. Green dug test pits in the Nohmul area in 1972.

The British Museum–Cambridge University Corozal Project began in 1973 and continued in 1974 and again in 1978. During this work, directed by Norman Hammond (then of Rutgers University), the site was mapped and small-scale excavations were undertaken. In 1979, a limited excavation of Structure 9 was conducted by Diane Z. Chase.

From 1982 through 1986, Hammond began a major investigation called the Nohmul Project. The ceremonial precincts of Nohmul were excavated, as were outlying areas (including raised fields), and some structural consolidation was undertaken. A host of scholars worked at Nohmul during this time.

Funding for the Nohmul Project came from the National Geographic Society, the British Museum, Rutgers University, Cambridge University, and other British museums and societies.

Connections

1. Orange Walk to San Pablo and then to Nohmul: 10.8 miles [17.4 kilometers] by paved road (:21), 1.1 mile [1.8 kilometers] by poor rock road (:09), 0.1 mile [0.2 kilometers] by cane field road (:01), then a short distance by foot trail and the climb to Structure 2 (:06). Total: 12.0 miles [19.3 kilometers] (:37).

2. Corozal to San Pablo; 20.1 miles [32.4 kilometers] by paved road (:31).

3. Belize City to Orange Walk; 54.3 miles [87.4 kilometers] (1:31).

Getting There

Nohmul is on private property and you must talk to the landowner, Estevan Itzab, who will either take you to the site or send you with one of his children. Itzab lives at the north end of San Pablo on the west side of the Northern Highway, directly across from the town's water tower (on the east side of the highway).

1. If you start from Orange Walk, you will pass by the cutoff for Nohmul (by 0.7 mile [1.1 kilometers]) on your way to Itzab's house. You then return to the cutoff.
Note: Most published information indicates that the cutoff from the highway to Nohmul is the road from San Pablo to Douglas (marked with a small sign). This is *not* the route we took. Our guide was Guillermo Itzab, son of the landowner, and he indicated a cutoff 0.5 mile [0.8 kilometers] south of the Douglas Road, at the north side of Keystone Restaurant. We questioned him about this, but he insisted that the route he showed us was the only current access to the site. When asked, he said that the road we took continued to the village of San Luís.

The rock road from the highway heads west and was rutted and muddy in a few spots due to recent heavy rains, and we needed to use four-wheel drive to get through. When the road is dry, a high-clearance vehicle would suffice. The next cutoff is a cane field road (actually no more than a narrow track) that heads north for 0.1 mile [0.2 kilometer]; you can park where the track ends. From there it is a short walk and then a steep climb to Structure 2.

2. From Corozal, take the Northern Highway south to the junction for Louisville, then go west to Louisville and south to Buena Vista and San Pablo. Pick up your guide and continue to Nohmul.

3. From Belize City, take the Northern Highway to Orange Walk and follow the directions for Connection 1 to reach Nohmul.

There is no food or drink at Nohmul, but there is the restaurant at the cutoff. Wear boots and allow 30 minutes to visit Nohmul.

You can reach San Pablo by bus, but none runs along the rock road to the site. When the road to Nohmul is dry, you could reach the site by taxi from Orange Walk—after you pick up a guide.

★
CUELLO
(KWAY-yoh)

Derivation:
   The site is named for the family who owns the land on which the site lies.
Location:
   Northern part of Orange Walk District, Belize.
Maps: 1 (p. 24) and 1C (p. 25)

The Site

Cuello is a small ceremonial center on the lands of the Cuello Brothers Distillery. The feature of interest for the visitor is Structure 350, which dates to the end of the Late Preclassic period. The structure is a small stepped pyramid, rising in nine tiers, with a projecting stair of eleven steps on the east side. The corners of the structure are deeply inset. At the rear there is a series of terraces that vary from curved to straight in plan. They are arranged so that they fan out from the rear corners of the structure. There are no indications of masonry construction atop the structure; perhaps it supported a superstructure of perishable material.

Excavations have shown that an earlier, partly demolished building lies within Structure 350. Later, Structure 35, built in the early part of the Early Classic period, encased Structure 350, but because of its poor preservation, Structure 35 was stripped away to reveal the earlier building. Structure 350 has been consolidated and was later whitewashed.

Structure 350 (and its earlier and later versions) lies near the southwestern edge of Platform Number 34. The platform covers more than an acre and rises 10 to 13 feet above ground level. The platform itself was raised and resurfaced many times beginning around 300 B.C.

A large area of Platform Number 34, in front of Structure 350, was excavated to bedrock. At the lowest levels, built at a time before the earliest construction of Platform Number 34 began, lay the remains of structures surrounding a sunken courtyard. The structures are simple, low, lime-plastered platforms that supported perishable buildings. The early structures date to early in the Middle Preclassic period.

Before the construction of Platform Number 34 began, the courtyard of the Middle Preclassic structures was filled with rubble and surfaced. A depression was left in

Structure 350, Cuello, view from the northeast. Late Preclassic period.

the rubble, into which was placed a mass burial of more than 20 individuals accompanied by ceramic vessels and carved bone tools. This burial was part of the ritual destruction of the early structures at about 400 B.C. Over it lies the earliest level of Platform Number 34.

When Platform Number 34 was first excavated, it was believed (on the basis of radiocarbon dates) that the early Middle Preclassic structures were older and that they dated to the Early Preclassic period (around 2200 B.C.). Later, other samples were tested for radiocarbon and the dates were revised to around 1000 B.C. So while Cuello may not be as old as originally thought, it may still be one of the earliest Middle Preclassic centers yet encountered in the Maya Lowlands.

Later remains have also been found at Cuello. To the northeast of Platform Number 34 is a pyramid and plaza group of Late Classic date. This area is uncleared and is behind a fence, inaccessible to visitors. The road to Platform Number 34, however,

passes by the west edge of the group. When you are leaving the site, if you look off to the right (east), you can spot some of the mounds that are part of this group.

Cuello was deserted at the end of the Classic period.

Recent History

The mounds at Cuello were known to local inhabitants of the area, but it was not until 1973 that Cuello was recognized by archaeologists as a Maya site, when Norman Hammond spotted it on an aerial photograph. He later confirmed its existence on the ground by examining ceramics from a bulldozed mound.

In 1974, the site was investigated by Joseph O. Palacio, then archaeological commissioner of Belize. The next year, Duncan C. Pring and Michael Walton, students working with Hammond, excavated and collected material for radiocarbon dating and began mapping the site. In 1976, Hammond spent six weeks excavating, and he returned in 1978, 1979, and 1980 for longer field seasons. His most recent work at Cuello was in 1987.

Funding for the work at Cuello came from the National Geographic Society, the British Museum, and Rutgers University. Many scholars were involved.

Connections

1. Orange Walk to Cuello: 3.1 miles [5.0 kilometers] by poor rock road (:13), then 0.5 mile [0.8 kilometer] by dirt road (:05).

2. Corozal to Orange Walk: 30.0 miles [48.3 kilometers] by paved road (:49).

3. Belize City to Orange Walk: 54.3 miles [87.4 kilometers] by paved road (1:31).

Getting There

1. From Orange Walk, head west on San Antonio Road (also called Yo Creek Road) to the cutoff for the Cuello Brothers Distillery (3.1 miles [5.0 kilometers]). Turn left and go 0.2 mile [0.3 kilometer] to the distillery, and stop to ask permission there to visit the site; someone will follow you.

From there, follow the road as it bears to the left and then to the right. Platform Number 34 is 0.3 mile [0.5 km.] from the distillery.

2. From Corozal, take the Northern Highway heading south to Orange Walk, then proceed as described.

3. From Belize City, head north on the Northern Highway to Orange Walk, then proceed as described.

You may visit the site only when the distillery is open. The hours are 9:30 A.M. to 5:00 P.M. on Monday through Saturday. It is closed on Sunday. It is not necessary to call ahead as is sometimes stated, but you must ask permission at the distillery before you enter the site.

Although the dirt road to the site is rutted, you can drive it in a standard vehicle if you go slowly. Allow 25 minutes to see Structure 350. There is no food or drink at the site.

You can also reach Cuello by taxi from Orange Walk. You can reach Orange Walk by bus from Corozal or Belize City.

★ ★ ★
LAMANAI
(lah-mah-NAHEE)
Indian Church

Derivation:
    Spanish rendition of the Maya
    for "Submerged Crocodile."
Original Name:
    Lamanai.
Location:
    East-central part of Orange
    Walk District, Belize.
Map: 1 (p. 24)
	The Site
	
	Lamanai is a delightful site. It has become one of the most visited sites in Belize, though it is not overwhelmed with tourists. The site lies on the west side of the New River Lagoon in an archaeological reserve that covers 1.5 square miles [3.9 square kilometers]. The major ceremonial precincts and minor residential structures are included in the reserve.
	
	    Crocodiles inhabit the New River and the lagoon (though I have never spotted

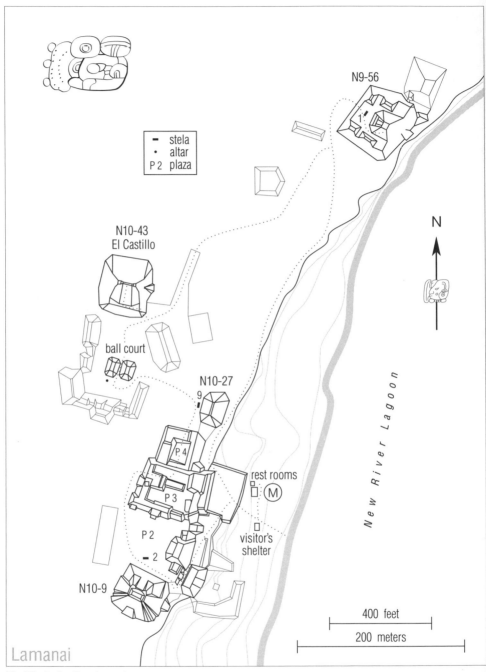

stela
altar
P 2 plaza

N9-56

1

N10-43
El Castillo

N

ball court

N10-27

9

P 4

rest rooms
M

P 3

P 2

visitor's
shelter

2

N10-9

New River Lagoon

400 feet

200 meters

Lamanai

Modified after Pendergast.

The front (west side) of Structure N9-56, Lamanai. Early Classic and early Late Classic periods.

any), and their depictions are found in the art of Lamanai.

The wide trails at Lamanai are unmarked but are kept well cleared, as are the areas near the major structures. Some of the architecture at the site has been consolidated. While a guide is not essential to get around, you may prefer to have someone along.

When you arrive at Lamanai by boat (the recommended access), you will dock near the southern end of the ceremonial sector. From there, follow the trail heading north (and paralleling the shore) for about 0.4 mile [0.6 kilometer] to Structure N9-56, the northernmost structure of interest to the visitor.

A basal stairway leads from the trail up a platform upon which Structure N9-56 is set back. Before you climb the stairway, take a look at the left (north) side of the plat-form; there are a few remains of stucco decoration, including a knot design that is especially clear. In front of Structure N9-56 is Stela 1, which probably dates to around A.D. 625 or somewhat earlier. It lies on its back and is protected by a thatch shelter. Though somewhat eroded, the image of an elaborately dressed, standing figure can still be discerned.

The final phase of Structure N9-56 dates to around A.D. 550 to 650. The most interesting features at the structure are two masks that decorate the west facade of a building constructed somewhat earlier than the final phase. The masks are on two levels on the south side of a central stairway. On the lower level, the mask is more than 15 feet high; it is well preserved. It represents a rather humanized face and is bordered by decorative elements. The headdress of the mask represents a crocodile. The mask on

Stone mask with a thin layer of stucco, on the south side, lower level, of Structure N9-56, Lamanai. Early Classic period.

the upper level of the building is not quite so well preserved; the face was broken away during later construction.

Unlike most masks in the Maya area, these are constructed of stone with only a thin layer of an unusual gray stucco as a coating. Generally masks are made of a rudimentary stone armature covered with thick stucco into which the details are carved. The masks date to the late fifth to early sixth centuries. Limited probing indicates that there are masks to the north of the stairway as well, but they have not been excavated.

Still earlier structures were found within N9-56, but they are not visible today. One has a mask similar to those at Cerros; it probably dates to around 100 B.C. A few portions of an even earlier structure were also found.

All of the additions to Structure N9-56 were made to the front (west side) of the building. During excavation, two tombs were discovered, one in the structure and another in a pit beneath a platform stair; both date to the Early Classic period.

In the Late Postclassic period, when Structure N9-56 was unquestionably in ruins, several small platforms were built at its base, and a reset Classic period stela was placed on the central platform.

You now retrace your steps along the trail for a short distance, then take a branch trail to the right; this leads to El Castillo (Structure N10-43), about 0.3 mile [0.5 kilometer] from Structure N9-56 by trail.

El Castillo is an enormous pyramid, rising 108 feet above the plaza level. It was first built around 100 B.C.; it is one of the largest securely dated Preclassic structures known in the Maya area. It was modified and rebuilt several times, but its impressive height was reached in the initial Preclassic con

The front (south side) of Structure N10-43 (El Castillo), Lamanai. Late Preclassic period with some Classic period additions.

struction phase. The last major addition to El Castillo was made around A.D. 600 to 700. The structure faces south, and part of the lower stairway of the earliest structure has been consolidated on that side. From the top of the stairway, a rocky trail leads to the summit. Near ground level, and to the right (east) of the stairway, are remains of a large mask that was part of the earliest construction.

A short distance to the south of El Castillo is a ball court, the only one encountered at Lamanai. It dates to around A.D. 900 to 950 and has a circular stone center marker. An offering recovered from beneath the marker contained ceramics and, surprisingly, 0.6 cubic inch (9.7 cubic centimeters) of mercury. David M. Pendergast, of the Royal Ontario Museum, who discovered the offering, states that this is the first reported occurrence of mercury in the Maya lowlands; he believes that it probably came from a Honduran source.

South of the ball court and off to the west (right) are remains of a carved stone monument. In the center of it there are three rows of glyphs, and on each end, seated figures in profile face the glyphs and each other.

From this area you head east to Structure N10-27, which has been excavated but not consolidated. Early on the very first day of the 1983 excavation season, the upper part of Stela 9 was discovered face down on a stairway at the front of the structure. Its lower part, still in situ, was found in the remains of a room at the top of the stairway. Today, the upper part of the stela is found face up under a thatch shelter, near where it was discovered. There is a small ladder that is part of the shelter and you can climb it to get head-on photographs of the stela.

Stela 9, depicting Lord Smoking Shell, Lamanai. A.D. 625.

Glyphs in an L-shaped panel on the upper left of the front of the stela (as you face it) indicate that Stela 9 dates to A.D. 625 and that it depicts Lord Smoking Shell of Lamanai; the occasion represented is probably an accession.

From Structure N10-27, follow the trail southward to Plaza 3 and its surrounding structures. This is a residential assemblage that dates from around the late ninth century to Late Postclassic times; it is composed of buildings surrounding courtyards. The masonry is mostly reused material from earlier structures, and some of the buildings have been consolidated. What you see today are steps and platform walls from various periods. Around A.D. 1025 the buildings were torn down and the materials were used to fill the courtyards to a depth of eight feet, creating a single large platform. A variety of

offerings found in the courtyard fill indicate that this monumental effort may have taken the better part of a century.

Again follow the trail south to Structure N10-9, another of Lamanai's massive pyramids. Initially constructed around A.D. 500 to 550, the structure is about 65 feet high. Like other buildings at Lamanai and elsewhere, it was altered over the years. A major modification took place around the eighth century. After that, and through the mid-eleventh century, there were only minor alterations.

Structure N10-9 rises in nine tiers and has a broad basal stairway on the north side, part of which has been consolidated. On either side of the stairway are large horizontal masks that are part of the initial Early Classic construction. During excavation, offerings were recovered (probably of Early Classic date) that included a jade mosaic mask, a pair of jade earplug flares, a carved jade pendant, and 571 obsidian cores, materials that had to have been imported. On the ground in front of the structure is Stela 2, once carved but now greatly eroded.

From Structure N10-9, the trail leads past a few ruined buildings, back to where you docked.

Lamanai has one of the longest histories known in the Maya area; it was continuously occupied from at least the Middle Preclassic period (around 500 B.C.), for which there is ceramic evidence, through the Classic and Postclassic periods and into the historic period until A.D. 1675 or later.

The earlier structures at Lamanai are more similar to those in the Petén than to those in northern Belize, as are the recovered offerings. Many of Lamanai's structures were rebuilt over the centuries, but late in the Classic period the ceremonial locus shifted to the southern part of the ceremonial sector. Rebuilding of the northern structures came to an end, and parts of that area

The front (north side) of Structure N10-9, Lamanai. Early and Late Classic periods.

were converted to residential use. Why this shift occurred is unknown.

Throughout its history Lamanai was involved in trade, and copper objects found in Postclassic burials came from Oaxaca, western and central Mexico, and lower Central America. Less is known about what Lamanai exported. It is also uncertain why Lamanai continued as an important center into and through the Postclassic period when other sites in the central lowlands had collapsed.

The early historic period at Lamanai began in A.D. 1570, when Catholic clergy arrived to erect a church. The apse was made of masonry while the nave was constructed of perishable materials, typical of *visita* churches, where there was no resident priest but where the clergy visited occasionally. A second church was built a little later. For this reason the site is also called Indian Church, a name still in use in Belize. The early historic period ended at Lamanai around 1675, with the last occupation of the church by apostate Maya. If you wish to see the remains of the church, it is 0.5 mile [0.8 kilometer] south of the back of Structure N10-9, and you should have a guide to take you.

Recent History

From A.D. 1675 onward, for 150 years, the history of Lamanai is largely unknown, although small groups of people probably inhabited the area because of the rich resources of the lagoon.

In the mid-nineteenth century, the area was given over to the production of sugarcane, and in 1868 a sugar mill imported from New Orleans was installed. This enterprise was later abandoned, probably around 1883, and for the following 90 years the area was exploited for timber. Mayas continued to settle at Lamanai, sometimes temporarily, along the shore of the lagoon, and the last village was destroyed in 1917.

Mask panel from the lower level of the north facade (east side) of Structure N10-9, Lamanai. Early Classic period.

Even after that, a few families lived or camped at the site until 1973.

The first person to investigate Lamanai as an archaeological site was Thomas Gann in 1917. In 1931 and 1934, Sir J. Eric S. Thompson passed Lamanai on his way to Hill Bank (on the south end of the New River Lagoon). He was headed to San José, where he excavated. He mentioned passing Lamanai but did not investigate the site. In the early 1960s, William R. Bullard, Jr., made surface collections and explored Lamanai, and another small surface collection was gathered in 1967 by Thomas Lee of the New World Archaeological Foundation.

Only in 1974 did substantial excavation begin at Lamanai. This work continued through 1985 under the direction of Pendergast; it was funded by the Social Sciences and Humanities Research Council of Canada, the Royal Ontario Museum research fund, and the Richard M. Ivey Foundation of London, Ontario, Canada. Thanks to Pendergast's efforts, there is now a wealth of information in the literature about Lamanai.

Connections

1. Orange Walk to Lamanai: 4.3 miles [6.9 kilometers] by paved road (:08), then about 20 miles [32.2 kilometers] by boat (approx 1:15).

2. Corozal to Orange Walk: 30.0 miles [48.3 kilometers] by paved road (:49).

3. Belize City to Orange Walk: 54.3 miles [87.4 kilometers] by paved road (1:31).

Getting There

1. There are a number of options for reaching Lamanai. On our second visit to the site we opted to go with Carlos Godoy, who

came highly recommended; we never regretted that decision.

Carlos lives in Trial Farm and docks his boat there (1.2 miles [1.9 kilometers] north of Orange Walk). From there he goes by river to the Tower Hill toll bridge, where he meets you at a prearranged time. We made arrangements with him the day before—and this is recommended. We drove from Orange Walk to the bank of the New River (by a dirt cutoff just before the toll bridge), where Chester Armstrong and his family live. You may safely leave your vehicle there—they will watch it for you. While there is no specific charge for watching your vehicle, a couple of dollars when you return would be appropriate and appreciated.

Carlos met us at the Armstrong compound with his boat. From there it took us 1:15 by boat to reach Lamanai, using a fairly large outboard motor. It would have taken longer, of course, with a smaller one. Carlos provides the boat and a boatman, a picnic lunch, an ice chest with soft drinks, rain gear, and his services for a tour of Lamanai. He is a pleasant and knowledgeable young man and an expert on orchids, which abound in the area. He will point them out to you on the river trip. He can also identify the bird life you will see along the way. You can contact Carlos through Barons Hotel in Orange Walk or call him at 03-22969.

Another tour operator is Herminio Novelo at phone number 03-22293 in Orange Walk. There are also boat operators near the toll bridge, one on each end of it. The one before the bridge (as you drive south from Orange Walk) is on the right. Look for a pond and picnic area. The one past the bridge has a small sign (on the right) advertising trips to Lamanai.

2. From Corozal, head south on the Northern Highway to Orange Walk, then proceed as described.

3. From Belize City, head north on the Northern Highway to Orange Walk, then proceed as described.

You can also drive to Guinea Grass or Shipyard (a Mennonite community) and hire a boat there. From Orange Walk it is 3.7 miles [6.0 kilometers] by paved road to the Guinea Grass cutoff (unmarked). This is 0.6 mile [1.0 kilometer] before the toll bridge. From the cutoff it is 5.3 miles [8.5 kilometers] by dirt road to Guinea Grass (:18) and an additional 3.5 miles [5.6 kilometers] to Shipyard (:20). The dirt road to Guinea Grass and Shipyard will be rutted and muddy in wet weather and it will be faster to go by boat from the toll bridge.

A truck reportedly leaves Orange Walk around 10:00 A.M. and goes to Guinea Grass and Shipyard. The problem with this option is that by the time you get there, arrange for a boat, and reach Lamanai, it would be midday at least. And I have seen nothing published about a *return* truck to Orange Walk. Taking a taxi from Orange Walk to Guinea Grass or Shipyard is a possibility, if you can arrange for its return to pick you up later.

The final option is to drive all the way to Lamanai from Orange Walk, through August Pine Ridge and San Felipe. This should not be attempted in wet weather as the dirt roads are poor. I have not tried this nor am I inclined to, so I cannot give exact distances or driving times. From maps it would appear to be about 36 miles [57.9 kilometers], and it would undoubtedly take longer than going to Lamanai by boat.

When we last visited Lamanai (in the rainy season), we saw a tour group who had driven in—except for the last mile, which they had to walk. From the knees down their trousers were covered with mud, and I imagine it wasn't a very pleasant walk. We also saw the road where it entered Lamanai just south of Structure N10-9, and to say it looked terrible would be an understatement. Obviously it would have bogged down even a vehicle with four-wheel drive.

There is no food or drink sold at Lamanai, but there is a thatch shelter where you can eat your lunch, and there are rest rooms. Camping is not allowed at the site. Allow 3 hours to visit Lamanai and wear boots if it has been wet.

If your transportation to Lamanai does not include a guide at the site, and you would prefer to have one, ask at the thatch shelter when you register.

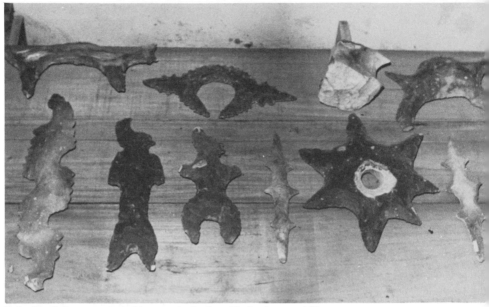

Eccentric flints excavated at Lamanai, displayed in the Lamanai Museum.

★ ★
LAMANAI MUSEUM

The Lamanai Museum is housed in a small building at the site. The collection includes a wide array of ceramic vessels stacked on wooden shelves. Included are incense burners, bowls, a cylindrical tripod with a lid, vases, and plates. There is a nice assortment of eccentric flints and a few pieces of stucco sculpture. All the items come from the site but none is labeled.

The lighting is sufficient to view the objects, but you will need flash to photograph them. Fortunately, this is permitted. Allow 20 minutes to view the collection, which is definitely worth seeing while you are at the site.

★ ★ ★

ALTUN HA
(ahl-TOON HAH)

Derivation:
Yucatec Maya for "Rockstone Pond," a rough translation of the name of a nearby village.
Location:
North-central part of Belize District, Belize.
Maps: 1 (p. 24) and 2 (p. 56)

The Site

Altun Ha is a medium-sized Maya center occupying an area of 2.3 square miles [6.0 square kilometers] on the periphery of the central Maya area. Some 450 to 500 buildings have been recorded there. Most of these are in a 0.4-square-mile [1.0-square-kilometer] area surrounding the central precincts. These precincts are made up of Plaza A, surrounded by Structures A-1 through A-7, and, adjacent on the south, Plaza B, surrounded by Structures B-1 through B-6. When you arrive at the site and park, you will see a trail that leads to Plaza A.

Plaza A was originally entirely plastered. The final surface is about 10 inches below the present ground level, but at least two earlier floors were discovered beneath the last one. Plaza A and its surrounding buildings seem to have formed the main ceremonial precinct until around A.D. 550 in the Early Classic period. At that time construction began around Plaza B.

You enter Plaza A from the northeast, just south of Structure A-7, an almost completely destroyed low mound. To the northwest is Structure A-6, which borders the north side of Plaza A; it is now a large, rectangular, grass-covered mound with a few remains of a stair in the center on the lower south side. The volume of the structure is an enormous 900,000 cubic feet. The pyramidal base was once topped by a superstructure that comprised two long narrow rooms, each with multiple doorways.

On the east side of the plaza is Structure A-1 (Temple of the Green Tomb), where at least seven construction phases were found, several of which are visible today. The substructure dates to the early sixth century and is one of the few visible Early Classic temple bases not covered by later construction. The slight curvature seen at the rear is reminiscent of that in the Early Classic Temple 5D-23 at Tikal. The superstructure of Structure A-1 shows later building additions. Most of the upper portion, however, has fallen into the lower part of the chamber. A tomb that dates to A.D. 550 to 600—the earliest burial in the central area of the site—was found inside this structure. Among its contents were nearly 300 jade objects, which gave the tomb and structure their names. Another interesting funerary item was the remains of a smashed codex. The paper base had disintegrated, and only the fragments of the painted stucco surface remained. Unfortunately, this rare find probably cannot be reassembled; neither can two others found at Altun Ha

Structure A-2 abuts A-1 on the south, although they were not originally connected. A-2 is a large, complex platform showing at least two construction phases but no evidence of a superstructure.

Bordering the south side of the plaza is Structure A-3, the smallest temple facing Plaza A. It rises in tiers and has a broad stairway on the north side. At ground level on each side of the stairway are remains of stone and stucco mask panels; there are a few remains of additional panels above these. At the top of the structure are the lower walls of a temple.

Structure A-5 (the Bowling Alley), on the east side of the plaza, is later and larger than A-1 but only slightly taller, and was ap-

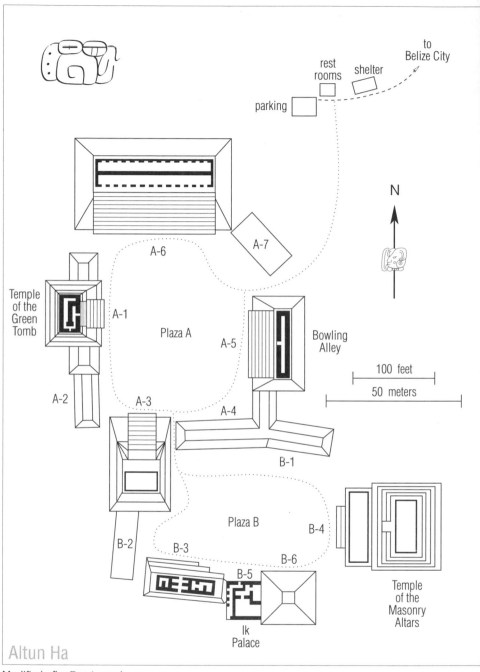

to
Belize City

rest
rooms

shelter

parking

N

A-7

A-6

Temple
of the
Green
Tomb

A-1

Plaza A

A-5

Bowling
Alley

100 feet

50 meters

A-2

A-3

A-4

B-1

Plaza B

B-4

B-2

B-3

B-5

B-6

Ik
Palace

Temple
of the
Masonry
Altars

Altun Ha

Modified after Pendergast.

Structure A-1 (Temple of the Green Tomb), Altun Ha, view from the southeast. Early Classic period.

parently built all at once. The extremely narrow single chamber on top gives the structure its name; it was probably used for ceremonial activities.

Structure A-4 forms the southeast corner of Plaza A. It is an L-shaped low platform that abuts Structure A-5. It originally abutted A-3 as well, but that portion of the building has been obliterated; the trail to Plaza B is at this disjuncture. An extension of A-1 (to the east) is believed to be a separate structure and is called B-1. It too is a low platform, though higher than A-1, and it has a slightly different alignment.

Plaza B differs from Plaza A in that the plaza floor was surfaced only once. The most important structure facing this plaza is B-4 (Temple of the Masonry Altars) on the east. At 58.5 feet, it is the tallest structure at Altun Ha, and it lies on top of the plaza floor—some remnants of which can be seen at the base of the structure. Here, again, are

remains of monumental sculpture in the form of mask panels. There are two masks on each side of the central stairway, one on each of the two tiers that abut the stairway. All four masks have large rectangular ear flares. The masks and stairway are on the front (west side) of the structure.

From 1965 through 1968, extensive excavations were carried out on B-4, and eight phases of construction were discovered. The latest six were in very poor condition and were removed. What you see today is Phase VII, dating to A.D. 600 to 650. The initial construction of the structure (Phase VIII), underlying the existing one, was begun around 550, at the time of the flooring of Plaza B. In Phase VIII, an altar was placed atop the temple and was followed by three later ones, giving the temple its name. The one you see today is from Phase VI, all that remains from that period.

During Phase VII, a tomb was con-

Remains of a mask panel on the north facade, east of the stairway, on the lower level of Structure A-3, Altun Ha. Late Classic period.

structed in the large stair block near the top of structure B-4. It contained a large jade head of Kinich Ahau, the sun god. This full-round sculpture, weighing 9.75 pounds, was discovered in 1968 and was the largest carved jade then known from the Maya area. Since then a larger but much cruder jade figure, weighing 12.5 pounds, was found at San Jerónimo in the Salama Valley of Guatemala's Baja Verapaz. The head of Kinich Ahau dates to A.D. 600 to 650 and is safely stored in a bank vault, but a replica is on display at the tourist board in Belize City. Since it is in a glass case, try a polarizing filter when you photograph it. The replica is definitely worth a look.

Another spectacular jade was found in B-4, a bas-relief plaque with a seated figure on one side and some rather crude glyphs on the other. It was part of a burial from Phase VI that was placed against the face of the stair block in the lower stairway. The plaque weighs over a pound, and the burial in which it was found dates to A.D. 650 to 700.

Structures B-3, B-5, and B-6 border the south side of the plaza and differ from B-4 and the structures around Plaza A. Structure B-3 is a platform that had at least two construction phases; there are remains of rooms on top. Structure B-5 (adjacent to the east of B-3) is believed to be a somewhat later extension of B-3. Known as the Ik Palace because of ventilator shafts in the form of a T or an *ik* symbol, B-5, like B-3, was a residential structure. Structure B-6 is a two-tiered platform with a stairway on the north; it may have been a ceremonial structure. Its form is unlike that of B-3 and B-5.

Structure B-4 (Temple of the Masonry Altars), the front (west) side, Altun Ha. Early part of the Late Classic period.

At the southwest corner of Plaza B is Structure B-2, which was greatly destroyed by local digging before it could be excavated. Recovered information was therefore limited, but it is known that B-2 was constructed in three phases and that the entire complex rests atop the plaza floor, indicating an initial construction around A.D. 600.

The pre-Columbian history of Altun Ha indicates that there was a fairly extensive settlement by perhaps 200 B.C. and that permanent buildings were erected by at least the first century B.C., although the main concentrations were not in the present central area, but south and east.

Work in the central precincts (Groups A and B) began around A.D. 300 and continued for 600 years, but there was a decline in the quality and size of construction during the last 150 years. A population of 8,000 to 10,000 occupied the site during its peak, but the central area's population was probably no more than 2,500. Altun Ha collapsed around 900 to 950, though it was not totally deserted.

There is evidence of occupation in the Postclassic period, during the tenth, thirteenth, and fourteenth centuries, but so far evidence is lacking for the eleventh and twelfth centuries. Although people lived at Altun Ha during the Postclassic and reused the old buildings, there were no new architectural endeavors.

The oldest major building at Altun Ha is Structure F-8 (Reservoir Temple), apparently started in A.D. 100 and added to until 200 or 250. It lies 0.4 mile [0.6 kilometer] south of Plaza B. I have not visited this structure, and indications are that it is not very impressive visually. Its name comes from a nearby reservoir, the ancient water supply for Altun Ha. There is no indication that the reservoir was the scene of sacrifices or offerings. It sits in an area covered with dense second-growth vegetation. If you want to visit F-8, ask to have someone take you when you enter the site and register.

There is one interesting point about Structure F-8 that merits mention. During excavation, a postinterment offering was

Detail of the mask panel on the north side of the west facade of Structure B-4 (Temple of the Masonry Altars), Altun Ha. Early part of the Late Classic period.

discovered above a tomb in the top of the structure. The offering contained a wide range of imported objects, including green obsidian eccentrics and blades, traceable directly to a Teotihuacán (Mexico) source. While it is not unusual to find evidence of Teotihuacán influence in the lowland Maya area, the dating of these objects to A.D. 150 to 200 is remarkable. Until this discovery the earliest evidence of contact between the lowland Mayas and Teotihuacán was found at Tikal and dated 250 or 300 years later. Evidence uncovered at Becan in Campeche, Mexico, also suggests contact with Teotihuacán around the time it is found at Altun Ha.

An unusual feature you will notice at Altun Ha is the absence of carved stelae. Only one broken stela—uncarved or unfinished—has been found at the site. It was located south of the central precincts.

Some tombs at Altun Ha contained shells from the Pacific, which suggests that the site may have been an important trading center in a network spread along the Caribbean coast.

Recent History

The reports of some questionable mounds in the area were investigated in 1957 by A. H. Anderson, who recognized the remains as an archaeological site. In 1961, William R. Bullard, Jr., studied some of the remains. In 1964, a full-scale investigation was undertaken by David M. Pendergast of the Royal Ontario Museum, Toronto, Canada. The site was selected because of its peripheral location in the Maya area, where little work had been done previously, and, reportedly, because of the discovery in 1963 of a carved jade plaque by local villagers who were quarrying at the site. Pendergast's excavations continued into 1971, and that year restoration work was begun by Joseph O. Palacio; it continued until 1976. In 1978, additional restoration was undertaken by Elizabeth Graham. The site is kept well maintained.

Connections

1. Belize City to Altun Ha: 30.0 miles [48.3 kilometers] by paved road (1:13), then 2.4 miles [3.9 kilometers] by rock and dirt road (:13).

2. Orange Walk to Altun Ha: 47.1 miles [75.8 kilometers] by paved road (1:22), then 2.4 miles [3.9 kilometers] by rock and dirt road (:13).

3. Corozal to Orange Walk (via Louisville): 30.0 miles [48.3 kilometers] by paved road (:49).

Getting There

1. From Belize City, head north on the Northern Highway for 18.6 miles [30.0 kilometers] to the junction of the New and Old Northern Highways. Take the Old Northern Highway (the right branch) and go 11.4 miles [18.3 kilometers] to the cutoff for Altun Ha. The cutoff is between miles 30 and 31 (although not all the mile markers are in place). The cutoff is marked with a sign for Altun Ha and indicates it is 2 miles—it is actually 2.4 miles [3.9 kilometers]. Turn left (west) at the sign and go 1.7 miles [2.7 kilometers] to an unmarked fork in the road. Take the right branch and continue 0.7 mile [1.1 kilometers] to the site's parking area.

Along the rock road to Altun Ha you will pass some small stands selling ziricote carvings.

2. From Orange Walk, take the Northern Highway heading south. When you come to the junction of the Old and New Northern Highways (0.9 mile [1.4 kilometers] after the Tower Hill toll bridge), take the new alignment on the right and continue 30.5 miles [49.1 kilometers] to where the highways rejoin. Turn left at the junction onto the Old Northern Highway and follow the directions for Connection 1. From Orange Walk it would be 12.0 miles [19.3 kilometers] shorter to take the Old Northern Highway directly to the Altun Ha cutoff (and this would actually take 11 minutes less in driving time), but because of the condition of the Old Northern Highway, the route described first is recommended.

3. From Corozal, take the Northern Highway heading south to Orange Walk, then proceed as described.

There is another possible stopover near Altun Ha if you prefer not to return to Belize City or Orange Walk. This is the Maruba Resort in Maskall on the Old Northern Highway; Maskall is 8.6 miles [13.8 kilometers] north of the Altun Ha cutoff.

Altun Ha is open from 8:00 A.M. to 5:00 P.M. daily; allow 1.5 hours for a visit. There are rest rooms and a large thatch shelter near the parking area. You register at the shelter and could use it to have a picnic lunch. Food is not sold at the site, but soft drinks are available at a house nearby. We also saw Wallace's Beer Parlor near the parking area, but it was closed at the time (late morning on a weekday). Perhaps it opens later.

Since the new alignment of the Northern Highway was put into use, there is no longer regular bus service along the Old Northern Highway. Tours to Altun Ha can be arranged through hotels or travel agencies in Belize City, or you can hire a private car and driver if you do not have your own vehicle.

SECTION 2

• • • •

CENTRAL BELIZE

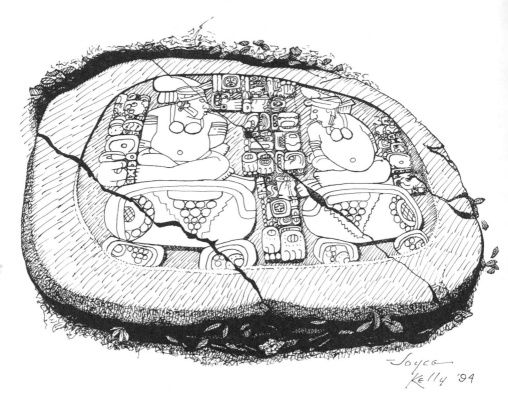

Altar 23, Caracol. A.D. 800.

GENERAL INFORMATION FOR SECTION 2, CENTRAL BELIZE

The best places to stay in central Belize are hotels in Belize City, Belmopan, Cayo (San Ignacio), and Dangriga (formerly Stann Creek). In this case "best places" means the most convenient places to stay (with good accommodations) when visiting the ruins covered in this book. Although Dangriga is not close to any of the ruins, it is a good stopover when traveling from Belize City or Belmopan to Punta Gorda or San Antonio in southern Belize. There are other places to stay, including hotels in Benque Viejo (spartan accommodations), and some nice lodges around Cayo (off the highway and varying distances from it by unpaved roads). All of the places just mentioned have restaurants, some connected with the hotels.

The Western Highway goes from Belize City to the Guatemalan border, 79.3 miles [127.6 kilometers], and is well paved throughout. The Hummingbird Highway starts at the Western Highway and goes 56.0 miles [90.1 kilometers] to Dangriga, where it ends. (Some maps show the part of this highway from Middlesex to Dangriga as Stann Creek Valley Road. Here, I am calling the entire road the Hummingbird Highway.) This highway was once paved, but over the years it has deteriorated. It is currently undergoing repair, and the first 12.0 miles [19.3 kilometers] from the Western Highway are in good condition; the remainder is only fair (at best), but may be improved by the time you get there.

Manatee Road is a rock road; at one time (for a short period) it was the preferred route between Belize City and Dangriga. Later, part of the road washed out during heavy rains. It connects with the Western Highway and the Hummingbird Highway. The southern part of the road—from the Gales Point junction to the Hummingbird Highway—is also called the New Belize Road. Total distance of the two roads is 36.4 miles [58.5 kilometers]. If you wish to use these roads, it would be best to check on their condition beforehand. In Belize City,

you might try asking at your hotel, at Z-Line Bus Service on Magazine Road, or at the Belize Tourist Board (53/76 Regent Street). In Belmopan, the Department of Archaeology would have current information.

Distances and driving times in central Belize are from the following reference points: (1) in Belize City, the Swing Bridge over Haulover Creek; (2) in Belmopan, the small traffic circle at Constitution Drive and Bliss Parade; (3) in Cayo, the Hawksworth Bridge over the Macal River; and (4) in Dangriga, the large "welcome" sign (next to a Texaco gasoline station) at the entrance to town.

In central Belize there are tour operators in Belize City, Belmopan, Cayo, and Dangriga; some specialize in archaeological and cultural tours.

Some of the more interesting items to look for when shopping are ziricote carvings and crafts made of reeds. The carved items come in the form of birds, shells, and boats. They are nicely done and fairly priced. These items can be found in shops in Belize City and the larger towns in central Belize. In San Antonio, Cayo District, the García sisters create and sell unusual slate carvings with Maya motifs.

From Belize City, airlines offer flights within the country to Corozal, Dangriga, Punta Gorda, and some of the offshore cays. There are also flights to Flores, Guatemala, the best access for Tikal.

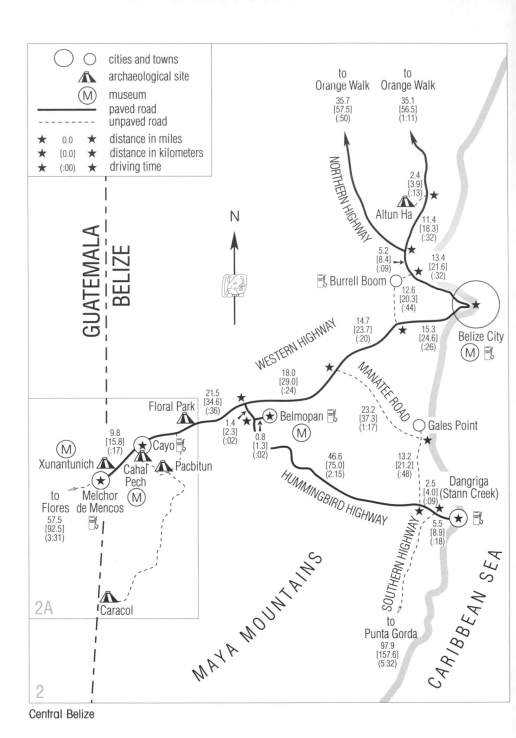

Central Belize

★ ★
BLISS INSTITUTE
(Belize Museum, Belize City)

The Belize Museum is housed in the Bliss Institute which serves a variety of functions. Although the museum's collection is small, it is of high quality. All the objects are labeled and all come from Caracol.

Stela 1 has a panel of incised glyphs at the bottom, on which the main figure and a subsidiary figure are standing. The rest of the stela is carved in low relief. Although the stela dates to A.D. 593, the principal figure has both feet pointing in the same direction, a trait generally seen on earlier monuments. The figure, who represents Ruler III (Lord Water) of Caracol, is richly attired and holds a long ceremonial bar at an angle in front of his body.

Altar 1 lies in front of the stela and has the same date. A giant ahau glyph is found on the altar, a rarity elsewhere but a feature for which Caracol is famous.

Altar 12 portrays two seated individuals facing each other, accompanied by glyphs. It dates to A.D. 818 (or 820 according to some authorities). Though broken, some of the carving on the altar is very clear. The altar was originally found set into a plaza floor; it was paired with a stela.

The last monument in the collection is Stone 28, a three-dimensional depiction of the sun god with a tenon on the back. This architectural decoration was found fallen from its place in 1950. It probably projected from a wall originally, or else formed part of the top of an *alfarda*.

The use of flash is allowed at the museum, and you will need it for photographing the monuments. Ambient light is adequate for viewing the collection. Allow 30 minutes to see and photograph the monuments.

The Bliss Institute is on the waterfront on Southern Foreshore, north of the junction with Bishop Street. It is open from 8:30 A.M. to noon and 2:00 to 8:00 P.M., Monday through Friday, and from 8:00 A.M. to noon on Saturday. It is closed on Sunday.

Altar 12, with two seated figures and glyphs, Caracol. A.D. 818 or 820. On display in the Belize Museum.

Stone 28, a depiction of the sun god with a tenon on the back, Caracol. Classic period. On display in the Belize Museum.

★ ★
BELMOPAN VAULT

Belmopan does not have a formal museum, though plans to build one are under way. In the meantime, some of Belize's archaeological treasures can be seen in the vault of the Department of Archaeology, in the basement of one of the government buildings in Belmopan.

The displays are principally ceramic vessels from all parts of the country, tightly packed on wooden shelves and unlabeled. The most interesting is a group of several vases from Hokeb Ha cave in Toledo District of southern Belize.

Hokeb Ha was first reported to authorities by Peace Corps volunteer Tim Kennedy; later, Barbara MacLeod confirmed the presence of ceramic vessels there. Shortly afterward, in June 1973, a salvage operation was undertaken by Joseph O. Palacio, who recovered 24 vessels—23 of which were complete or almost complete—as well as fragments of other vessels. Included were polychrome cylindrical vases, slipped and painted jars, polychrome bowls, and *insensarios*. One of the finest pieces is vessel number 7, a polychrome cylindrical vase with two seated figures separated by glyphs. The vase is in pristine condition and the quality of its painting is superb. The action portrayed may have

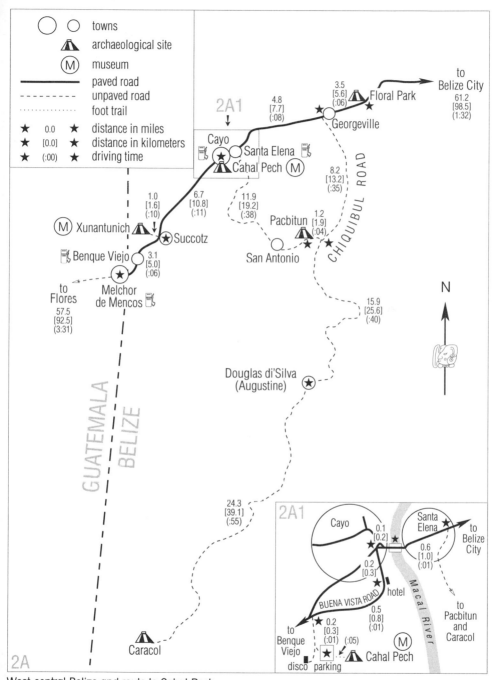

West-central Belize and route to Cahal Pech

an association with rainmaking. You will not want to miss seeing this exceptional item.

To visit the Belmopan Vault, you must make an appointment two days ahead of time (phone 08-22-106). The vault is available to visitors from 1:30 to 4:30 P.M. on Monday, Wednesday, and Friday.

Allow 20 minutes to view the collection.

FLORAL PARK

Derivation:
    Named for Floral Park Estates, which owns the land on which the site lies.
Location:
    North-central part of Cayo District, Belize.
Map: 2 (p. 56) and 2A (p. 59)

The Site

Floral Park is a small ceremonial group composed of two conical mounds joined by an irregular crescent-shaped plaza. The mounds are adjacent to the Western Highway on the north side. The more southerly Mound B (closest to the highway) is 18.4 feet high, while the taller Mound A rises 19.7 feet. The mounds lie on a natural ridge, and the plaza was formed when the limestone bedrock of the ridge was leveled.

It is believed that the mounds are pyramidal substructures that once supported buildings on top.

The site is worth a five-minute stop and a couple of photographs if you are passing right by on your way to or from Xunantunich.

Recent History

Floral Park is one of several sites reported upon in *Prehistoric Maya Settlements in the Belize Valley,* published by the Peabody Museum of Harvard University in 1965. The authors are Gordon Willey, William R. Bullard, Jr., J. B. Glass, and James C. Gifford. The site was mapped and a plan of it is included with the text. No extensive excavation has been undertaken at Floral Park.

Connections

1. Cayo to Floral Park: 8.3 miles [13.4 kilometers] by paved road (:14).

2. Belmopan to Floral Park: 15.4 miles [24.8 kilometers] by paved road (:26).

3. Belize City to Floral Park: 61.2 miles [98.5 kilometers] by paved road (1:32).

Getting There

1. From Cayo, head east on the Western Highway to the site.

2 and 3. From Belmopan or Belize City, head west on the same highway. If you approach from one of the last two places, you will cross a bridge and then begin a slight climb. The mounds are just beyond on the right side of the highway. Another landmark is the Riverwalk Nursery across the highway from the mounds.

★ ★
CAHAL PECH
(kah-HAHL PEHCH)

Derivation:
  Mopan and Yucatec Maya for
  "Place (or City) of Ticks."
Location:
  Northwestern part of Cayo
  District, Belize.
Maps: 2 (p. 56) and 2A/2A1
  (p. 59)

The Site

The name Cahal Pech was given to the site—
no doubt for good reason—in the 1950s
when the land around it was used for pasture. The site is on a hill that overlooks the
town of Cayo (San Ignacio), and it lies on
the west bank of the Macal River. Cahal
Pech is a medium-sized site covering somewhat more than six acres [0.02 square kilo-
meter]. There are at least 34 structures at
the site, both pyramids and range-type buildings, as well as two ball courts (uncleared).
The structures are mostly arranged around
seven plazas. An altar and six plain stelae
have been discovered at Cahal Pech.

Part of the site is nicely cleared and
some of the structures have been restored,
while others are overgrown. You enter the
site at the northeast corner, which puts
you in Plaza B, the largest at the site. Structures B-2, B-1, and B-3 border the plaza on
the east; they have been partly excavated
but are unrestored. One burial found in
Structure B-1 contained obsidian blades,
ceramic vessels, and a jade and shell mosaic mask. This royal burial dates to
around A.D. 600 to 800. Structure B-1, the
center building in the group, is the tallest,
and with Structures B-2 and B-3 forms a
variant of an "E-Group" complex. These
types of complexes were first identified in
Group E at Uaxactún and consist of several
buildings on an east-west alignment, used

for astronomical purposes. See "Uaxactún"
for more details.

On the south side of Plaza B is Structure B-4, made up of a tiered platform with
a central stair. Two unusual, geometric stuc-
coed masks flank each side of the stairway.
There were several construction phases in
Structure B-4; the first was from 900 to 600
B.C. The restored phase seen today dates to
600 to 300. From the top of the structure
you can look down into the small, unexcavated Plaza G to the southwest.

At the southwest corner of Plaza B is
the entrance to Plaza F, which has remains
of several structures that have been partly
restored on the west and north sides. There
are doorways on two levels on the left and a
vaulted passage on the right. In between, a
stairway zigzags up to higher levels, and this
will get you to Plaza E and its surrounding
structures. In this area of Cahal Pech the
structures are compacted around three
plazas, but if you follow the steps and trails
you will not miss anything.

Structure E-1, on the east side of Plaza
E, has two doorways, one of which has a
stepped vault. This entrance leads to a single vaulted room with a large masonry
bench and a few remains of red paint. This
structure has been restored, and what you
see today was probably built around A.D.
700 to 800. It covers an earlier structure
that perhaps dates to around 500 to 700. It
is believed that the later structure (the one
you see today) may have been a private
shrine; the other buildings around Plaza E
probably served as elite residences. On the
north side of Plaza E, a stairway descends to
plaza level.

From Structure E-1 you climb to the
north and follow a trail that descends to
Plaza A. On the south side of the plaza is
Structure A-1, 77 feet high and the tallest at
Cahal Pech; the center part of its front
(north side) has been partly restored. Structure A-1 is a tiered pyramid with a single,

Stucco mask on the north facade of Structure B-4, east of the stairway, Cahal Pech. Middle Preclassic period.

long, vaulted room on the north side, a few steps above plaza level. The room contains a long decorated bench that was originally painted red. There was never a temple on top of Structure A-1. The structure as seen today dates to the fifth or sixth century A.D. and completely covers an earlier Late Preclassic building, discovered during excavation. Trails on either side lead to the summit of the building.

Structure A-4, a vaulted, multiroom, range-type building, is on the west side of the plaza. It was excavated but has not been restored. Found above the floor of one of its rooms were several ceramic vessels that seem to have been deliberately smashed, perhaps during a sort of "termination ritual" upon the abandonment of the site around A.D. 800. Along the north side of Structure

A-4 is a long corridor at plaza level with remains of a vault at the west end.

The east side of Plaza A is bordered by Structure A-2, a range-type building with a double row of vaulted rooms. The structure has been partly restored; it has central stairways facing both Plaza A (on the west) and Plaza B (on the east). The building seen today is the third construction phase; below it is a structure dating to around A.D. 600 to 700, and below that is the first phase, a Preclassic platform that probably supported a building of perishable materials.

The exit from Plaza A is through the center of Structure A-2, via the stairways that connect with Plaza B. The most interesting part of Structure A-2 is the east side (facing Plaza B). On this side you can see the stepped platform (restored) that sup-

Structure to the west of Plaza F, Cahal Pech. The stairway in the center leads to Plaza E and its surrounding buildings.

ports the structure and the remains of the walls of rooms. The center part of the building is more intact (or is more fully restored), and above the lintel of the doorway is a simple, rectangular, projecting medial molding.

When you arrive at Cahal Pech and enter Plaza B at its northeast corner, you can look across the plaza and see Structure A-2. If you wish, you can go there first and tour the site in the reverse order from that just described.

Ceramic and architectural studies show that Cahal Pech was continuously occupied from around 900 B.C. through A.D. 800. Its greatest periods of development were the Late Preclassic and the middle of the Classic, with less architectural activity during intermediate Early Classic times. During the Middle and Late Preclassic periods, Cahal Pech may have been the primary cen-

ter of the region, since no other site in the central Belize River valley had architecture on a comparable scale at that time. In Early Classic times the importance of Cahal Pech seems to have diminished, while that of Buena Vista (4 miles [6.4 kilometers] to the west) increased. By A.D. 500 to 700, Cahal Pech had once again instituted major architectural undertakings that continued until 800, when the site was abandoned. At least two burials were made after its abandonment by people still living in the area.

Recent History

Although residents of the area no doubt knew of the existence of Cahal Pech, the first work at the site was that of Linton Satterthwaite of the University Museum, University of Pennsylvania. He did some

The east facade of Structure A-2, as seen from Plaza B, Cahal Pech. Late Classic period.

preliminary mapping and excavation but never published a complete report of his work; he did mention the site briefly in a 1951 publication.

In 1953 through 1955, during a settlement study of the Belize River valley, Gordon Willey of Harvard University visited Cahal Pech, and in 1965 he described the site. He undertook no excavations.

A. H. Anderson, the first archaeological commissioner of Belize, visited Cahal Pech several times during the 1960s, and in 1969, after his death, Peter Schmidt took over the post. Schmidt investigated looting at Cahal Pech and conducted a salvage operation, concentrating on the royal tomb in Structure B-1.

Between 1970 and 1985, Cahal Pech fell prey to looters, and concern about these destructive activities felt by the San Ignacio (Cayo) Town Board and the Cayo Branch of the Belize Tourism Industry Association ultimately led to the first major archaeological investigation, begun in 1988. This work was organized by Jaime J. Awe and was conducted by him, Mark D. Campbell, and others. The work was funded by the Canadian Commission of UNESCO and Trent University; it included the drafting of a detailed map and excavation of several of the large structures. In 1989, Awe and Campbell wrote a preliminary guide for Cahal Pech, and later, stabilization of some of the structures was undertaken by Joseph W. Ball.

Connections

1. Cayo to Cahal Pech: 0.8 miles [1.3 kilometers] by paved road (:02), 0.2 mile [0.3 kilometer] by rough rock road (:01), then a few hundred feet by foot trail (:05).

2. Belmopan to Cayo: 23.7 miles [38.2 kilometers] by paved road (:40).

3. Belize City to Cayo: 69.5 miles [111.8 kilometers] by paved road (1:46).

Getting There

1. When you cross the Hawksworth Bridge at Cayo heading west, follow the traffic pattern counterclockwise around a triangular plaza. Then take Buena Vista Road heading south and then west for 0.7 mile [1.1 kilometers] to the cutoff for Cahal Pech (marked with a sign). Turn left at the cutoff and proceed uphill. Shortly before you reach the parking area for Cahal Pech, the rock road you are on curves to the right. Leave this road and take a cutoff on the left, onto a narrower rock road, and continue to the parking area, just past the museum. This last part is very rutted but can be driven in a standard vehicle if you take it slowly. From the parking area, follow the trail to the entrance to the site. There is a fork near the end of the trail; take the right branch to enter Plaza B.

2 and 3. From Belmopan or Belize City take the Western Highway to the Hawksworth Bridge at Cayo and follow the directions just given.

Allow 45 minutes to visit Cahal Pech. There is no food or drink at the site, but you are on the outskirts of Cayo where both are available. A nearby disco has cold drinks; you can spot its large thatch roof as you drive the last part of the road to the site. If, when you approached Cahal Pech, you had followed the road as it curved to the right (instead of taking the left cutoff indicated earlier), you would end up at the disco.

You can reach Cahal Pech by taxi from Cayo.

The caretaker of Cahal Pech does not have a particular station at the site; as you roam around he will find you and ask you to sign the registration book. Sometimes he is found perched atop Structure A-1, the coolest spot at Cahal Pech. Can you blame him?

★ ★ ★

XUNANTUNICH

(shoo-nahn-too-NEECH)

Derivation:

Yucatec Maya for "Maiden of the Rock" or "Stone Lady"; a free translation.

Earlier names:

1. Benque Viejo, Spanish for "Old Bank" or "Old Business Settlement," referring to a lumber camp where logs are thrown into the river. According to Teobert Maler, the word *benque* is apparently not used outside Belize.

2. Mount Maloney.

Location:

Extreme western part of Cayo District, Belize.

Maps: 2 (p. 56) and 2A (p. 59)

The Site

Xunantunich is one of the largest ceremonial centers in the Belize River valley, but as Maya sites go, it would be considered of medium size. The major ceremonial precincts are impressive, however, and they occupy more than 22 acres [0.09 square kilometers]. Beyond that, residential structures are found radiating for several miles into the surrounding area.

Some ceramics found at the site date to the Late Preclassic period, and some structures at Xunantunich date to the end of the Early Classic or the beginning of the Late Classic. Most of the currently visible remains are of Late Classic date. Evidence indicates that during the tenth century A.D. there was a disruption at Xunantunich, and that in the Postclassic period the site was reoccupied while the structures were in ruins.

When you drive to the site from the

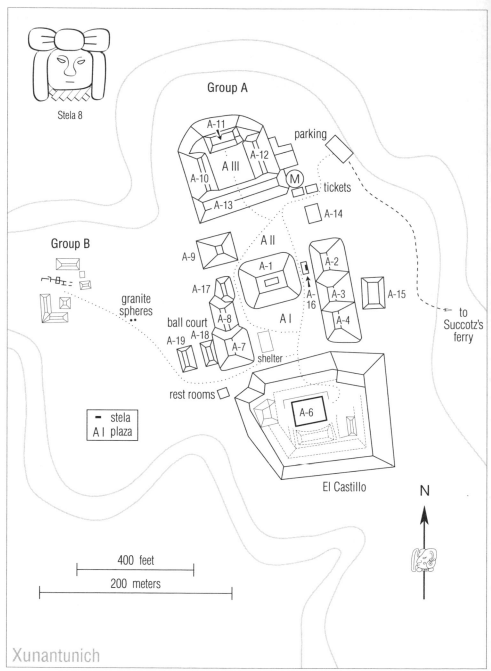

Stela 8

Group A

A-11

A-12

A III

A-10

parking

M

tickets

A-13

A-14

Group B

A II

A-9

A-1

A-2

granite
spheres

A-17

A-16

A-3

A-15

ball court

A-8

A I

A-4

A-19 A-18

A-7

to
Succotz's
ferry

shelter

rest rooms

A-6

— stela
A I plaza

El Castillo

N

400 feet

200 meters

Xunantunich

Modified after "Discover Belize."

Structure A-16, with a plain stela and altar, Xunantunich. The stela and altar date to the Classic period, the structure to the Postclassic.

east, you get a couple of good views before you arrive. Keep an eye out toward the right (north) whenever the road climbs a bit (after Cayo and before Succotz). The towering Structure A-6 (El Castillo) is plainly visible on the horizon and worth a couple of telephoto pictures. If you approach from the Guatemala side, you also get a good view— just as you leave the Belize immigration office—since the road climbs a little before descending to the town of Benque Viejo.

The central area of Xunantunich is laid out around three plazas, A I, A II, and A III, which are aligned in a north-south row, A I being the most southerly. The plazas were formed by leveling the limestone ridge on which the site was constructed. About 20 mounds or structures border these plazas.

You enter the site at the northeast corner of Plaza A II, near a building where you register. Next to this is the small Xunantunich Museum. When you head south from there, you will first pass the small Structure A-14 on your left; this is a platform with a stair on the west side and a mound on top. From there you can see (to the southwest) Structure A-1, the central pyramid with a stairway on the north; the structure is currently being excavated, and no doubt more of it will become visible as work progresses.

Follow the path heading south between Structure A-1 (on the right) and Structures A-2, A-3, and A-4 (on the left). In front of Structure A-2, the northernmost of this group, is the small Structure A-16, which has been excavated and consolidated. It is composed of two rooms, one behind the other, with a step up to the rear chamber. The lower walls of the structure are in place, and the rear chamber houses a plain stela. At the back of the front chamber a plain altar was excavated (just below floor level), beneath which was found a cache of small chipped flints and obsidian blades. The stela dates to the Classic period and perhaps was once painted. It is believed that

The front (north side) of Structure A-6 (El Castillo), Xunantunich. Late Classic period.

the altar dates to the same period. The stela and altar originally stood in front of the base of Structure A-2, totally unencumbered. They were later enclosed by Structure A-16 in the Postclassic period.

Continue south past Structure A-3 and then to A-4, which is being excavated on the west side. Just to the southwest is El Castillo, the real gem of the site, which forms the southern boundary of Plaza A I. El Castillo is the tallest, largest, and most interesting building at Xunantunich. Its present height is a very respectable 127 feet, and it is estimated that its roof comb was originally 10 feet higher. From the plaza, climb the partly consolidated stairway to the top of the first terrace, then take a trail to the left (east) and continue to that side of the building. This will get you to a fantastic stucco frieze. In typical Maya fashion, this frieze was covered with later construction. The decoration originally extended around the other sides of the building as well, but was destroyed by the action of roots and weather.

The existing frieze has been restored, and the elements displayed are masks of the sun god and other motifs symbolic of astronomical matters; the moon and Venus are prominently represented. You will want lots of photos here—including details. You can get good overall shots of the frieze from a slightly lower level. When you climb to the frieze, you will need a wide-angle lens, as it is impossible to back off from it more than a few feet. You then return to the north side of the structure and take a branch path that goes to the upper temple. The final access is by a wooden stairway. The top temple is later than that with the stucco frieze, and in

The stucco frieze with astronomical symbols on the east side of Structure A-6 (El Castillo), Xunantu-nich. Late Classic period.

the time of the ancient Mayas it would not have been possible to see both at the same time, because the lower temple was filled in and covered before the top temple was constructed.

From El Castillo there are delightful views of the surrounding lush jungle—notable for its abundance of graceful cohune palms. This is also a good vantage point for taking photos of the rest of the site, which extends north.

From the temple atop El Castillo, descend to Plaza A I. There is a thatch shelter nearby; it once housed the three carved stelae from the site, but they have been moved to the new site museum. Stela 9 dates to A.D. 830 and is the only one that has been securely dated.

All three carved stelae were found on the south side of Structure A-1. Several plain stelae and altars are found in Plazas A I and A II. One carved altar is known from

Xunantunich, but it was sent to the British Museum in 1924 by Thomas Gann. The shelter has benches and tables; it is a nice place to have a picnic lunch.

Leave Plaza A I at its southwest corner and follow the trail to the west, passing the south end of a ball court (Structures A-18 and A-19). They are simply mounds today. Then follow the trail to the northwest, along the west side of Structure A-19, and continue to Group B. About midway along the trail, you will see two granite spheres of unknown significance.

Group B is composed of seven small structures believed to have been middle-class residences (rather than elite residences) because of their location. Some have been excavated but not consolidated. Return to Plaza A I the way you came, turn left (north), and go to Plaza A II. At the north end of this plaza is a raised area with four structures surrounding Plaza A III,

Detail of the stucco frieze on the east side of Structure A-6 (El Castillo), Xunantunich. Late Classic period.

about 10 feet higher than the other plazas. A stairway leads up the platform to the excavated and consolidated Structure A-13, which borders the south side of Plaza A III. Structure A-13 is a long range-type building; it was residential, as were the other structures surrounding Plaza A III. Beyond the plaza (to the north) is Structure A-11, which rises on a pyramidal base. The structure on top has also been consolidated.

Recent History

Like some other sites in Belize, Xunantunich was first investigated by Gann, the colony's medical officer, in 1894 and 1895. In 1905, Teobert Maler visited the site during his extensive work in the southern Maya lowlands. His work was published by the Peabody Museum of Harvard University in 1908. Maler called the site Benque Viejo because of the nearby town, and that name is found in the earlier literature.

Gann returned in 1924 for additional work, and in his book, *Mystery Cities,* published in 1925, he related that he first learned that the site was locally called Xunantunich from the natives in the area.

In 1938, Sir J. Eric S. Thompson excavated in Group B and established a ceramic chronology for the Late Classic period at Xunantunich. In 1949, A. H. Anderson rediscovered the remains of the stucco frieze on El Castillo that had previously been noticed by Gann; in 1950, Linton Satterthwaite excavated a portion of it.

During the 1959–60 season, excavation was conducted by Euan MacKie of England's Cambridge University Museum of Archaeology and Ethnology. Anderson continued uncovering the stucco frieze during the same time. This impressive decoration was partly reconstructed by Joseph O. Palacio in 1971, and its consolidation was completed by Elizabeth Graham in 1978 and 1979. Several other structures were consolidated by Peter Schmidt in 1968 and 1971.

Even though Xunantunich has had a

Stela 8, Xunantunich. Late Classic period. Now on display in the Xunantunich Museum.

full-time guard since 1967, looting occurred there in 1979 in Group B. When this was discovered, salvage operations in the area were undertaken by David M. Pendergast and Graham. Additional salvage work was supervised by Harriot Topsey in 1980.

In 1992, a major excavation effort was begun by Richard Leventhal of the University of California at Los Angeles, and the project is expected to continue for a few years.

Connections

1. Cayo to Xunantunich: 6.7 miles [10.8 kilometers] by paved road (:11), then 1.0 mile [1.6 kilometers] by rough dirt road (:10).

2. Belmopan to Cayo: 23.7 miles [38.1 kilometers] by paved road (:40). Total Belmopan to Xunantunich: 31.4 miles [50.5 kilometers] (1:01).

3. Belize City to Cayo: 69.5 miles [111.8 kilometers] by paved road (1:46). Total Belize City to Xunantunich: 77.2 miles [124.2 kilometers] (2:07).

Getting There

1. From Cayo, take the Western Highway heading west to the village of Succotz, where a hand-cranked ferry will take you across the Mopan River. There is a sign at the ferry landing. From the far side of the river the dirt road heads uphill to the parking area for Xunantunich. The first part of the road is steep and rutted, but it can be negotiated in a standard vehicle if you drive very slowly. A high-clearance vehicle would be better if you have the choice.

The ferry operates from 8:00 A.M. to 5:00 P.M. and can take only one vehicle at a time; there is a five-ton limit. The ferry also transports passengers without vehicles. If you are driving your own vehicle, be extremely careful when you approach Succotz; you will drive over a few large speed bumps (not all of which are marked) before reaching the ferry landing. If you hit them at anything faster than a crawl, you could damage your vehicle. At the very least you would get a serious jolt. There are also speed bumps past the ferry landing, so watch out for those too if you are heading to Guatemala or are coming in that way.

2 and 3. From Belmopan or Belize City, head west on the Western Highway to Cayo, then follow the directions just given.

Buses pass the ferry landing and can drop you off there; then you can walk to the site. If you choose this option, carry a canteen of water with you; the hike up to the site will take about 30 minutes and there is no food or drink at the site. You could also taxi to Xunantunich (or to the ferry landing) from Cayo, or look into a conducted tour (from Cayo, Belmopan, or Belize City).

Allow 2 hours to visit Xunantunich. There are rest rooms at the site near the northwest corner of El Castillo.

★

PACBITUN

(pahk-bee-TOON)

Derivation:
 Mopan Maya for "Stones Set in Earth."
Location:
 Northwestern part of Cayo District, Belize.
Maps: 2 (p. 56) and 2A (p. 59)

The Site

Pacbitun is a compact, medium-sized Maya center with a core area of about 36 acres [0.15 square kilometers], on which at least 40 masonry structures have been recorded. Three plazas (A, B, and C) are aligned on an east-west axis, and two others (D and E) are found to the north. Two *sacbeob* have also been recorded at the site, though these are in overgrown areas and are not seen by visitors today. Beyond the core area, house mounds extend for 1.3 miles [2.0 kilometers] around the site, and to the west and north for twice that distance.

Only Plaza A and its six surrounding structures are cleared, but this is the most interesting part of the site; clearly it was the most important area in ancient Maya times.

Structure 1 is a pyramid temple and the tallest building at Pacbitun. When it reached its final construction phase it is estimated to have stood 54 feet high. It is on the east side of Plaza A and faces west. It is flanked by Structure 4 (on the north) and Structure 5 (on the south), which also face west onto Plaza A. The three structures

The front (east side) of Structure 2, Pacbitun, view from the northeast. Terminal Classic period.

have been excavated, and all show at least five construction phases, dating from the Late Preclassic period through Terminal Classic times.

Structure 1 had a single vaulted room on its summit, with central doorways on its front (west) and rear (east) walls. When cleared, the lower walls were intact but the vault had fallen. It is estimated that the height of the vaulted chamber was about 13 feet; this would have brought the structure to the 54 feet mentioned earlier. The lower part of the summit temple has been consolidated, and a rocky path leads to it, up the west side of the pyramidal base. The base has not been consolidated.

Structures 4 and 5 each also had a one-room temple on top, but they have not been consolidated. These two structures, as well as Structure 3 (on the north side of the plaza) and Structure 6 (on the south side of the plaza) appear as rubble mounds today.

Plaza A is the most elevated of the five at Pacbitun, and at least four plaster floors covering the entire plaza have been found. They date from the Middle Preclassic through the Early Classic period. Plaza A was formed when the Mayas considerably altered a natural hilltop, making it taller and broader.

Structure 2, the most interesting for visitors, is on the west side of Plaza A and faces east. Its east side has been consolidated. The structure rises in tiers and has a central stairway; there are remains of the lower walls of a one-room temple on top. Structure 2 had four major structural phases, beginning in the Late Preclassic and ending with the Terminal Classic period.

Structure 2, along with Structures 1, 4, and 5 on the opposite side of Plaza A, form a variant "E-Group" complex. This type of complex, first identified at Uaxactún many years ago and later at other sites, has astronomical significance. See "Uaxactún" for details.

Two burials at Pacbitun, one in Structure 1 and another in Structure 2, held the remains of elite Maya women. Each was accompanied by musical instruments. There were flutes, figurine ocarinas, a drum, and two flute-maracas, all made of fired clay. Most were found in fragments; it is believed that musicians played them in the funeral rites of the deceased and then deliberately broke them before placing them in the tombs. Some of the instruments have been reconstructed and can be played. Other elaborate burials and caches have also been found at Pacbitun.

There are remains of 19 monuments (stelae and altars) at Pacbitun, but they are poorly preserved. Some have been dated to the Early Classic period, and others to the Late Classic, based upon stratigraphic evidence or upon burials or caches with which they were associated. The one exception is Stela 6, found in fragments but retaining some of its carving, including the first part on an Initial Series date. Enough remains for the stela to be dated to around A.D. 475. We were told that the monument had been reburied for protection.

The monuments visible to the visitor today are all eroded (or were never carved). One broken stela and an altar are in the center of Plaza A, and another stela is at the base of Structure 5.

There is a thatch shelter just off the northeast corner of Plaza A, and from there you can look at the rather overgrown remains of two mounds (on a lower level) that form a ball court, the only one known at Pacbitun. The playing alley was searched for possible ball court markers, but none was found.

Pacbitun was first settled in the Middle Preclassic period around 900 B.C. It later grew and flourished until it was abandoned around A.D. 900.

Recent History

Pacbitun was known to the residents of the nearby village of San Antonio for many years, but it was brought to the attention of the Belize government only in 1971, when a new road was being constructed nearby. The site was then registered by Peter Schmidt, who at that time was the archaeological commissioner of Belize. Schmidt conducted a preliminary survey of the site but did not carry out any excavations.

In 1980, a surface survey of Pacbitun was carried out during a reconnaissance of terraced hills in western Belize. This was conducted by Paul F. Healy of Trent University (Canada) and others.

Healy returned in 1984 for a short field season during which four test pits were dug in the core area of the site. The results indicated that Pacbitun had a lengthy history. In 1986 and 1987, for four months each year, the Trent University–Pacbitun Archaeological Project conducted extensive excavations, directed by Healy. At the end of each season, consolidation of the structures was undertaken.

Several reports were issued by Healy in 1988 and 1990, including one about the musical instruments found in the two graves.

Connections

1. Cayo to Pacbitun (via San Antonio): 0.6 mile [1.0 kilometer] by paved road (:01), 11.3 miles [18.2 kilometers] by rough rock road (:37), then a few hundred feet by fair dirt track (:03). Total: 11.9 miles [19.2 kilometers] (:41).

2. Cayo to Pacbitun (via Chiquibul Road): 4.8 miles [7.7 kilometers] by paved road (:08), 9.4 miles [15.1 kilometers] by rough rock road (:39), then a few hundred feet by fair dirt track (:03). Total: 14.2 miles [22.8 kilometers] (:50).

3. Belmopan to Chiquibul Road: 18.9 miles [30.4 kilometers] by paved road (:32). Total Belmopan to Pacbitun: 23.8 miles [45.5 kilometers] (1:14).

4. Belize City to Chiquibul Road: 64.7 miles [104.1 kilometers] by paved road (1:38). Total Belize City to Pacbitun: 74.1 miles [119.2 kilometers] (2:20).

Getting There

From Cayo to Pacbitun there are two routes, the first is a little shorter.

1. Leave Cayo heading east on the Western Highway and go 0.6 mile [1.0 kilometer] past the Hawksworth Bridge to a cutoff on the right (south). This is in Santa Elena, and there is a sign at the junction marked for "Caracol." The sign faces east (for traffic heading west), so when traveling east you will have to look for it. Turn right at the junction and continue uphill a short distance to an unmarked fork in the road. Take the left branch and continue to Cristo Rey, San Antonio, and the cutoff for Pacbitun (marked with a small sign). Turn left (north) and continue to the thatch shelter at the northeast corner of Plaza A, where you can park.

2. From Cayo, head east on the Western Highway to Chiquibul Road, which joins the Western Highway just west of Georgeville. There are signs at the junction for Hidden Valley Falls and Pacbitun, but they face the other way. Turn right (south) onto Chiquibul Road and go to the cutoff for San Antonio. Turn right again and proceed to the cutoff for Pacbitun, then right again to reach the site.

3 and 4. If you are approaching from Belmopan or Belize City, the route via Chiquibul Road is the better choice. From either place, head west on the Western Highway to Chiquibul Road, then follow the directions for Connection 2.

Either route to Pacbitun will take you over rutted rock roads, and although you can make it in a standard vehicle, one with high clearance would be preferable. Having your own vehicle is the best way to reach the site. Otherwise you could hire a taxi in Cayo, but this would be rather expensive. Another possibility would be to check at Eva's Restaurant and Bar in Cayo. Trips to points of interest can be arranged there.

There is no food or drink at Pacbitun. Allow 30 minutes for a visit; try to get there in the morning when the front of Structure 2 is best lighted. Petronila Tzul and her family live near the ruins and are the guardians. She or a family member will come over once you have arrived, tell you about the site, and ask you to sign a registration book. It is not necessary (as is often stated) to stop along the road between San Antonio and the cutoff for Pacbitun at the house of Mr. Tzul (Petronila's nephew) to ask permission to visit the site, since Pacbitun now has guardians.

★ ★ ★
CARACOL
(kah-rah-KOHL)

Derivation:
Spanish for "Snail."
Location:
Southwestern part of Cayo District, Belize.
Maps: 2 (p. 56) and 2A (p. 59)

The Site

Caracol is a site that truly can be described in superlatives. Investigations over the last decade attest that Caracol was enormous; it is the largest site in Belize and one of the largest in the entire Maya area. Its core area covers 14.9 square miles [38.5 square kilometers], and greater Caracol covers 34 square miles [88.1 square kilometers]. The site's sustaining area encompassed more than 121 square miles [313.4 square kilometers].

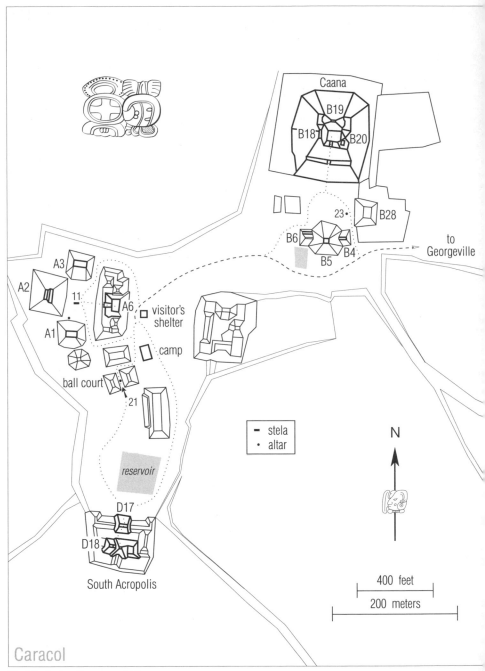

Caana

B19

B18   B20

B28

23·

B6   B4

B5

to
Georgeville

A3

A2

11·

A6   visitor's
shelter

A1

camp

ball court

21

stela
altar

N

reservoir

D17

D18

South Acropolis

400 feet

200 meters

Caracol

Modified after Chase and Chase.

The front (north side) of Structure D18, showing the entrance to a tomb, Caracol. Late Classic period.

The site had its peak between A.D. 650 and 700, in the Late Classic period. At this time, around 36,000 structures were occupied (of which more than 3,000 have been carefully recorded), and the population is estimated to have been 150,000, only slightly less than the current estimate of 200,000 for the entire country of Belize today. The tallest structure in ancient or modern Belize is Caana (Sky Place), found at Caracol; it rises 138 feet. The site also has a long occupational record, from around 300 B.C. in the Late Preclassic period to around A.D. 1150 in the Postclassic. Seven *sacbeob* are known at Caracol, five of which radiate from the center of the site; some extend more than 1.5 miles [2.4 kilometers]. The total distance known to have been covered by the various *sacbeob* was 22.4 miles [36.0 kilometers] in 1994, and more are expected to be found in the future. There are also vias (streets) at the site, some of which connect to a *sacbé*. There is more.

Many hieroglyphic texts have been found at Caracol, on stone monuments (stelae, altars, and ball court markers) and on artifacts, capstones, and wall facades. From these texts, epigraphers have been able to establish a preliminary dynastic sequence for Caracol that includes a dozen or more rulers who reigned from at least A.D. 495 through 859. The discovery of new texts and the continuing study of those already known may eventually provide information on earlier rulers. During its history, Caracol defeated Tikal and Naranjo in war events.

The epicenter of the site—which contains most of the largest structures—is what visitors to Caracol see today. As you drive to the site you will find a parking area near the archaeological camp, and nearby a thatch shelter for visitors. Across the entrance

Altar 21 (ball court marker), Caracol, commemorating Lord Water's successful war event against the ruling lineage of Tikal in A.D. 562.

road from the shelter (to the west) you will see the back of Structure A6.

From the visitor's shelter, a trail heads south to the South Acropolis. Along the way you pass one of Caracol's ancient reservoirs, used today as a water supply by the staff and workers at Caracol. At the South Acropolis there has been some consolidation of Structures D17 and D18. You climb the north side of Structure D17, over a stepped trail, to a single long narrow room on top. There are low benches on each end of the room (east and west), and central doorways on the north and south sides. From here there are good views of Structure D18 just to the south. You then climb down the south side of Structure D17 to a courtyard and up the north side of D18. The upper level of the structure appears today as two buildings with a passageway between them; they share a single pyramidal base. Two tombs can be visited, one in each of the upper structures. The tomb on the east has a

bench that can be photographed, as light comes in from the top. Part of the vault near the entrance to the tomb is intact. Two interments were found on the bench, and the accompanying grave goods date the burial to the early part of the Late Classic period.

You now return the way you came, to the north side of Structure D17, and take another trail to the Group A ball court. The most interesting feature here is not the two unconsolidated mounds that form the court but a central, circular ball court marker called Altar 21. Although broken and partly eroded, it is an extremely important monument; it was discovered in 1986 and records, among other things, that in A.D. 562, Caracol's Ruler III (Lord Water) conducted a successful war event against the ruling lineage of Tikal. The ball court marker is protected by a thatch shelter; this is a good spot to try off-camera flash. From here you return to the visitor's shelter and lunch break.

Structure A3, on the north side of the plaza in A Group, Caracol, view from the southeast. Late Classic period.

After lunch, again follow the trail a short distance to the south, then turn west and then northwest and enter the Main Plaza of Group A. The structures around this plaza are some of the largest at Caracol, and early on this area was recognized as being very important. Some of the structures have been systematically investigated.

The plaza is surrounded by Structures A1 through A8. Structure A3, at the north end of the plaza, and A6, one of five on the east side of the plaza, have been partly consolidated. Structure A2, on the west side of the plaza, rises 66 feet above plaza level. When the top of the structure was investigated, Stela 22 (A.D. 633), with a hieroglyphic text composed of 140 glyph blocks, was discovered; it is the longest hieroglyphic text in Belize. The stela is still in place atop Structure A2.

Structure A3 rises 52 feet above plaza level, and a stepped-stone path leads to the top. The summit structure has two rooms, one behind the other, with a single central doorway connecting the two through the medial wall. The front room had three doorways. A burial in a chamber with capstones was excavated beneath a bench in the front room of the building. A single skeleton was found accompanied by 18 pounds of obsidian and 88 pounds of chert; eight Late Classic ceramic vessels were also found. One of the capstones of the tomb was painted with six glyphs and carried a calendar round date, tentatively placed at A.D. 696. The last glyph is the Caracol Emblem Glyph, which suggests that the interred was a member of the ruling lineage of Caracol.

Structure A6 stands in the center of a huge platform that borders the east side of the plaza; it is the tallest in the group of five

The rear (east side) of Structure A6, Caracol. Late Classic period.

buildings. Below Structure A6 are earlier constructions, and the whole was in use for more than a thousand years. The earliest construction dates to A.D. 70 and the latest to 1100. During excavation, caches containing exotic goods were discovered; one included 0.24 cubic inches (4 cubic centimeters) of mercury. On top of Structure A6 there is a single range of three rooms and a single exterior doorway facing east onto the plaza. This structure is also known as the Temple of the Wooden Lintel, for one found in the building. From plaza level a path leads part way up the base of the structure; from there the upper stairway has been consolidated and gives access to the building on top.

There are a number of altars and stelae in the plaza, but most are fairly eroded. The most interesting are a giant ahau altar (at the south end of the plaza) and Stela 11 (in the center of the plaza). The stela depicts a principal standing figure (holding a ceremonial bar) accompanied by a dwarf near his feet. The stela dates to A.D. 800.

You leave the plaza at its northeast corner, loop to the south, and connect with the entrance road. From there you follow the road in an easterly direction and pick up a trail that enters the Main Plaza of Group B at its southeast corner. When you turn left and enter the plaza, you will be facing the breathtaking Caana, the most impressive structure at Caracol. On your way to Caana, stop for a look at Altar 23, which lies on the east side of the plaza in front of Structure B28.

Altar 23, one of the largest at Caracol, is fairly well preserved. It depicts two bound and seated captives facing each other; there is a panel of glyphs between the figures and other glyphs at the side of each figure. The two individuals are named in the glyphic text, which further states that the one on the right (as you face the altar) is a divine lord from the polity of Ucanal (in today's Guatemala and about 16.2 miles [26.0 kilometers] from Caracol). The prisoner on the left is also a lord, from a polity so far unidentified. The altar commemorates the capture of the two lords, and it was installed

Altar 23, showing two bound lords, Caracol. A.D. 800.

by Hok' K'awil, one of Caracol's important rulers. The altar was discovered in 1989 and dates to A.D. 800.

Now proceed to Caana. This massive pyramid has three more pyramids—of quite respectable size—rising from its summit and bordering three sides of a summit plaza. Structure B18 is on the west, B20 is on the east, and the tallest, B19, is in the center and to the north. Only the top parts of two of these (B18 and B20) are visible from ground level. All three structures are being excavated. Along the south face of Caana are two levels with ranges of rooms spanning the width of the structure. Both are divided by the central stairway (partly consolidated) that ascends Caana on the south side. One range of rooms is about midway up the pyramidal base of Caana; the other is at the summit. The stairway flattens as it goes through each of the ranges of rooms,

and evidence indicates that these flattened areas were once covered with vaulted passageways. Both ranges of rooms were originally vaulted and contained benches.

Excavations in the summit structures and below the surface of the summit plaza have uncovered stone masks, stucco decorations (both in place and fallen), earlier structures, painted capstones, and rich tombs, as well as a carved circular ahau altar. The final phase of Caana dates to the Late Classic period, but Early Classic structures lie buried below. A late addition on the top of Caana was a crude wall and associated broken censers. Carbon from the censers gave a mean radiocarbon date of A.D. 1175 ± 120, the latest documented date at the summit of Caana.

Directly opposite Caana, and bordering the south side of the Main Plaza in Group B, are Structures B4 (on the east), B5 (in the

The front (south side) of Caana, the tallest structure in ancient or modern Belize, Caracol. Late Classic period.

center), and B6 (on the west). Structure B5 is the tallest of the group and is unconsolidated. The flanking wings have been consolidated (B6) or partly consolidated (B4). Structure B6 consists of a two-room building fronted on the north (plaza side) with a broad stairway of a few steps. The latest use of this structure was in the Terminal Classic period, as shown by recovered ceramics and radiocarbon dating. You can climb the central Structure B5 for a good head-on view of Caana; from this vantage point you can see all three of Caana's upper pyramids.

Recent History

Caracol was discovered in 1937 by Rosa Mai, a logger looking for mahogany. Later that year the existence of the site was reported to the government of Belize (then British Honduras). In 1938, A. H. Anderson, then archaeological commissioner of Belize, visited Caracol for two weeks. It was he who named the site Caracol because of its winding access road. (Another theory holds that the site was named Caracol because of the many snails found there.) During his stay, Anderson recorded information on most of the structures around the Main Plaza in Group A and on nine monuments. His excavations were limited; he and Mai exposed the intact wooden lintel in Structure A6, and Anderson dug near Stelae 13 and 14 in front of Structure A4, where he found censer fragments.

Linton Satterthwaite of the University Museum, University of Pennsylvania, investigated Caracol in 1950, 1951, and 1953. He was accompanied by Anderson for all three seasons. During these field seasons, mapping was done, some excavations were undertaken, and some of the stelae and altars were removed from the site. Some were sent to the University Museum while others were removed to the Bliss Institute in Belize City, where they can be seen today. The monuments remaining at Caracol were recorded. Some of Satterthwaite's work was published in 1951 and 1954, but he died before completing the volume on Caracol's monuments. Carl Beetz finished this volume and it was published in 1981, co-authored by the two men.

Anderson returned to Caracol in 1954, 1956, and 1958. Among other things, he cleared the summits of Structures D17 and D18 in the South Acropolis and excavated one of the tombs in D18. Some of Anderson's work was published in 1958 and 1959. Unfortunately, his notes were mostly destroyed in 1961 when Hurricane Hattie hit Belize City, so there has been no complete publication of his investigations.

In part of his study of Maya agricultural practices, Paul F. Healy of Trent University in Canada investigated the core area of Caracol. He recorded extensive terrace systems and a high settlement density. His work appeared in the early 1980s.

In 1985, the Caracol Project began (after two short earlier visits to study the feasibility of working at the site and to do some reconnaissance). This ongoing and extensive project is directed by Diane Z. and Arlen F. Chase of the University of Central Florida. An incredible amount of information has been recorded during the project, far too much to list here. It may be said, however, that all of the clearing seen at Caracol, as well as the consolidation of the structures, were accomplishments of the Caracol Project. Funding came from private donations, the government of Belize, the United States Agency for International Development, the National Science Foundation, and the Harry Frank Guggenheim Foundation.

Three important monographs concerning Caracol have been published by the Pre-Columbian Art Research Institute. Monograph 3, *Investigations at the Classic Maya City of Caracol, Belize: 1985–1987*, appeared in 1987; it was authored by the Chases. In 1994, they edited Monograph 7, *Studies in the Archaeology of Caracol, Belize*, which included studies by a number of scholars. Monograph 8 was released in 1996. It is titled *Investigations at Caracol, Belize: 1988–1993* and was written by the Chases. Other papers on specific subjects dealing with Caracol have appeared elsewhere.

Connections

1. Cayo to Caracol (via Chiquibul Road): 4.8 miles [7.7 kilometers] by paved road to Chiquibul Road (:08), 8.2 miles [13.2 kilometers] by rough rock road (:35), then 40.2 miles [64.7 kilometers] by good rock road (1:35). Total: 53.2 miles [85.6 kilometers] (2:18).

2. Belmopan to Chiquibul Road: 18.9 miles [30.4 kilometers] by paved road (:32). Total

Belmopan to Caracol: 67.3 miles [108.3 kilometers] (2:42).

3. Belize City to Chiquibul Road: 64.7 miles [104.1 kilometers] by paved road (1:38). Total Belize City to Caracol: 113.1 miles [182.0 kilometers] (3:48).

Getting There

To visit Caracol you *must* get a permit from the Department of Archaeology in Belmopan or the Forestry Station in Douglas di'Silva. In the future Caracol may become an open site, but until then, a permit is required. I recommend that you get your permit in Belmopan where you can learn the condition of the road from the Western Highway to the site and whether it is open all the way; this is important, especially in the rainy season.

1. From Cayo, head east on the Western Highway to Chiquibul Road (at the western edge of Georgeville) and turn right (south). There are signs at the junction for Hidden Valley Falls and Pacbitun, but they face the other way. The part of Chiquibul road from the highway to the junction with the road to San Antonio is rutted and rough (8.2 miles [13.2 kilometers]). Go straight ahead at this junction—from there to Caracol the road is better. Shortly after this junction you come to a gate where you stop and register.

From there, go on to Douglas di'Silva (formerly Augustine). You take a left turn as you enter, and soon you will come to the Forestry Station, where you must get your permit signed or pick one up. Then go straight ahead to leave (heading south), and follow the road to the epicenter of Caracol, where you will be asked to relinquish your permit.

There are several cutoffs along the way after you pass the one for San Antonio, not all of which are marked. If you take what looks like the best road you will do all right. At some of the junctions there are signs for Caracol—reassuring. Between Douglas di'Silva and Caracol, you cross the Macal River on a low, cement, one-lane bridge.

This is where the water-tank truck fills up to help supply Caracol during dry spells. If it is filling up when you arrive, you will have to wait for it to finish and leave. There is no way to pass it.

Another route from Cayo to Caracol is the San Antonio Road to Chiquibul road. It is about the same distance and will take about the same time. The difference is that on this route you go over a rough rock road for a longer distance and a paved road for a much shorter distance. I prefer the first route.

2 and 3. From Belmopan or Belize City, head west on the Western Highway to Chiquibul road, turn left and follow the directions for Connection 1.

Other stopovers closer to Caracol are lodges on Chiquibul Road that you will pass along the way to the site. Mountain Equestrian Trails is on the east side of the road and a short distance from it. Blancaneaux Lodge is farther along on the west side of the road. Farther yet is a cutoff on the east for Hidden Valley Falls; partway there you will find Hidden Valley Inn. Last is Pine Ridge Lodge on the west side of the road; it is the closest to Caracol. The lodges and the cutoff for Hidden Valley Falls are marked with signs.

When it is dry, you can reach Caracol in a standard vehicle—if you drive the rutted part very slowly—although a high-clearance vehicle would be better. If your vehicle is air-conditioned, you will be able to keep the windows closed, which will be a plus because the rock road will be dusty. In wet weather you may need four-wheel drive.

If you are without a vehicle or would prefer having someone take you to Caracol, ask at Eva's Restaurant and Bar in Cayo. There is a sign posted indicating that they can arrange trips to Caracol. If you have a party of four (or more) it is not prohibitively expensive. You could also check with travel agencies and hotels in Cayo, Belmopan, or Belize City for conducted tours, or ask at the lodges mentioned earlier. Prices for tours and transportation are reportedly quite variable.

Whichever way you plan to reach Caracol, you *must* provide your own food and drink (including water). Nothing is available at the site. You must also be sure you have enough gasoline to get there and back. There is no gasoline available once you leave the Western Highway. Visitors are not allowed to stay overnight at Caracol. Camping is allowed at Douglas di'Silva if you get prior permission from the Forestry Department.

The best time to visit Caracol is in the early part of the year, February through May, with March or April being the best. The roads are more likely to be dry at that time.

Allow four hours to visit Caracol; this will allow time for a lunch break. If possible, bring along an ice chest with water and cold drinks. There is a good ice house in Santa Elena, 0.5 mile [0.8 kilometer] east of the Hawksworth Bridge, on the south side of the Western Highway, where you can fill it.

Visiting Caracol is an interesting experience, although it is a long and rather tiring trip of at least 8.5 hours. If you have enough stamina, you could make a side trip to see Pacbitun as well. This would add another 44 minutes to the trip (to get there, visit, and return to Chiquibul Road). It would be best to do this on your return from Caracol; concentrate your efforts on reaching Caracol in the morning. When you are returning from Caracol and reach the cutoff for San Antonio, turn left and go to the cutoff for Pacbitun. See "Pacbitun" for details.

There are three other attractions along the road to Caracol. One, Hidden Valley Falls, is on a spur road off Chiquibul Road. The others are the Río On Pools and the Río Frío Caves (near Douglas di'Silva). All sound interesting but would best be left for another trip. There would not be enough time to combine them with a trip to Caracol in a single day.

SECTION 3

• • • •

SOUTHERN BELIZE

North side of Stela 18, Uxbenka. Early Classic period.

GENERAL INFORMATION FOR SECTION 3, SOUTHERN BELIZE

When visiting the archaeological sites in southern Belize, the stopovers are hotels in Punta Gorda, where there are also restaurants, and Bol's Hilltop Hotel (the only hotel) in San Antonio. The latter is the most convenient.

The rooms at Bol's are small—with shared baths—but the place has a certain charm and the management is accommodating. The hotel will serve meals if you ask ahead of time. There is also a separate two-room unit behind the hotel that rents by the month. When it is unoccupied, you can negotiate with the owner for its rental for a night or two. This unit has lots more space and cross ventilation, which the other rooms do not. It also has a private detached bath. The unit is sparsely furnished, but if you are prepared to sling your hammock, I think you will find staying there an interesting experience.

Other places to eat in southern Belize are Roy's, along the road to San Antonio, at the junction with the road to Blue Creek, and a restaurant next to (north of) the Shell gasoline station at the junction of the Southern Highway and the road to San Antonio.

The Southern Highway starts at the Hummingbird Highway, 5.5 miles [8.9 kilometers] east of Dangriga, and continues south for 84.9 miles [136.6 kilometers] to a junction with the road to San Antonio (where there is the aforementioned Shell station). From there the Southern Highway heads southeast and continues for 13.0 miles [20.9 kilometers] to Punta Gorda, where it ends.

The Southern Highway is a rock and dirt road that can be poor in the rainy season, though it is usually kept passable. The rock and dirt road that goes to San Antonio is narrower than the Southern Highway, but its condition is similar.

Distances and driving times in southern Belize are from the following reference points: (1) in Punta Gorda, there is no *exact* reference point; I have not driven the part of the Southern Highway from the junction with the San Antonio road to Punta Gorda, but the distances shown on Maps 3 and 3A should be fairly accurate; (2) in San Antonio, the town church, along the main road and across the road from Bol's Hilltop Hotel.

There is a tour operator in Punta Gorda, and one can get flights from there connecting with Belize City.

The only place in Belize where I have seen anything like a traditional costume was in Toledo District, primarily in San Antonio. It is worn by the older Maya women and includes an ankle-length full skirt and an unusual blouse, wide at the bottom, with a hand-embroidered band at the top. The women of San Antonio are noted for their embroidery, and you will have ample opportunities to buy some, including the blouses and small, colorful Maya calendar wall hangings. The women of the village also make and sell small baskets that are finely and tightly woven. If you stay in San Antonio, they will find you to offer their wares.

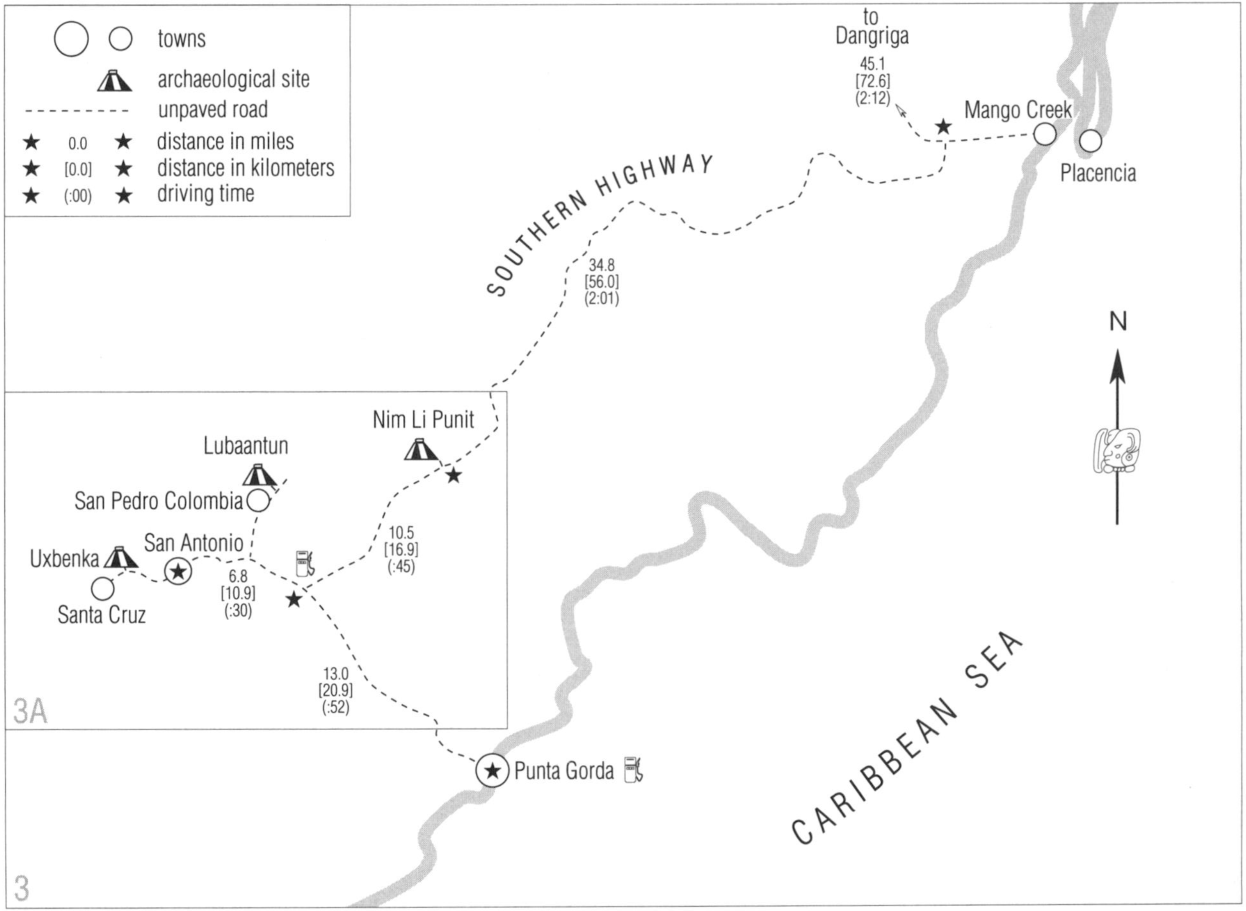

Legend

○ ○	towns
⬛▲	archaeological site
- - -	unpaved road
0.0	distance in miles
[0.0]	distance in kilometers
(:00)	driving time
★	
★★	
★	

N ←

to
Dangriga
45.1
[72.6]
(2:12)

Placencia

Mango Creek

SOUTHERN HIGHWAY

34.8
[56.0]
(2:01)

Nim Li Punit

Lubaantun

San Pedro Colombia

San Antonio

Uxbenka

Santa Cruz

10.5
[16.9]
(:45)

13.0
[20.9]
(:52)

6.8
[10.9]
(:30)

Punta Gorda

CARIBBEAN SEA

3A

3

Southern Belize

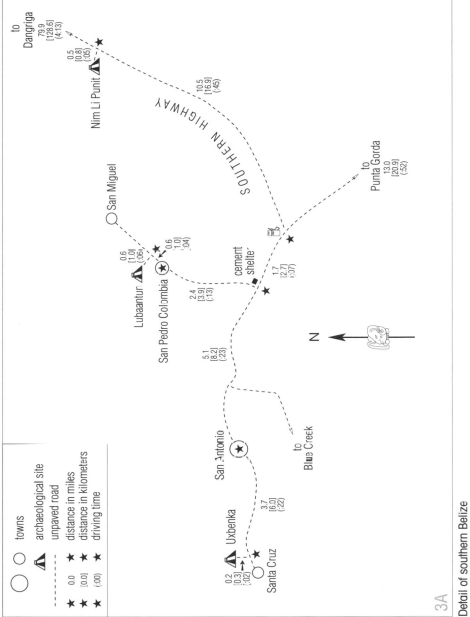

○ ◯ towns

◮ archaeological site

- - - - - unpaved road

★ ★ ★	distance in miles
★ ★ ★	distance in kilometers
★ ★ ★	driving time

★	0.0
★	[0.0]
★	(:00)

to
Dangriga
79.9
[128.6]
(4:13)

0.5
[0.8]
(:05)

Nim Li Punit ◮ ★

10.5
[16.9]
(:45)

○ San Miguel

SOUTHERN HIGHWAY

Lubaantun ◮ ★ 0.6
[1.0]
(:06)

0.6
[1.0]
(:04)

San Pedro Colombia ⊛

2.4
[3.9]
(:13)

cement shelter ■

1.7
[2.7]
(:07)

★

to
Punta Gorda
13.0
[20.9]
(:52)

5.1
[8.2]
(:23)

N

San Antonio ⊛

to
Blue Creek

3.7
[6.0]
(:22)

Uxbenka ◮ ★

0.2
[0.3]
(:02)

Santa Cruz ○

3A

Detail of southern Belize

★ ★
NIM LI PUNIT
(NEEM LEE poo-NEET)

Derivation:
Kekchi Maya for "Big Hat."
Location:
Central part of Toledo District,
Belize.
Maps: 3 (p. 88) and 3A (p. 89)

The Site

Nim Li Punit is a minor ceremonial center lying on a ridge in the foothills of the Maya Mountains. It is made up of three groups (East, West, and South), but only the South Group is open to visitors; this is the most interesting group by far. The plaza of the South Group is well cleared and easy to get around, but the structures surrounding it have been only partially cleared.

From the parking area, follow a clear trail to the west and then to the south. The trail goes through an unrestored ball court (the only one known at the site), where an uncarved circular stone center marker is in place. Continue south to the plaza of the South Group and register at the large thatch shelter.

Nim Li Punit is known for its stelae; 25 have been found at the site, of which at least six are carved. The two most impressive are under the large thatch shelter, lying on their backs. Stela 14 is 31 feet long, including its uncarved butt (it is one of the tallest known Maya stelae), and is very narrow. It is fairly well preserved and depicts a single, richly garbed figure in the middle, with panels of glyphs above and below. It dates to A.D. 790 but was never erected. One theory holds that this was because the sculptor made an error in carving the glyphs, so that the time cycles did not correlate correctly. The elaborate headdress worn by the figure is the "Big Hat" that gives the site its name.

Nearby is Stela 15, which dates to A.D. 721, the earliest date known from Nim Li

Punit. A principal figure and two subsidiary figures are represented; they are almost totally surrounded by glyphs. This stela is also fairly well preserved.

The other stelae are mostly along the periphery of the plaza of the South Group, and those that are carved have their own thatch shelters. The most notable are Stela 1 (A.D. 741), with two rather eroded figures, a mask panel below, and glyphs above, and Stela 2, broken and partly defaced. Three figures are represented on Stela 2, and below is a profile mask panel. As you tour the plaza you will see two other carved but eroded stelae.

In the northwest corner of the plaza, resting in a sort of pit a little below present ground level, is a large rectangular stone slab; it is carved with a single ahau glyph and the numeral eight near one end. From there a short climb to the north will get you to an excavated royal tomb. The tomb was used several times, and the remains of five individuals have been identified. Grave goods included carved jade pendants, incised bone, jaguar teeth, and remains of 40 ceramic vessels. What you see today is simply a stone-lined crypt set into the ground.

The architecture at Nim Li Punit has not been consolidated but it is the same type of cut slab construction at that seen at Lubaantun. The tallest structure at Nim Li Punit is on the west side of the plaza; it rises about 40 feet above plaza level and has a stairway on the east (plaza) side.

The site was occupied during the Late Classic period, the same time as was Lubaantun, and the Nim Li Punit stelae date from A.D. 721 to 790 or 800. They are made of local sandstone, a material also used in the construction of the buildings. At its peak Nim Li Punit had a population of 5,000 to 8,000. The South Group was the site's ceremonial precinct; the East and West groups were used for civic purposes and as elite residences.

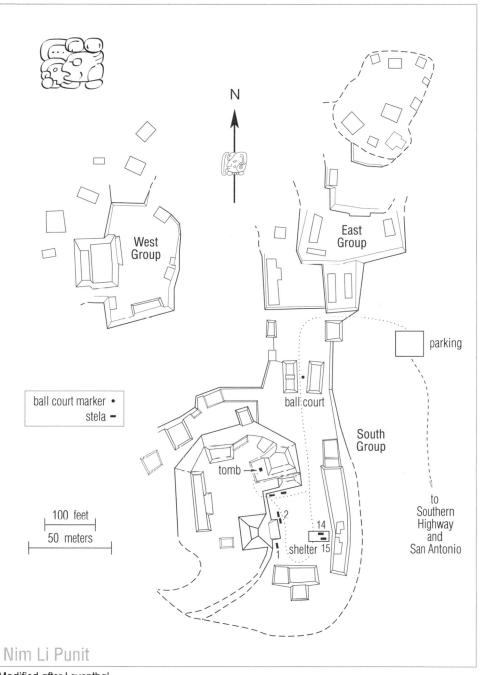

N

West Group

East Group

parking

ball court marker •
stela —

ball court

South Group

tomb

to Southern Highway and San Antonio

100 feet
50 meters

2

14

1   shelter 15

Nim Li Punit

Modified after Leventhal.

The principal figure on Stela 15, Nim Li Punit. A.D. 721.

Recent History

Nim Li Punit was accidentally discovered in 1976 by oil company workers who, while bulldozing a trail, cut into a peripheral mound. The existence of the site was reported to the Department of Archaeology of Belize, and Joseph O. Palacio, then Archaeological Commissioner, dispatched staff member Jaime J. Awe to conduct a reconnaissance. Shortly afterward, Norman Hammond, who had been working in northern Belize, conducted a three-day investigation of what is now called the plaza of the South Group. At Palacio's request, Hammond prepared a preliminary map, did a couple of test excavations in the plaza, and turned several monuments to examine the carvings.

In 1981, L. J. Jackson and Heather McKillop visited the site and found evidence of defacement of some of the stelae—principally Stela 2—and a looter's pit. They inventoried the damage and alerted the Department of Archaeology.

In 1983, the Southern Belize Archaeological Project began under the direction of Richard Leventhal; it continued for several years. During this work, test pits were excavated and the elite tomb was discovered, as were the East and West groups. The site was also mapped.

Connections

1. San Antonio to Nim Li Punit: 17.3 miles [27.8 kilometers] by rock and dirt roads (1:15), then 0.5 mile [0.8 kilometer] by rough track (:05).

2. Punta Gorda to Nim Li Punit: 23.5 miles [37.8 kilometers] by rock and dirt roads (1:37), then 0.5 mile [0.8 kilometer] by rough track. (:05).

3. Dangriga to Nim Li Punit: 5.5 miles [8.9 kilometers] by paved but poor road (:18), 74.4 miles [119.7 kilometers] by rock and dirt roads (3:55), then 0.5 mile [0.8 kilometer] by rough track (:05). Total: 80.4 miles [129.4 kilometers] (4:18).

4. Belize City to Dangriga via the Hummingbird Highway: 104.0 miles [167.5 kilometers] by paved road (some poor) (3:54). Total Belize City to Nim Li Punit (with a stop at Dangriga): 184.4 miles [296.9 kilometers] (8:12). Total Belize City to Nim Li Punit (direct): 173.4 miles [279.1 kilometers] (7:36).

Getting There

1. From San Antonio, head east for 6.8 miles [10.9 kilometers] to the Shell station at the junction with the Southern Highway. From there head north along the Southern Highway for 10.5 miles [16.9 kilometers] to the cutoff for Nim Li Punit, which is marked with a small sign indicating that it is 0.75 mile [1.2 kilometers] to the site. Happily, it is only 0.5 mile [0.8 kilometer]. Turn

left (west) and continue—slowly—to the parking area. This last stretch is rough and you should have a high-clearance vehicle to drive it. The road first goes up, then descends and curves to the left, and then climbs again to the parking area. From there it is about a three-minute walk, with a slight climb, to the site.

2. From Punta Gord,a head west for 13 miles [20.9 kilometers] to the junction with the San Antonio road (Shell station) and follow the directions just given.

3. From Dangriga, head west on the Hummingbird Highway to the junction with the Southern Highway. Turn left (south) and follow the Southern Highway to the cutoff for Nim Li Punit. Turn right (west) and proceed to the parking area.

4. From Belize City, head west on the Western Highway to its junction with the Hummingbird Highway. Turn left at the Hummingbird Highway and follow it to Dangriga.

The large thatch shelter is the only facility at the site; there is no food, drink, or rest room. When we registered we asked the caretaker if the use of flash was permitted to photograph the two stelae sheltered there. After a pause he said, "No." Perhaps this was the first time the question had been posed. There was no sign indicating that flash was prohibited.

Allow one hour to visit Nim Li Punit.

There is no direct public access to the site, but buses pass the cutoff going between Belize City (and Dangriga) to Punta Gorda. If you plan to walk from the cutoff to the site, carry a canteen of water. If you are not driving your own vehicle, you can reach the site from Punta Gorda in a rental vehicle or with a hired vehicle and driver.

★ ★ ★

LUBAANTUN

(loo-bah-ahn-TOON)

Derivation:
 Yucatec Maya for "Place of Fallen Stones."
Earlier name:
 Río Grande, a name used until 1924.
Location:
 Central part of Toledo District, Belize.
Maps: 3 (p. 88) and 3A (p. 89)

The Site

Famous since the early twentieth century, Lubaantun is one of the largest sites in southern Belize. Its ceremonial precincts cover almost 15 acres [0.06 square kilometer] and are surrounded by a settled area of 1.2 square miles [3.1 square kilometers]. The site lies on top of a ridge above the Colombia River (on the south) and small tributary streams (on the east and west). Lubaantun is composed of architectural remains surrounding 18 plazas. The five main plazas are arranged along a north-south axis and are numbered from the south (Plaza I) to the north (Plaza V). The structures at Lubaantun are mostly stone platform-pyramids—some of which are enormous—that originally were topped with perishable structures. This style of architecture is also found at the nearby sites of Nim Li Punit and Uxbenka, but it is unusual in the corpus of Classic Maya construction, in which vaulted masonry superstructures are more common. There are two ball courts at Lubaantun and huge stone retaining walls that form terraces around the site.

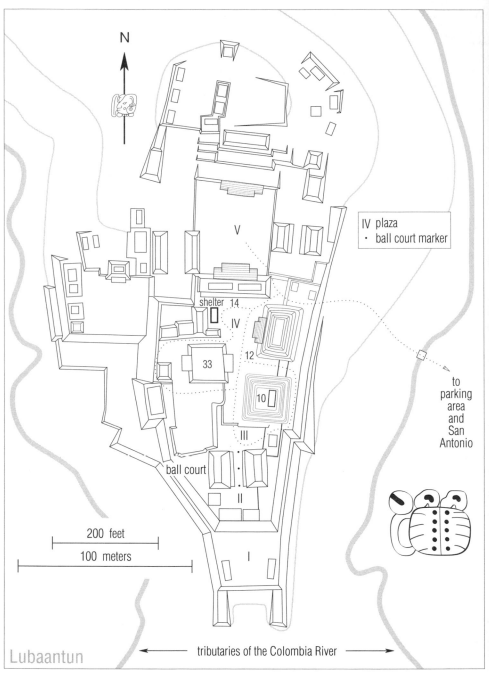

N

IV plaza
· ball court marker

V

shelter 14

IV

33

12

10

III

II

ball court

·

I

200 feet

100 meters

to
parking
area
and
San
Antonio

Lubaantun

tributaries of the Colombia River

Modified after Hammond.

The front (west side) of Structure 12, Lubaantun. Late Classic period.

In the site's early history, construction was of trimmed but undressed stone. Later, a finer-quality stone was used that was superbly worked into large slabs, set without the use of mortar. Both styles of construction can be seen at the site today.

Another unusual feature is the lack of stelae at Lubaantun. This is surprising considering the size and obvious importance of the site. The only carvings known from Lubaantun are three fairly eroded ball court alley markers (discovered in 1915 and moved to the Peabody Museum of Harvard University) and two semihuman faces carved in relief on wall blocks (also removed from the site). But while there is no fine sculpture or architectural detail at Lubaantun, the sheer massiveness of the structures is impressive and makes a visit worthwhile.

From the parking area for Lubaantun you can see some of the monumental constructions across the tributary stream. Head downhill to the stream and walk across a ce-

ment foot bridge, then climb to the site following a stepped foot trail to Plaza IV and a thatch shelter where you register.

The cleared area of the site extends from Plaza V on the north to Plaza III on the south and also includes some areas to the west of Plaza IV. Structure 14 borders both the north side of Plaza IV and the south side of the sunken Plaza V, to which a monumental stairway descends. It is worth climbing down to Plaza V to photograph the stairway. There is another stairway on the north end of Plaza V, and beyond are some ceremonial and residential structures that are not cleared. Return now to Plaza IV, the core of the site in terms of its growth, and probably its religious core as well. The three major religious structures (and the largest buildings at the site) surround Plaza IV, with Structures 12 and 10 on the east and Structure 33 on the west.

Structure 12 is 31 feet tall and has a stairway on the west side, facing the plaza.

The east facade of Structure 33, Lubaantun, showing two stages of construction. Late Classic period.

The corners of the structure are rounded, but the unevenness of the courses of stone, best observed along the front (west side), is due to uneven settling of the structure. This is seen in other buildings at the site as well.

Structure 33 is a little over 17 feet tall; it lies to the southwest of Structure 12, and two building phases can be seen at once, thanks to excavation. The earlier phase is the inner east wall; the outer section was built later.

To the southeast of Structure 33 is Structure 10, the largest at Lubaantun. It is 33 feet tall and has a basal area of over 8,000 square feet. It also has rounded corners and rises in several tiers; its plan is square.

By continuing south you come to the southern ball court, where the carved center markers were found. Today the ball court appears as two grass-covered mounds

on either side of a grassy playing alley. There is very little clearing south of the ball court.

From the ball court head north, then west, then north again, and finally east; this will bring you back to the north part of Plaza IV, where you started. Along this circuit you will see smaller but interesting residential and ceremonial structures, some of which rise in small steps. Other remains are stairs ascending platforms. As you near the end of the circuit, you will pass a wall (on your right) that is a good place to observe the finely cut stone for which Lubaantun is noted. You will also see L-shaped and T-shaped stones that interlock to provide structural stability.

Many of Lubaantun's structures were successively rebuilt over time, even though the site was occupied only during the Late

Detail of the rounded southwest corner of Structure 10, Lubaantun. Late Classic period.

Classic period, from no earlier than A.D. 700 to no later than 900, and probably only from 730 to 860. This is an extremely short time span for a major Classic Maya center; many were occupied for 1,500 years or more.

Many delightful mold-made clay whistle figurines have been excavated at Lubaantun. They depict the Manche Chol Mayas who founded the site and show people engaged in activities from playing ball to grinding corn.

Recent History

Lubaantun was discovered around 1875 by residents of the old Toledo settlement near Punta Gorda. The first study of the site was undertaken in 1903 by Thomas Gann, the colony's medical officer, who was sent there to investigate. He explored the area around Plaza IV, drew a sketch plan, and submitted a report to the governor.

Gann's account came to the attention of Raymond E. Merwin, who, in 1915, visited Lubaantun (called Río Grande at the time) for the Peabody Museum. Merwin excavated in the southern ball court and discovered the three carved markers.

In 1924, Gann returned to the site with Frederick A. Mitchell-Hedges and Lady Richmond Brown, and they cleared and photographed the central part of the site. It was at this time that the site was named Lubaantun. The three returned the following year and carried out some excavations, and Gann drew an expanded plan of the site.

In 1926, Thomas A. Joyce, whose interest was aroused by Gann's work, led the first British Museum expedition to British

Detail of some finely cut and fitted stones, laid without the use of mortar, Lubaantun. Late Classic period.

Honduras (Belize), during which he investigated Lubaantun. He mapped the site and made a number of excavations. In the same year (or in 1927, according to some accounts) Mitchell-Hedges was at Lubaantun with his adopted daughter, Anna, who, on her seventeenth birthday, discovered a rock crystal skull. Three months later the lower jaw of the skull was found a short distance away. It has been determined that the skull and jaw were carved from the same piece of rock crystal and that the jaw was later detached.

The skull has been the object of a good deal of controversy; one theory holds that Mitchell-Hedges may have deliberately planted the skull for his daughter to find. The skull was first publicly displayed in 1972 and 1973 at the Museum of the American Indian, Heye Foundation. The date of the skull is unknown. For more on this in-

famous skull, see *Pursuit of the Ancient Maya,* by Richard Brunhouse.

On the next British Museum expedition (1927), Sir J. Eric S. Thompson and J. Cooper Clark joined the staff, and both excavated in various parts of the site. Burials containing worked jade, eccentric flints, and figurine fragments were found. During this season Thompson discovered the site of Pusilha, southwest of Lubaantun and near the Guatemalan border. The three following British Museum expeditions concentrated on Pusilha and the surrounding area.

In 1970, major excavations were undertaken at Lubaantun by Norman Hammond and his staff. The fieldwork was funded by the British Academy, the British Museum, the University Museum of Archaeology and Ethnology at Cambridge, the Peabody Museum, the Pitt-Rivers Museum at Oxford University, and the Wenner-

Gren Foundation for Anthropological Research.

In 1971, Hammond concentrated on locating and relocating sites in southern Toledo District, and his findings from both field seasons were published by the Peabody Museum in 1975 under the title *Lubaantun: A Classic Maya Realm.* His work has greatly expanded our knowledge of Lubaantun.

Connections

1. San Antonio to Lubaantun: 8.7 miles [14.1 kilometers] by rock and dirt roads (:46), then a few hundred feet by foot trail (:05).

2. Punta Gorda to Lubaantun: 18.3 miles [29.5 kilometers] by rock and dirt roads (1:22), then a few hundred feet by foot trail (:05).

3. Dangriga to Lubaantun: 5.5 miles [8.9 kilometers] by paved but poor road (:18), 90.2 miles [145.2 kilometers] by rock and dirt roads (5:10), then a few hundred feet by foot trail (:05). Total: 95.7 miles [154.1 kilometers] (5:33).

4. Belize City to Dangriga: See that connection under "Nim Li Punit." Total Belize City to Lubaantun (with a stop at Dangriga): 199.7 miles [321.6 kilometers] (9:27). Total Belize City to Lubaantun (direct): 188.7 miles [303.7 kilometers] (8:51).

Getting There

1. From San Antonio, head east for 5.1 miles [8.2 kilometers] to the junction for San Pedro Colombia. There is no sign at the junction but there is a small cement shelter—apparently for passengers waiting for buses. Turn left (north) at the junction and go 2.4 miles [3.9 kilometers] to the San Pedro Colombia church (on your left). Just past the church the road forks (and is unmarked); take the right branch and go 0.6 mile [1.0 kilometer] to the cutoff for Lubaantun (marked with a small sign) and turn left. From there it is 0.6 mile [1.0 kilometer] to the parking area for the site.

2. From Punta Gorda, head northwest for 14.7 miles [23.6 kilometers] to the junction for San Pedro Colombia. Turn right (north) and follow the directions for Connection 1.

3. From Dangriga, head west on the Hummingbird Highway to its junction with the Southern Highway. Turn left (south) and continue to the junction with the road to San Antonio. Turn right and go 1.7 miles [2.7 kilometers] to the junction for San Pedro Colombia. Turn right (north) and follow the directions for Connection 1.

4. See "Getting There" under "Nim Li Punit."

Allow 1.5 hours to visit Lubaantun. There is no food or drink at the site, but cold drinks are available at some small stores in San Pedro Colombia that you will pass along the way to the cutoff for Lubaantun. At the time of our visit there were no rest rooms at the site, although there were plans for installing them.

Lubaantun is open from 8:00 A.M. to 5:00 P.M. daily, and you can reach it without a guide. If you prefer having someone along, ask at Bol's Hilltop Hotel in San Antonio or check with your hotel in Punta Gorda or Dangriga. You could also ask around in San Pedro Colombia. The affable caretaker of Lubaantun will be happy to show you around the site, and you will see more with him along. He will also be happy to sell you a copy of a Lubaantun whistle figurine.

Buses traveling between Punta Gorda and San Antonio pass the junction for San Pedro Colombia but do not run to the village itself. Vehicles or vehicles with drivers can be hired in Punta Gorda to reach the site.

★ ★
UXBENKA
(oosh-behn-KAH)

Derivation:
Mopan Maya for "Old Village,"
"Old Place," or "Ancient Place."
Location:
West-central part of Toledo
District, Belize.
Maps: 3 (p. 88) and 3A (p. 89)

The Site

Uxbenka is a small ceremonial center set on top of a knoll, the southern side of which was shaped, terraced, and faced with cut stone in ancient Maya times. Twenty-two stelae have been discovered at the site, at least seven of which are carved. Most are found in the plaza on the flat top of the knoll; two others you will see on the way up.

You park near the base of the knoll, and nearby you will see Stela 19. The stela is all glyphic and dates to A.D. 780; it is somewhat eroded and has some missing edges. From here you climb the south face of the knoll to a medial terrace, where you will find Stela 18. It is badly fragmented, but a portion of the middle section is well preserved. It depicts the head and upper torso of a figure holding a ceremonial bar. The curled position of the right hand and the nose bead indicate that the carving is of

The middle fragment of Stela 18, north side, Uxbenka. Early Classic period.

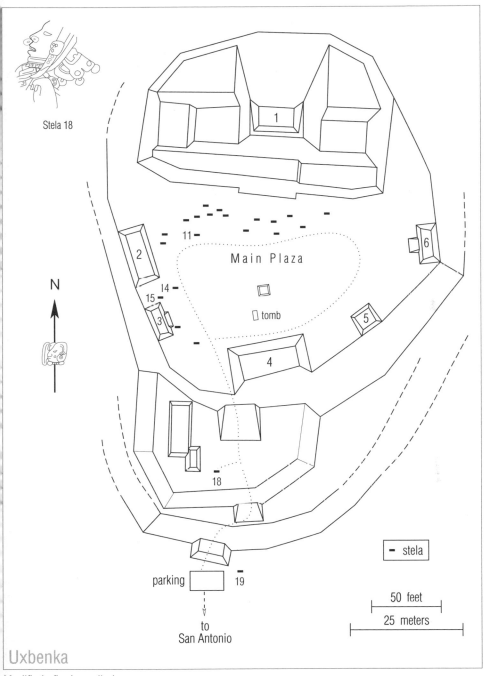

Stela 18

N

Main Plaza

tomb

1

2

11

14
15
3

6

5

4

18

parking 19

to
San Antonio

— stela

50 feet

25 meters

Uxbenka

Modified after Leventhal.

The front (south side) of Structure 1, Uxbenka, with a row of stelae aligned in front. Late Classic period.

Early Classic date. Two glyphs accompany the figure but are greatly eroded.

From here you continue up the next terrace to the Main Plaza, which is surrounded by the remains of six structures. (At the time of our visit, the plaza had recently been cleared of weeds, and it was easy to get around. Reportedly, it is sometimes overgrown. The structures are only partly cleared.)

Structure 1 is about 26 feet high and is the tallest at the site; it borders the north side of the plaza. Structures 2 and 3 are on the west side of the plaza, and the stelae are arranged in front of them and Structure 1. As you proceed clockwise from the south end of the plaza (where you entered), you will come to another all-glyphic monument (Stela 15), broken and fairly eroded and protected by a thatch shelter. Projecting from the same shelter is a nearly intact carved monument, but it is almost entirely eroded. Nearby are two carved fragments; one has scroll-type designs, and on the other, the left arm and the back of a headdress are clearly carved.

You will see other fragments, some greatly eroded, as you continue. Another stela, lying on the ground and also greatly eroded, has a single column of glyphs running down the center.

In front of Structure 1, near its west end, the butt and lower section of a stela is still in the ground, but at an angle. A fleshless skull seems to be depicted on the stela's lower section. Most of the remaining monuments have fallen (a few butts are still upright), and sections of some of the stelae have scaled off.

The architecture at Uxbenka is of the cut slab style also seen at Lubaantun and Nim Li Punit; this can best be observed on

Detail of the row of stelae in front of Structure 1, Uxbenka, view from the west. Late Classic period.

parts of the front (south side) of Structure 1, behind the stelae. This construction style seems to occur only at sites in southern Belize.

The last feature of interest in the plaza is a tomb near the south end (in front of Structure 4, which borders that edge of the plaza). The tomb is sunk into the plaza and is lined with cut stone slabs.

From the edges of the plaza there are delightful views of the countryside and the village of Santa Cruz below.

Recent History

Uxbenka was discovered in 1984 when Plácido Ash, the caretaker of Nim Li Punit, investigated reports of looting near Santa Cruz village; he found two carved stelae.

At that time, Richard Leventhal (then

of the State University of New York) was directing the Southern Belize Archaeological Project and was given permission by the Department of Archaeology of Belize to investigate the site. During a stay of a few days, he turned monuments—with the help of the British army—to check for carvings on the undersides, excavated the tomb, and drew a provisional map. The surrounding area was not thoroughly examined, but preliminary studies indicate that there was a fairly extensive settlement. Leventhal says that the site had been previously noted by Norman Hammond, who, however, did not see the stelae plaza.

Two of the stelae at Uxbenka have been dated stylistically to around A.D. 396 by Linda Schele, and these are two of the earliest dated monuments known so far in Belize. Two other stelae at Uxbenka are dated to A.D. 780.

Most of the other sculpted stelae do not retain enough definable carving to be dated.

Connections

1. San Antonio to Uxbenka: 3.7 miles [6.0 kilometers] by rock road (:22), then 0.2 mile [0.3 kilometer] by rough track (:02).

2. Punta Gorda to Uxbenka: 23.5 miles [37.8 kilometers] by rock road (1:44), then 0.2 mile [0.3 kilometer] by rough track (:02).

3. Dangriga to Uxbenka: 5.5 miles [8.9 kilometers] by paved but poor road (:18), 95.4 miles [153.5 kilometers] by rock and dirt roads (5:32), then 0.2 mile [0.3 kilometer] by rough track (:02). Total: 101.1 miles [162.7 kilometers] (5:52).

4. Belize City to Dangriga: See that connection under "Nim Li Punit." Total Belize City to Uxbenka (with a stop at Dangriga): 205.1 miles [330.2 kilometers] (9:46). Total Belize City to Uxbenka (direct): 194.1 miles [312.4 kilometers] (9:10).

Getting There

1. From San Antonio, head west for 3.7 miles [6.0 kilometers] to the cutoff for Uxbenka (unmarked). The cutoff is 0.3 mile [0.5 kilometer] *before* the village of Santa Cruz. Turn right (north) at the cutoff and drive—slowly—to the parking area at the base of the site.

2. From Punta Gorda, head northwest, then west to San Antonio and proceed as described.

3. From Dangriga, head west on the Hummingbird Highway to the junction with the Southern Highway. Turn left (south) onto the Southern Highway and continue to the junction with the road to San Antonio. Turn right (west) at the junction and go to San Antonio, then proceed as described.

4. See "Getting There" under "Nim Li Punit."

You should have a guide to reach Uxbenka. Ask at Bol's Hilltop Hotel in San Antonio. Buses from Punta Gorda go only as far as San Antonio. You can rent a car in Punta Gorda or hire a vehicle with a driver. If your driver is not familiar with Uxbenka, you can ask in San Antonio on your way through. Under no circumstances should you try to go to Uxbenka unaccompanied. The caretaker is not always on duty at the site—there are few visitors—and roaming around on your own is frowned upon.

If you cannot get a guide in San Antonio, you could go to Santa Cruz and ask for one there, then return to the cutoff and on to the site.

There is no food or drink, nor are there facilities of any kind at Uxbenka. Allow 40 minutes for a visit.

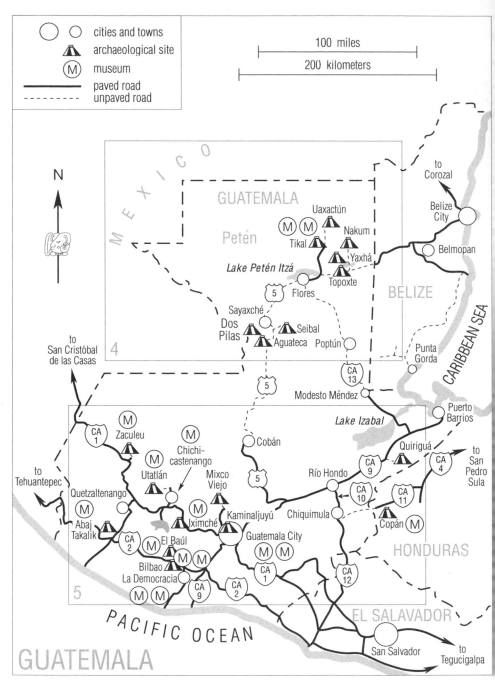

Guatemala, showing areas delimited by the sectional maps.

GENERAL INFORMATION
FOR GUATEMALA

Guatemala covers 42,042 square miles [108,889 square kilometers], and its estimated population in 1992 was 9,768,000. The country is bordered on the west and north by Mexico, on the east by Belize, the Caribbean Sea, Honduras, and El Salvador, and on the south by the Pacific Ocean. The southern part of Guatemala is composed of the mountainous highlands and the Pacific coastal plain; the northern part is made up of the Department of Petén, the jungly lowlands.

Guatemala City, the country's capital, has a population of about 2 million; it is in the highlands, the most densely populated part of the country.

Many cities and towns in Guatemala have long names, but shortened forms are used locally. Guatemala City is simply Guate; Chichicastenango is Chichi; Huehuetenango is Huehue; and Quetzaltenango is Xela (the name for the city used by the Quichés). Buses are generally labeled with these short forms.

Guatemala has the largest percentage of indigenous people (Indians who follow traditional ways) of any of the Central American countries. They wear their traditional dress, which is handwoven and extremely colorful. Although Spanish is the official language of the country, Mayan languages are spoken as well.

All visitors to Guatemala must have a passport. Citizens of the United States do not need a visa if they fly to Guatemala, provided that they stay no longer than three weeks. For visits longer than that, or if they drive to Guatemala, a visa is required. Citizens of some other countries need a visa while others do not. Since entry requirements are subject to change, it would be wise to check with the nearest Guatemalan consulate, in advance, for current regulations, and to obtain a visa ahead of time if required.

The unit of currency in Guatemala is the quetzal (Q in front of the number). The exchange rate varies, but, as a guide, it was 5.8 quetzales to one dollar in United States currency in 1995. Major credit cards are accepted at the moderate and better hotels and at many restaurants and shops. United States dollars are also widely accepted.

SECTION 4

• • • •

NORTHERN GUATEMALA

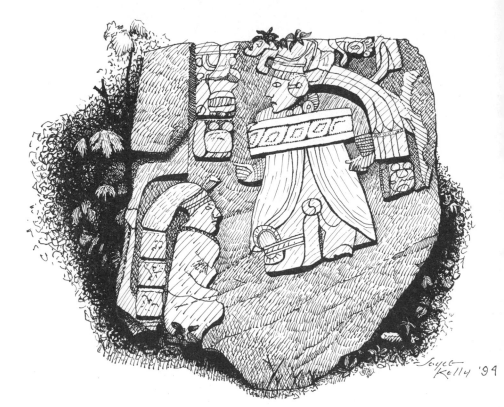

Stela 5, recording the date A.D. 771, Seibal. Probably erected in 780.

GENERAL INFORMATION FOR
SECTION 4, NORTHERN GUATEMALA

There are a number of places to stay when visiting sites in the Department of Petén in northern Guatemala. Those that are pertinent here are Flores, Sayaxché, Punta de Chimino, El Remate, Tikal, and Lake Yaxhá. Most visitors fly from Guatemala City to Flores and explore the area from there. Actually, Flores is an island in Lake Petén Itzá, joined to the mainland by a causeway. The mainland towns of Santa Elena (on the east) and San Benito (on the west) meet near where the causeway from Flores joins the mainland. Most visitors lump the three towns together as Flores, while residents make the distinction among them. For instance, the airport is in Santa Elena. The best hotels are in Santa Elena and on the island of Flores, but there are also some in San Benito.

While you are in Flores, there are three monuments you might like to see, all in the main plaza—in the center of town and at the high point of the island, west of the church. This pleasant plaza has raised beds of vegetation and benches for relaxing. Two of the monuments are propped up in the beds. One is the upper fragment of Stela 2 from Ixlu, a site near the east end of Lake Petén Itzá. It dates to A.D. 879 and portrays a main figure (badly eroded) and four fantastic smaller figures; the one on the upper left (as you face the stela) is particularly well preserved. The other monument is an oval altar carved with glyphs on its top surface; a Tikal Emblem Glyph is included in the text. The third monument is on the west side of the plaza, more or less at ground level, on a low cement base. This badly eroded monument was found being used as a paving block in a street in Flores until it was rescued by Sylvanus G. Morley in 1915. It is called Flores Stela 1 and it dates to A.D. 869; it is protected by a thatch shelter. Some monuments that we saw years ago in Flores and Santa Elena were later moved to Guatemala City.

There are a couple of modest hotels in Sayaxché; the old time favorite is the Guayacán, on the south side of the Río Pasión. A car ferry takes you across the river and lands a short distance to the east of the hotel. If you have taken a bus to the river, launches can get you across it. Sayaxché is the best stopover for Seibal, and it can be used as a base for visiting the Petexbatún sites.

Punta de Chimino is a peninsula that juts into Lake Petexbatún (see Map 4D, p. 000); access is by boat from Sayaxché. The Posada de Mateo is located there. This is reportedly a beautiful, eco-tourist paradise, with deluxe cabañas, hot water, ceiling fans, gourmet meals, and cold drinks. It is operated by John and Aurora Schmidt, who also run Petén Express, a tour company that can arrange visits to the Petexbatún sites, Seibal, and other sites farther away. They provide guides and camping equipment where necessary.

Both the posada and the tour company can be contacted by mail through a courier service (Fanny's, 24 Calle 0-78, Zona 4, Guatemala City, or by FAX 502-9-500505).

The posada would be a good base for visiting Dos Pilas and Aguateca. The small archaeological site of Punta de Chimino is nearby; it is noted for its enormous moated wall. I have not visited this site, but no doubt it would be worthwhile when you are staying at the Posada de Mateo.

In El Remate (1.0 mile [1.6 kilometers] north of El Cruce), there are three possibilities. La Mansión del Pájaro Serpiente is a pleasant place run by the helpful Nancy and Jorge Salazar. It sits on the side of a hill facing the east end of Lake Petén Itzá. The hotel is on the east side of the paved road that goes from Flores to Tikal, 1.0 mile [1.6 kilometers] north of the junction at El Cruce. At 0.3 mile [0.5 kilometer] north of the hotel, a rock road branches off and heads west along the north shore of Lake Petén Itzá; after 2.0 miles [3.2 kilometers] it passes El Gringo Perdido Campground,

Northern Guatemala

4

Legend:

○ towns
○ archaeological site
Ⓜ museum

paved road
unpaved road
foot trail

0.0 distance in miles
[0.0] distance in kilometers
(:00) driving time

★ ★ ★

MEXICO

GUATEMALA

BELIZE

Petén

Usumacinta River

Salinas (Chixoy) River

Pasión River

Lake Petén Itzá

Flores

El Cruce / Topoxte

Tikal
21.9
[35.2]
(:36)

Uaxactún
14.4
[23.2]
(:47)

Nakum

Yaxhá

CA 13

39.7
[63.9]
(3:00)

Melchor de Mencos

to Belize City
79.3
[127.6]
(2:03)

to Poptún and Guatemala City

CA 13

14.7
[23.7]
(:21)

3.1
[5.0]
(:10)

5

4A

4C

4B

4D

Seibal

Sayaxché
11.0
[17.7]
(1:05)

5

39.7
[63.9]
(2:24)

Dos Pilas

Aguateca

to Cobán

N

where there are also bungalows. A bit farther along the road is the deluxe (and expensive) Camino Real Tikal. These last two are in the Cerro Cahui Wildlife Reserve, where visitors can enjoy nature trails.

At Tikal there are four choices. There is a free campground at the end of the entrance road, across from the visitors' center. It provides cooking facilities and simple plumbing. There are three hotels on the other side of a cross road. From east to west they are the Tikal Inn (near the old air strip), the Jaguar Inn (just east of the Tikal Museum), and the Jungle Lodge (on a spur road to the west of the Tikal Museum). All the hotels are relatively modest but adequate. Sometimes they are filled with tour groups, so try to arrive early to get a room, or reserve one ahead of time from Flores or Guatemala City.

On the south shore of Lake Yaxhá is Campamento El Sombrero, idyllically situated and capably run by Juan José de la Hoz and his wife, Gabriela. The rooms are pleasant, though small, and there are detached baths. There is no hot water or electricity, but kerosene lamps are provided in the evening. A large thatched roof shelters the dining area, where Gabriela serves excellent meals. Prices for rooms and food are reasonable. Visitors who wish to sleep in their vehicles can park there for a small fee, which includes use of the baths and dining area. On the north shore of the lake, near the ruins of Yaxhá, a government operated camp has been opened. Lake Yaxhá is the best stopover when visiting Topoxte, Yaxhá, and Nakum.

Meals are available at all of the places listed, but you must make prior arrangements at the Posada de Mateo and Campamento El Sombrero.

The only paved road in the Petén is the one from Flores to El Cruce (Highway CA 13) and its continuation to Tikal (unnumbered). The continuation of Highway CA 13, heading east from El Cruce to Melchor de Mencos and the Belize border, is rough rock. Highway CA 13 also extends to the southeast from near Flores to Highway CA 9. From the junction near Flores to Modesto Méndez (103.7 miles [166.9 kilometers]), it

is rough rock. The road then enters the Department of Izabal and is paved to the junction with Highway CA 9 (43.8 miles [70.5 kilometers]). Highway CA 9 is paved to Guatemala City (156.1 miles [251.2 kilometers]). Highway 5 from Flores to Sayaxché is also rough rock. Buses run along all of these roads. Highway 5 continues south from Sayaxché and connects with highways in the Guatemala highlands. There is no scheduled bus service along the first part of the route, although trucks will sometimes pick up passengers. I have never found a reason to try this road, and all indications are that it is quite poor, especially where it goes through low-lying swampy areas. Clearly, it would be a long and arduous trip to reach the highlands this way. The condition of the roads leading to the archaeological sites is covered in the text pertaining to those sites.

Distances and driving times to sites in the Petén are from the following reference points: (1) in Flores, the junction of the causeway with the mainland in Santa Elena; (2) in Sayaxché, the ferry landing on the Río Pasión; (3) in El Remate, the Mansión del Pájaro Serpiente; (4) in Tikal, the *glorieta* (small traffic circle) near the visitors' center; and (5) in Lake Yaxhá, the gate at the national park service (CONAP) camp on the isthmus between Lakes Yaxhá and Sacnab.

The best way to get around the Petén, especially if you plan to visit all or most of the sites described in this book, is in a private vehicle. Vehicles of various types—some with four-wheel drive—can be rented at the airport in Santa Elena and from some hotels and travel agencies in Santa Elena and Flores.

Travel agencies in Santa Elena and Flores can arrange tours (with a driver) to some of the sites. If you start from Guatemala City, package tours are available, principally to Tikal, though others can be arranged. There are daily flights between Guatemala City and Flores–Santa Elena.

There is little to shop for in the Petén, and what is found there comes mainly from the Guatemala highlands. At Tikal, near the Tikal Museum, there are shops selling handwoven textiles.

In the part of the Petén covered in this section, gasoline is not as readily available as it is in the highlands. There are stations in the Flores–San Benito–Santa Elena area, at Libertad (on Highway 5 between Flores and Sayaxché), at Sayaxché, Melchor de Mencos, and, on the Petén Highway (the southern part of CA 13), near Río Dulce and at San Luís. Gasoline is not available at Tikal.

A gas pump symbol is used on Maps 4 and 4D to pinpoint possible gasoline stops; Libertad is not shown on these maps.

YAXHÁ
(yah-SHAH)

Derivation:
  Yucatec Maya for "Green Water." Named for Lake Yaxhá.
Original name:
  Yaxhá.
Location:
  East-central part of the Department of Petén, Guatemala.
Maps: 4 (p. 112) and 4A/4A1 (p. 116)

The Site

Yaxhá, one of the largest sites in Guatemala, covers several square miles on a ridge overlooking the north shore of Lake Yaxhá. The site was occupied from the first through the tenth centuries A.D. and was found to have a greater density of structures than most other lowland Maya sites (about 36 percent greater density than Tikal). More than 500 structures have been mapped at the site, including several immense pyramid-temples and monumental acropolis-like building complexes. A Twin-Pyramid Complex was discovered at Yaxhá, the only one known outside Tikal. Of some 40 stelae found at Yaxhá, about half are carved. In addition to the structures, there are four causeways (sacbeob) and several streets (vias), the first to be found at a lowland Maya site. Some of the causeways and plaza areas have been cleared and are identified with small signs.

Consolidation of Yaxhá's Structure 216 (also called Temple 1) has begun; most of the rest of the buildings are simply rubble mounds that are mostly overgrown, though the size of some of them is impressive.

When you visit Yaxhá, you will see more in less time if you have a guide. If you have not brought someone along, the guardian will be happy to show you around.

The parking area for Yaxhá is just south of Plaza C, and you enter the site from the southeast corner of the plaza. On the east side of the plaza are remains of carved but broken and eroded Early Classic stelae, protected by thatch shelters. As you approach from the south, you come first to Stela 5, then Stela 4 (the best preserved of the group), and then Stela 3. Stela 5 is very eroded, but it has been stylistically dated to A.D. 357; it is the earliest known monument at Yaxhá. Stela 4 portrays a standing figure with both feet facing in the same direction (to the viewer's left). To the left of the knees are two glyphs, and in a panel below the feet of the figure is a grotesque head (possibly a representation of Itzamná) with a squarish earplug. Of Stela 3, only the panel of the base remains; it is similar to the lower panel of Stela 4. These three stelae and others at Yaxhá show certain traits that are related to the early Izapan style.

You now leave Plaza C at its northwest corner, where it joins the Lincoln Causeway; follow the causeway to Plaza D, which is bordered on the south by the South Acropolis. A trail with poles for steps ascends the north side of the acropolis to the top. From there you can look down into one of the rooms

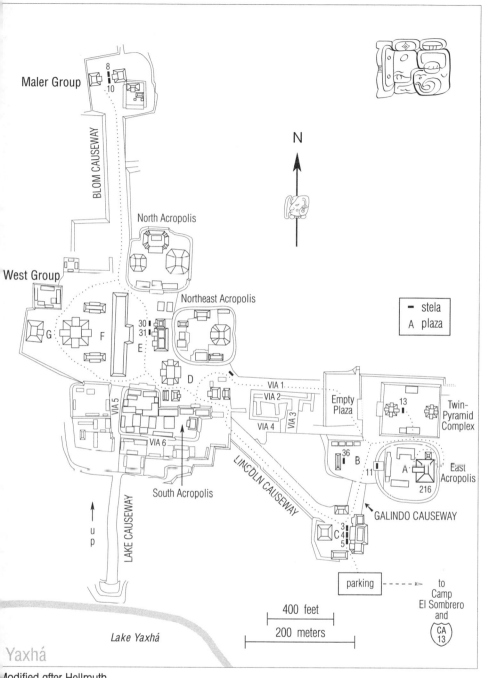

Maler Group

8
10

BLOM CAUSEWAY

North Acropolis

West Group

Northeast Acropolis

G
F
E
30
31

D

N

- stela
A plaza

VIA 1
VIA 2
VIA 3
VIA 4

Empty
Plaza

13

Twin-
Pyramid
Complex

VIA 5
VIA 6

South Acropolis

36
B

11

A

216

East
Acropolis

LINCOLN CAUSEWAY

GALINDO CAUSEWAY

LAKE CAUSEWAY

up

3
C 4
5

parking ----▷ to
Camp
El Sombrero
and

CA
13

400 feet

200 meters

Lake Yaxhá

Yaxhá

Modified after Hellmuth.

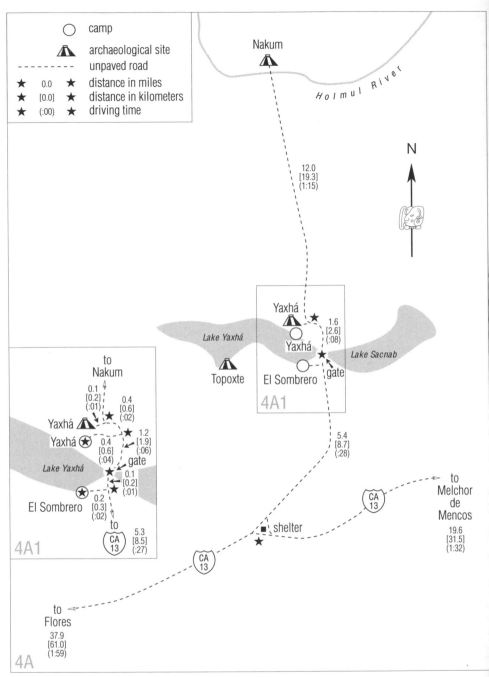

Routes to Topoxte, Yaxhá, and Nakum

where part of the vault has collapsed. You now descend to Plaza D and head west and then north to Plaza E.

There are two stelae in Plaza E. You come first to Stela 31, an ornate, Late Classic monument portraying a figure with an enormous headdress on its major fragment; smaller fragments lie nearby. The simpler Stela 30, of Early Classic date, is found in two fragments a little to the north of Stela 31.

From Plaza E, head north along the Blom Causeway to the Maler Group, where there are two more stelae. You reach Stela 10 first; only the bottom part of this Early Classic monument remains. Stela 8, a little to the north of Stela 10, appears to be of Early Classic date, and again only the bottom part of the stela is left.

You now return along the Blom Causeway and head west to enter Plaza G. On one of the large mounds on the plaza, a little of the original stonework can be discerned. From here you turn east and return to

Stela 4, showing Izapan traits, Yaxhá. Early Classic period.

Plaza D. In the northeast corner of the plaza is a large eroded stela. Next you walk east along Via 1, the longest and widest street at Yaxhá. The east end of Via 1 connects with the Empty Plaza; from there you head south and then east along the side of the Twin-Pyramid Complex. (See "Tikal" for a description of this type of complex.) A side trail turns north (with a short climb) and gets you into the complex itself. Of interest here is Stela 13, which lies at the base of the West Pyramid on its east (plaza) side. Stela 13 is fragmented, but much of its carving is well preserved, including a column of glyphs that record a Calendar Round date. This date has been interpreted as A.D. 793, the latest known at Yaxhá.

Leave the complex the way you entered and continue east along its base to the rear of the East Acropolis. Here you climb the base of the acropolis and enter Plaza A. On the east side of the plaza, facing west, is the immense Structure 216. It rises in tiers, and there are remains of a temple on top that bring the building to a total height of over 100 feet. It is the tallest and most impressive structure at Yaxhá; when consolidation is completed, it will be truly spectacular.

You now climb down the East Acropolis the way you came, head west along the base of the Twin-Pyramid Complex, and turn left (south) to enter Plaza B. On the east side of the plaza is the interesting and fairly well-preserved Early Classic Stela 11. It depicts a frontal view of Tlaloc, the Mexican deity. He is shown in the guise of a warrior or war god (holding a spear and a shield), rather than in his better-known as-

A fragment of Stela 13 in the Twin-Pyramid Complex, Yaxhá, A.D. 793.

pect as a rain god. The style of the stela is a variation of that of Teotihuacán. Other representations of Tlaloc are found on stelae at Tikal and Copán. Stela 11 lies on its back beneath a thatch shelter, but you can climb up behind it to get a head-on photograph; you will need a wide-angle lens.

Across Plaza B is Stela 36, erect but greatly eroded. Behind the stela is an overgrown structure where excavators found a building of unknown date with six round columns. This is a rare feature for a Maya site in the southern lowlands but is common in Puuc buildings in Yucatán and at some Mexican sites such as Teotihuacán.

From Plaza B, head south on the Galindo Causeway to Plaza C, where you started your tour. About 200 yards (183 meters) from Plaza C is a carving on bedrock of unknown date; it is made up of meandering lines. Depend on your guide to get you there.

Recent History

In 1904, after completing his work at Topoxte, Teobert Maler was rowing across Lake Yaxhá toward the hamlet on its east end. During the journey he scanned the forest on the north shore and became aware of "an extended chain of elevations appearing here and there." Convinced that these were the remains of an ancient city, he began explorations immediately. The Peabody Museum of Harvard University published his findings in 1908. Sylvanus G. Morley and Frans Blom visited the site briefly, and it was partly mapped in the 1930s by architect William Lincoln. In the 1960s, Merle Greene Robertson and Ian Graham documented the stelae.

In 1970, Nicholas M. Hellmuth directed a project at Yaxhá, sponsored by the Foundation for Latin American Anthropological Research; it lasted for four seasons. Assisting in this work were Guatemalan ar-

The front (west side) of Structure 216, Yaxhá. Late Classic period. The structure is undergoing consolidation.

chaeologists C. Rudy Larios, who discovered the Twin-Pyramid Complex, and Miguel Orrega Corzo, who mapped part of the site and conducted excavations.

In 1987, Juan Antonio Sillar and Oscar Quintana conducted a systematic study of a number of sites in the Petén, including Yaxhá. They recorded architectural deterioration and made recommendations to protect the remains. Some of their recommendations have been implemented, and in the early 1990s consolidation of Structure 216 began.

Connections

1. Lake Yaxhá to Yaxhá (ruins): 1.7 miles [2.7 kilometers] by rock road (:09).

2. El Remate to Lake Yaxhá: 1.0 mile [1.6 kilometers] by paved road (:02), then 25.5 miles [41.0 kilometers] by rock road (1:56). Total El Remate to Yaxhá: 28.2 miles [45.3 kilometers] (2:07).

3. Flores to Lake Yaxhá: 17.8 miles [28.6 kilometers] by paved road (:31), then 25.5 miles [41.0 kilometers] by rock road (1:56). Total Flores to Yaxhá: 45.0 miles [72.3 kilometers] (2:36).

4. Tikal to Lake Yaxhá: 21.9 miles [35.2 kilometers] by paved road (:36), then 25.5 miles [41.0 kilometers] by rock road (1:56). Total Tikal to Yaxhá: 49.1 miles [79.0 kilometers] (2:41).

Getting There

1. From the gate at the CONAP camp on Lake Yaxhá, head north and then west on the rock road to the parking area for Yaxhá

Stela 11, the Tlaloc Stela, Yaxhá. Early Classic period.

ruins. You will pass the cutoff for Nakum 0.1 mile [0.2 kilometer] before you reach the parking area for Yaxhá.

2, 3, and 4. To reach Lake Yaxhá from the other three connections, go first by paved road to El Cruce. This is south of El Remate and Tikal, and east and then north of Flores. At El Cruce, take the rock road (Highway CA 13) heading east to the Lake Yaxhá cutoff. The cutoff is marked with a sign for the CONAP camp, and there is a shelter for bus passengers at the junction as well. Turn left (north) at the junction and proceed to Lake Yaxhá on another rock road. After 1.0 mile [1.6 kilometers] you will come to a particularly bad spot in the road, at the top of a hill. This is due to an underground spring that keeps the road wet in this area most of the time. If it has been rainy to boot, you will need four-wheel drive to get through. There are a few other rutted areas after that, but they are not as bad. In any case, it would be best to have a high-clearance vehicle.

At 0.1 mile [0.2 kilometer] before you reach the gate at the CONAP camp, you will see a small sign marking the left (west) cutoff for Campamento El Sombrero. It is 0.2 mile [0.3 kilometer] to El Sombrero, the best place to overnight when visiting Yaxhá, Topoxte, and Nakum.

There is no food or drink at Yaxhá ruins, though both are available at El Sombrero; at least bring cold drinks along to the ruins. Allow 3 hours to visit Yaxhá, which can also be reached by boat from El Sombrero. If you also want to see nearby Topoxte, a boat from El Sombrero is your best bet. A boat trip to both sites can be arranged.

If you prefer having a guide to reach Lake Yaxhá and the ruins, check with travel agents in Flores–Santa Elena. Buses pass the Yaxhá cutoff but do not travel the road to the lake and the site. Few vehicles travel this road.

★ ★
TOPOXTE
(toh-pohsh-TEH)

Derivation:
Yucatec Maya name for a bush
bearing hollow seeds, according
to Teobert Maler.

Location:
East-central part of the
Department of Petén,
Guatemala.

Maps: 4 (p. 112) and 4A (p. 116)

The Site

The archaeological site of Topoxte occupies
three small islands in the western part of
Lake Yaxhá, and each island has its own
name. The largest is Topoxte (on the east);
Paxte is in the center, and Cante is on the
west. There are few remains on the last two
islands, and what follows pertains basically
to Topoxte Island.

From the boat landing on the west side
of Topoxte Island, it is a short walk up a
gentle slope to the main ceremonial precincts, which occupy the highest part of
the island. These precincts encompass 4.3
acres, but minor structures—mainly house
mounds—cover much of the island. The
best preserved ceremonial structures border
the east and north sides of a plaza; on the
west the ground slopes downward as a terrace to a lower level. The low bush has been
cleared from the plaza and it is easier to get
around than it was in years gone by.

Structure C (the Main Temple) is the
southernmost structure on the east side of
the plaza and is the most interesting. Most
of the walls of this two-room temple are
standing, though the beam-and-mortar roof
has collapsed. The temple rests on top of a
stepped pyramidal base that rises in four
tiers and is approached by a western stair.
Structure C was originally completely plastered, and a few remnants of this surface

still remain. The structure is undergoing
consolidation.

Structure D (north of Structure C) is
poorly preserved, but at its base, on the west
side, are a couple of small plain stelae and
altars protected by thatch shelters. Other
plain monuments lie nearby.

North of Structure D is Structure E,
which has some remains of standing architecture, as does the nearby Structure G, on
the north side of the plaza. Structures D, E,
and G are all one-room buildings, each with
two rectangular masonry columns at the entrance to the superstructure; all three buildings rest atop platforms.

There are remains of other buildings
on various terrace levels, but most are in ruinous condition. Structure A—impressive
for its size—is worth a look. It is a tall pyramidal mound located on a lower level than
the plaza, 50 yards [45.9 meters] to the
southwest of Structure C.

Two carved but eroded stelae were reported on the slope on the west side of the
plaza, but we were unable to locate them.
(Two other carved stelae are reported on
Cante Island.)

Topoxte is considered a Late Postclassic site, and its visible architecture dates to
that period, but it was also occupied in earlier times. There is ceramic evidence, including figurines, for a heavy occupation
during the Late Preclassic period and continuing into the Early Classic. There was a
falloff during Late Classic times. Veneer masonry—used in a retaining wall and dating
to the Late Classic—was discovered, however, on Topoxte Island. During the Preclassic and Classic periods Topoxte was probably subordinate to the major center of
Yaxhá across the lake.

The carved stelae are of Late Classic
date and are assumed to have been reused
by occupants of the site during the Late
Postclassic. It is thought that the stelae ei-

Structure C, undergoing consolidation, Topoxte. Late Postclassic period.

ther came from Yaxhá or relate to the earlier occupation period at Topoxte.

Some details of the architecture at Topoxte—square columns in doorways, stairway *alfardas* with vertical upper zones, and beam-and-mortar roofs—are also characteristic of Late Postclassic Maya architecture on the east coast of the Yucatán Peninsula, while other features at Topoxte appear to be local developments. Late Postclassic figurine censers found at Topoxte are also closely related to those produced in Yucatán and Quintana Roo, Mexico, during the same period. The plain stelae are also Late Postclassic, and at least some originally bore designs in stucco.

Recent History

Juan Galindo, one-time governor of the Petén and an early visitor to Palenque and Copán, was the first to report structures on Topoxte Island. In 1831 he wrote a letter to the Society of Antiquarians of London that included information about the site; the society published his letter in 1834. There is some question about whether Galindo personally visited the site or relied on reports of someone in his employ. Included in the letter is a description of Structure C, mentioned as a "five-story tower," apparently in reference to its four-tiered base plus the temple on top.

In 1904, Teobert Maler visited Topoxte. He photographed Structure C and made a map of the plaza; his work was published by the Peabody Museum of Harvard University in 1908. On brief visits, the site was subsequently investigated by Sylvanus G. Morley in 1914 and by Frans Blom in 1924. Two biologists, Cyrus Lundell and L. C. Stuart, visited Topoxte in 1933 and discovered the four carved stelae. They also produced a new map of the main group and gave letter designations to the structures.

The most intensive work at the site was that conducted by William R. Bullard, Jr., and published by the Peabody Museum in 1970. Bullard visited Topoxte briefly in 1956 and made additional visits in 1958 and 1959. In 1960 he spent two and a half weeks at the site with two workmen. They dug trenches in various parts of the site to collect ceramic specimens, and Bullard photographed the structures. No extensive excavation was undertaken, however, nor was any restoration attempted. Although Topoxte had been known to archaeologists for many years, until Bullard's investigation it was not known that the remains were of Late Postclassic date.

In 1974, Nicholas M. Hellmuth mapped Topoxte; he was sponsored by the Foundation for Latin American Anthropological Research. In the same year, Cante Island was mapped and test excavated by the Central Petén Historical Ecology Project. In the early 1990s, Guatemalan archaeologists undertook the clearing of the plaza and consolidation of some of the structures.

Connections

1. Campamento El Sombrero (on Lake Yaxhá) to Topoxte: about 2.6 miles [4.2 kilometers] by boat (:15), then a short distance by foot trail (:03).

2. El Remate to Campamento El Sombrero: 1.0 mile [1.6 kilometers] by paved road (:02), then 25.6 miles [41.1 kilometers] by rock road (1:57).

3. Flores to Campamento El Sombrero: 17.8 miles [28.6 kilometers] by paved road (:31), then 25.6 miles [41.1 kilometers] by rock road (1:57).

4. Tikal to Campamento El Sombrero: 21.9 miles [35.2 kilometers] by paved road (:36), then 25.6 miles [41.1 kilometers] by rock road (1:57).

Getting There

1. At Campamento El Sombrero you can hire a boat with an outboard motor and a boatman to take you to Topoxte Island. From the boat landing at Campamento El Sombrero it is a pleasant short ride west to the island. Your boatman will carry rain gear in case it is needed and will lead you to the site after you land at the island.

2, 3, and 4. See "Yaxhá" for detailed directions on reaching Lake Yaxhá.

When we first visited Topoxte in 1976, the lake was at a very low level; Topoxte Island was actually a peninsula and we were able to walk there. A couple of years later there was a flood, and the lake level rose dramatically. Since then the only access to Topoxte has been by boat.

The tremendous fluctuation of the lake level, over and above minor seasonal variations, has been often noted—but never explained. In any case, reaching Topoxte by boat is a great deal easier and more pleasant than walking there.

Allow about 45 minutes to visit Topoxte. There is no food or drink at the site but these are available at Campamento El Sombrero. You may want to bring cold drinks along in the boat.

NAKUM
(nah-KOOM)

Derivation:
Yucatec Maya for "House (Place) of the Gourds."
Location:
East-central part of the Department of Petén, Guatemala.
Maps: 4 (p. 112) and 4A (p. 116)

The Site

Nakum is a relatively large, major ceremonial center with a good deal of standing architecture. Trails at the site and many plaza areas have been nicely cleared, giving the site a parklike ambience. It is not difficult to walk around, but you will see more having someone guide you.

Some of the structures are uncleared and others only partly cleared. In preparation for consolidation, scaffolding has been erected around many of the buildings, partially obscuring them. So although Nakum is a delightful site to visit, for the moment it is not as photogenic as one might wish. I would still encourage anyone to go if the opportunity presents itself.

There are two principal groups at Nakum, connected by a *sacbé;* the southern group is by far the more interesting. This group is composed of the Great Plaza, with structures on all four sides, and to the south, the raised Main Plaza, with numerous courts and structures. There are additional structures to the east of these two areas. The Périgny Sacbé starts at the northwest corner of the Great Plaza and heads north for 950 feet [285 meters] to another huge plaza in the north group. If time is limited, concentrate on the south group.

You enter the site from the west, at the southwest corner of the Great Plaza. There is an interesting display of orchids on benches and on the ground near the entrance. From there, head north to Temple C, a steep pyramidal base with a few remains of a one-room temple on top. Temple C faces east onto the plaza and is now mostly rubble, but there are a few of the original steps in place on the east side of the base, about midway up. At plaza level, in front of the structure, is Stela C, the best preserved carved monument at Nakum. It has a single column of glyphs running down the center, surrounded by a plain area, and a simple border on each side. This Late Classic monument was erect when discovered and remains so today. The stela leans a bit to the side, and its glyphs are not parallel to the sides but are almost vertical. One theory is that the glyphs were carved after the stela was erected and had assumed a leaning position.

On the north side of the plaza is the greatly ruined and mostly uncleared Structure B, a pyramidal mound as seen today. At its base are the remains of plain altars and plain, fallen stelae.

Temple A, on the east side of the plaza, is the best known and most interesting structure at Nakum. It is the tallest structure in a row of five mounds, and it has the only superstructure in the group. The other mounds have flat tops and never supported masonry temples. Only Temple A in this group has been cleared. When discovered, the front (west) wall of Temple A had already fallen. What early photographs of the temple show is actually the medial wall, with three doorways that enter a rear corridor. Of particular interest were the north and south doorways, which had rounded arches, a unique feature for a Maya site. They were not true Roman arches with a keystone but were cast rather crudely into this shape, no doubt with wooden supports from below. The center doorway was rectangular and was topped by five massive beams of zapote to form a lintel. Unhappily, in recent years the south doorway completely collapsed, along with most of the central doorway.

The rear corridor of Temple A is less than two feet wide; restoration drawings show that the front corridor would have been a little wider. Neither corridor, however, is as wide as the medial wall is thick. This feature is also found at Tikal and other sites in the Petén.

Above the medial wall of Temple A is a roof comb that was originally ornamented with masks and other designs in stucco. These are the only decorations on Temple A, except for a simple medial molding and cornice.

At plaza level, six plain stelae and their accompanying plain altars were found in front of Temple A and its two lateral mounds. Some can be seen today, protected by thatch shelters.

The south side of the Great Plaza is bounded by the long Structure D, with a double range of rooms. The structure is overgrown.

You now exit the Great Plaza at its southeast corner and head a short distance to Temple V. This structure faces west and is composed of a base with a one-room temple on top and two low, lateral mounds on the west adjoining the north and south sides of the base. The base of the structure (and some others at Nakum) is unusual in that the sides are nearly vertical; a sloping pyramidal base is more common in Maya architecture. The front of the temple is gone, but part of the rest of it is still standing.

From here head to Temple U, which lies to the south. Temple U also has only one room, but its base takes the more usual pyramidal form. Part of the temple remains intact, and the side wall of the stairway ascending the base is still visible on the north. The base has been partly cleared of trees, but no other architectural features are visible. At the foot of the stairway is Stela U, carved but eroded. The best preserved part of the stela is near the top, where feathers

Stela C, with a single column of glyphs, Nakum. Late Classic period.

that were part of a headdress can still be discerned.

A short distance to the west of Temple U is the Main Plaza Acropolis, which rises about 35 feet above the level of the Great Plaza. The acropolis is immense and roughly square in plan, measuring about 500 feet on a side. Entry to the acropolis is on its south side, and on the way there you will pass its retaining wall, a good deal of which remains. The Main Plaza Acropolis supports the remains of many courts and numerous structures. Small hand-painted signs indicate the number of some of the courts or plazas. One of the most impressive structures of the Main Plaza Acropolis is the massive mound of the Inner Acropolis. This mound rises about 50 feet above the level of the Main Plaza and has a multichambered building (Structure 62) on top, near the south end.

Temple A, showing the remains of a rounded arch (on the left) in the medial wall of the building, Nakum. Late Classic period.

Structure 62 rises yet another 30 feet to the highest point reached by any of Nakum's structures. One of the chambers of Structure 62 can be entered, though there is not a lot to see. The east side of the Inner Acropolis had two tiers of rooms, a few remains of which can be seen today.

Other structures of interest on the Main Plaza Acropolis are N, Q, E, and F. Temple N is at the southwest corner of the Main Plaza, facing east. It is made up of a main temple with six rooms resting on a base with nearly vertical sides. There are two separate and smaller one-room annexes on the east. An unusual feature in the main temple is a circular window in the northern wall that connects with one of the interior rooms.

Structure Q lies along the eastern edge of the Main Plaza across from the east side

of the Inner Acropolis. It is about 150 feet long with a single range of rooms. Its front (west side) has fallen but the inner vaults of the two northernmost rooms are partly intact. One of the rooms has a stepped vault, and the other has some remains of plaster bearing graffiti.

The rear of Temple E is partly standing; it rests on a pyramidal base that is rubble today. At the rear (west side), Temple E is abutted by Structure F. The back (north) wall of Structure F has a single-course medial molding, above which are remains of a carved mask, one of the very few architectural decorations found at Nakum.

Because of an imminent rainstorm (and poor road conditions on the way into Nakum), we elected not to walk the Périgny Sacbé to visit the northern part of the site—

Remains of a carved mask on the back (north) wall of Structure F, Nakum. Late Classic period.

one of our rare bouts of prudent behavior. All information suggests that the only features to be seen in the north section are low mounds, a totally ruined pyramid-temple, and one mostly ruined range-type structure.

The structures and monuments seen at Nakum today date to the Late Classic period, but since no extensive excavations have been undertaken, we do not know when the site was first occupied.

Recent History

French Count Maurice de Périgny discovered Nakum in 1905 during his expedition to the area. The site was previously known to chicle gatherers, but Périgny was the first to report it to the outside world. He returned during a 1909–1910 expedition under the auspices of the Ministry of Public Instruc-tion and the Geographic Society (both of France). During this expedition he spent six weeks at Nakum; he principally occupied himself with clearing the structures—a formidable task—so that they could be photographed. His efforts in clearing left him little time for excavation.

Members of the Peabody Museum Expedition of 1909–1910 heard reports of Nakum from several sources and decided to visit the site. Gentlemen that they were, when they learned that Périgny was on his way to Nakum, they changed their plans so that Périgny, the real discoverer of Nakum, "might not be anticipated in his plans." The Peabody Museum also delayed publishing its report on Nakum until Périgny's work had appeared.

Shortly after Périgny's departure from Nakum, the Peabody Museum expedition visited the site for almost a month in early 1910. They gave great credit to Périgny for having cleared the site, because it made their work comparatively easy. In 1913, Alfred M. Tozzer wrote a preliminary study of Nakum, a result of the work he and Raymond E. Merwin had undertaken. A map was produced and the site was exhaustively photographed. This study, including the map and photographs, was published by the museum and is still a major source of information on Nakum.

In 1971, Nakum was filmed for three days by a crew brought in by Guatemalan archaeologist Miguel Orrego Corzo, who saw evidence of looting and destruction.

In an effort to salvage information, the Foundation for Latin American Anthropological Research sent an expedition to Nakum in 1973 to photograph the site and to map part of it. The north part of the site was mapped by Nicholas M. Hellmuth, while students of the Yaxhá summer field school, working on the south part of the site, recorded additions to the map that had originally been published by the Peabody Museum.

In 1987, an architectural reconnaissance of sites in the Petén was undertaken by Juan Antonio Sillar and Oscar Quintana. They documented deterioration of the sites and made recommendations for protection, noting which measures were urgently needed. Several recommendations were made for Nakum.

In 1991 and 1992, part of the site was cleared, and in preparation for consolidation, the scaffolding was erected and protective thatch shelters were placed above some of the structures and monuments.

Connections

1. Lake Yaxhá to Nakum: 1.6 miles [2.6 kilometers] by rock road to the Nakum cutoff (:08), then approximately 12.0 miles [19.3 kilometers] by dirt road (1:15).

2. El Remate to Lake Yaxhá: 1.0 mile [1.6 kilometers] by paved road (:02), then 25.5 miles [41.0 kilometers] by rock road (1:56). Total El Remate to Nakum: 40.1 miles [64.5 kilometers] (3:21).

3. Flores to Lake Yaxhá: 17.8 miles [28.6 kilometers] by paved road (:31), then 25.5 miles [41.0 kilometers] by rock road (1:56) Total Flores to Nakum: 56.9 miles [91.6 kilometers] (3:50).

4. Tikal to Lake Yaxhá: 21.9 miles [35.2 kilometers] by paved road (:36), then 25.5 miles [41.0 kilometers] by rock road (1:56) Total Tikal to Nakum: 61.0 miles [98.1 kilometers] (3:55).

Getting There

You must have a guide to reach Nakum. Check with Juan José de la Hoz at Campamento El Sombrero on the south shore of Lake Yaxhá. The cutoff to El Sombrero is 0.1 mile [0.2 kilometer] *before* (south of) the gate at the CONAP camp on the lake. The cutoff heads left and goes 0.2 mile [0.3 kilometers] to El Sombrero. Juan José has a sturdy four-wheel-drive vehicle, and having him take you to Nakum in it is the best way to reach the site. He will also give you a tour of Nakum.

1. From the gate at Lake Yaxhá head north toward the ruins of Yaxhá and go to a junction marked with a small sign for Nakum. Turn right at the junction and continue to Nakum. The distance is about 12.0 miles [19.3 kilometers]; I was unable to record it exactly because the odometer on the vehicle in which we were traveling was inoperable.

The dirt road to Nakum is poor at best, and you must have a vehicle with four-wheel drive to reach the site. When it has been wet, the road can become impassable even for vehicles so equipped. Check with Juan José or with someone at the CONAP camp about the current condition of the road before attempting to reach Nakum.

2, 3, and 4. See "Getting There" for "Yaxhá" for detailed directions on reaching Lake Yaxhá from the other three connections.

If you are starting from Flores and would prefer to have a guide for the entire trip, check with travel agencies there. Keep in mind, however, that driving from Flores to Nakum and back to Flores will take more than 7.5 hours (6.5 of which will be on poor roads); then add the time you will need to visit the site. This would be a grueling day.

Allow two hours to visit the south part of Nakum, and if you plan to walk to and visit the north part of the site add another hour.

Although a guardian and some workmen live at Nakum, they are not prepared to provide food and drink; bring your own. Wear boots if the weather has been wet.

★ ★ ★ ★
TIKAL
(tee-KAHL)

Derivation:
A traditional name of unknown meaning, according to William R. Coe. "Place Where Spirit Voices Are Heard," according to Teobert Maler.

Original name:
Possibly Yax Bal or Yax Balam, according to Linda Schele and David Freidel.

Location:
Northern part of the Department of Petén, Guatemala.

Maps: 4 (p. 112) and 4B (p. 131)

The Site

Tikal is, in a word, overwhelming; it is truly a world-class site. The sheer number and massiveness of its buildings leave one with open mouth.

According to William R. Coe, in the small section (about 6.7 square miles [16.0 square kilometers]) of central Tikal that has been mapped, more than 3,000 separate constructions were recorded, including temples—five of them more than 125 feet tall—palaces, and shrines. Over 200 stone monuments—stelae and altars—both carved and plain were found in and about the ceremonial precincts. It is possible that some 10,000 earlier constructions lie beneath the buildings already mapped. Structures were built at Tikal for more than 1,100 years, and stone monuments were erected for nearly that long. Tikal eventually grew to cover an area of about 25 square miles [64.7 square kilometers]. The population estimate for the site during its peak in the Late Classic period is about 100,000 people who lived there on a permanent basis.

The pre-Columbian history of Tikal dates back to at least 600 B.C. Pits cut down to the bedrock below the North Acropolis revealed traces of occupation from that time forward, although the earliest buildings date only as far back as 300 B.C.

Because of the tremendous recent advances in epigraphy, a great deal more is known about the politics and dynastic sequences of many Maya sites than was known in the not-too-distant past. The political history of Tikal is far too long to recount here. New information is appearing and new interpretations are being offered all the time. A few points, however, should be mentioned.

According to Linda Schele and David Freidel, Tikal was ruled by a single dynasty throughout its history; it had 39 successive rulers. During Classic times there was abundant interaction among polities within the Petén—and with some sites farther afield. Texts at other sites record information about Tikal, and vice versa. The early part of the Early Classic period saw rivalry between Tikal and Uaxactún, and one of Uaxactún's rulers took captives from Tikal. Later, one of Tikal's warlords conquered Uaxactún at a time in the Early Classic pe-

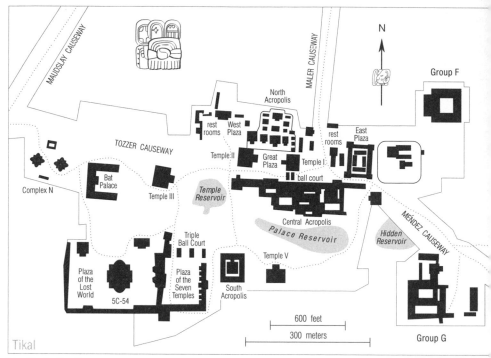

Tikal

Modified after Coe.

riod when the scope of warfare amplified. Early in the Late Classic period Caracol defeated Tikal, and shortly afterward an offshoot of the royal lineage of Tikal founded Dos Pilas.

Alliances were forged between individuals of different polities through marriages, and shifts in power took place among the polities. The sites of Naranjo (Guatemala) and Calakmul (Mexico) were also involved in the history of Tikal. For more information on these intriguing and complex affairs— some yet to be completely resolved—the following publications can be recommended: *Hieroglyphs and History at Dos Pilas,* by Stephen D. Houston (1993), *Classic Maya Political History,* edited by T. Patrick Culbert (1991), *A Forest of Kings,* by Schele and Freidel (1990), and, even though a new list of rulers is being worked out, *The Rulers of Tikal,* by Genevieve Michel (1989).

Many of the structures in the central precincts of Tikal and some in more outlying areas have been consolidated or restored or both, and this enhances their grandeur. The length of time you have at Tikal and whether you have your own vehicle will determine how you can see the site most efficiently, so I will not recommend a specific tour but will simply describe the various groups and their relative locations. I *do* recommend that you get a copy of *Tikal: A Handbook of the Ancient Maya Ruins,* second edition, 1988, by William R. Coe, available in the Tikal area and at book stores in Guatemala City. This excellent guide provides more details about the site than it is possible to give here.

The heart of Tikal is found in the Great Plaza and its surrounding structures. The plaza is bounded on the north by the North Terrace and, above this, the North Acropolis, on the east by Temple I, on the south by the Central Acropolis, and on the west by

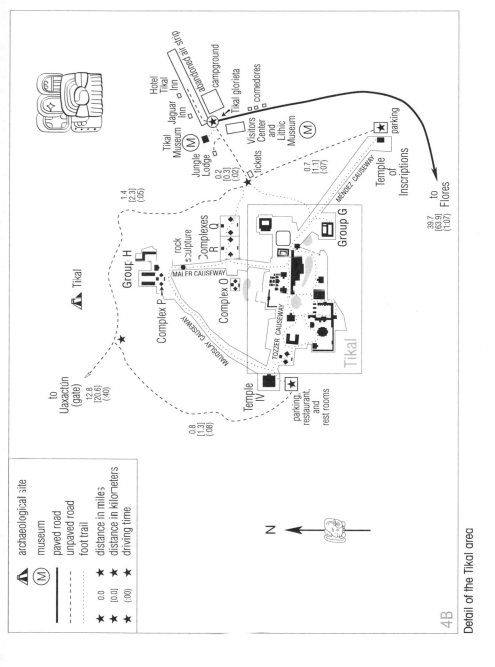

Legend:

△ archaeological site
Ⓜ museum
— paved road
------- unpaved road
·········· foot trail

distance in miles ★ 0.0
distance in kilometers ★ [0.0]
driving time ★ (:00)

N ←

Map labels:

Hotel Tikal
Jaguar Inn
abandoned air strip
campground
Tikal glorieta
comedores
Tikal Museum Ⓜ
Jungle Lodge
tickets
Visitors Center and Lithic Museum Ⓜ
Temple of Inscriptions parking
to Flores
MÉNDEZ CAUSEWAY
0.2 [0.3] (:02)
0.7 [1.1] (:07)
39.7 [63.9] (1:07)
1.4 [2.3] (:05)

△ Tikal

Group H
Complex P
rock sculpture
Complexes R Q
MALER CAUSEWAY
Complex O
MAUDSLAY CAUSEWAY
TOZZER CAUSEWAY
Group G
Tikal
Temple IV
parking, restaurant, and rest rooms

to Uaxactún (gate)
12.8 [20.6] (:40)
0.8 [1.3] (:08)

4B

Detail of the Tikal area

The North Acropolis as seen from Temple I, Tikal, view from the southeast. Early and Late Classic periods.

Temple II; most of the structures face the plaza itself. Many stelae and altars are found in the Great Plaza and the adjoining North Terrace, and a great deal of time can be profitably spent in this one area. Some of the stelae have been moved to the Lithic Museum in the visitors' center, and others are covered with thatch shelters.

The Great Plaza is now a grassy area kept closely clipped, but it was originally plastered. Four plaster floors dating from 150 B.C. to A.D. 700 are found just a little below the present surface.

In the North Acropolis, a hundred buildings lie buried—one on top of the other. This interesting but confusing complex contains fine examples of Early Classic temple construction. One of the finest is the small Temple 5D-23, the center structure on the west side of the upper level of the acropolis.

Other vestiges of Early Classic construction in the North Acropolis are the underlying structures and mask decorations of 5D-22 (the north central structure) and 5D-33 (the central structure on the south). Do not miss the masks. During excavation and restoration, part of the last construction phase of 5D-33 was dismantled.

Temple I, 145 feet tall, was built around A.D. 700. It is a steep climb to the top over worn limestone steps that can be slippery in damp weather, which is most of the time. A chain has been installed that facilitates the climb. This is actually a construction stairway that was used while the temple was being built. Later, a grander one was superimposed and used for ceremonies after the temple was completed. Only a small portion of this final stairway still exists at the base of the pyramid.

The temple on top is composed of three chambers, one behind the other, and each of the three doorways is spanned by a multibeamed zapote lintel. The lintel above the doorway to the outer chamber is plain (as are all the lintels on outer doorways at Tikal), but the others are carved. There are four beams in the lintel of the middle doorway, two of which are original; the others were removed in the nineteenth century and their whereabouts are unknown. The beams of the lintel from the third (innermost) doorway were also removed; they are in the British Museum in London and the Museum für Völkerkunde in Basel. Epoxy resin casts made from molds of these originals have been installed in the places of the latter. The carvings on the lintels at Tikal portray rulers of the site, and accompanying glyphs record historical events.

It has been estimated that a structure the size of Temple I could have been built in two years. Taken into account in this estimate were the construction methods employed and the availability of materials and labor.

The front (west side) of Temple I and stelae and altars in the Great Plaza, Tikal. Late Classic period.

In the early 1990s, Temple I was undergoing additional consolidation, and while this work was in progress visitors were not allowed to climb the structure. Perhaps by the time you get there work will have been completed and climbing the structure will once again be permitted. Marvelous views are to be seen from the top of Temple I.

The Central Acropolis is another rather confusing assemblage of buildings that, like the North Acropolis, grew over many centuries. The two differ, however, in that the buildings of the Central Acropolis are more the palace type (range type) arranged around courts, whereas those of the North Acropolis are of the pyramid-temple style. Plan to spend some time in the Central Acropolis investigating its many interesting buildings. Do not miss the Five-Story Palace (Structures 5D-52 and 5D-50), with its spindle-shaped vault beams. Most of the visible remains of the Central Acropolis date to the Late Classic period.

Interesting graffiti are found in some rooms of the Central Acropolis, particularly in the so-called Maler's Palace (Structure 5D-65) on the south side of Court 2. Another interesting but sometimes overlooked structure is 5D-43, near the northeastern end of the Central Acropolis and facing the

The Central Acropolis, Tikal, view from the northeast. Late Classic period.

East Plaza Ball Court. This Late Classic platform and temple show an architectural style that is reminiscent of Teotihuacán. It is one of three such structures found at Tikal, and the only one that has been restored. Other evidence of influence from central Mexico is found at Tikal in some Early Classic pottery and, more notably, in Stela 32 (now in the Tikal Museum) depicting the face of Tlaloc. Studies show that Tlaloc had at least dual aspects. One is that of the well-known rain god, but another represents a war god. Stela 32 apparently depicts this latter aspect of the deity, which is differentiated from the former by the inclusion of tassels or spearheads in the headdress. Teotihuacán influence appears at Tikal in the Early Classic period.

The small Great Plaza Ball Court (restored) is found between Temple I and the Central Acropolis. It seems strange that Tikal, one of the largest sites known, would have such a small ball court.

Temple II—125 feet tall—is the most completely restored of all the tall pyramid-temples and is, therefore, the easiest to climb. It dates to around A.D. 700. There are three chambers in the temple on top, with doorways spanned by lintels. Only in the middle doorway was the lintel carved. One of the five original beams that formed the lintel is in the American Museum of Natural History in New York.

For best photography in the area, I suggest climbing Temple I in the morning (when this is once again allowed) for front-lighted shots of Temple II. Do the reverse in the afternoon. The two flanking acropolises have good light most of the day.

West of the North Acropolis is the West Plaza. Of interest here are some stelae and altars, not all of which have been reerected. A short distance to the south and southwest of the Great Plaza are a number of structures accessible by foot trails. Some, but not all, of the buildings have been partly restored. Temple V—almost 190 feet tall—is still covered by jungle vegetation, unlike the

Structure 5D-43, showing Mexican influence, Tikal, view from the northeast. Late Classic period.

other four tall pyramid-temples, which have been restored to some degree. Immediately west is the South Acropolis, which has not been excavated.

West of the South Acropolis is the Plaza of the Seven Temples, with some structures in a good state of preservation. The central temple on the east side of the plaza (5D-96) has been restored and is decorated with a skull-and-crossbones motif on its rear (east) facade. This temple and the other six in the row give the plaza its name. There is also some standing architecture on the south and west sides of the plaza. An unusual triple ball court bounds the plaza on the north.

Again to the west is the Late Preclassic Pyramid 5C-54, surely one of the largest structures in Mesoamerica when it was built. It sits in the middle of a plaza called

the Plaza of the Lost World, and the structure itself is sometimes called the Lost World Pyramid. It stands almost 100 feet tall and originally had stairways on all four sides. The most important one is on the west, and this side of the structure has been restored. There has been less restoration of the other sides. The west stairway is flanked by terraces and huge masks (under thatch shelters). On the east side of the plaza is a row of several structures; near the middle of the row are the consolidated and partly restored Structures 5D-86 (a Late Classic building) and 5D-87 (the stairway of which has also been restored). During the excavation of 5D-86, the Early Classic Stela 39 was discovered where it had been redeposited during the Late Classic period in a room of the building. This stela is now in the Lithic Museum.

Temple II, Tikal. Late Classic period. Part of the North Terrace and the North Acropolis are on the right. The roof combs of Temple III (left) and Temple IV (center) rise above the tropical vegetation.

To the west of the Lost World Pyramid is the small Structure 5C-53, which has been excavated; it remains partly cleared. This is a platform without a superstructure but with stairways on all four sides. The use of moldings and the style of construction indicate influence from Teotihuacán. The platform was built around A.D. 600.

To the north of the platform is the restored Structure 5C-49, a large pyramidal base with a broad stairway on the south and remains of temple walls on top.

To the north of the Plaza of the Lost World (and reached by an unmarked trail) is the Bat Palace, also called the Palace of the Windows. This building has two stories; there is a double range of rooms in the first story and a single range in the upper story. The upper range has been consolidated, and

much interesting graffiti is found throughout the structure. There are some low windows in the structure that give it its second name.

A bit to the east of this is Temple III—180 feet high—and the climb, though a somewhat difficult one over roots and rubble, is worth it both for the view and for the carved zapote lintel inside the temple on top. Temple III, believed to date to A.D. 810, is composed of two tandem chambers. The lintel over the inner doorway is almost completely intact. If you wish to photograph the lintel, I recommend an early morning climb; light enters the doorway at that time. Do not hesitate to lie on your back and shoot straight up. You will probably be the only one there at the time. A wide-angle lens and fast film will be helpful.

To the west of Temple III, and past the

Pyramid 5C-54 (Lost World Pyramid), west side, Tikal. Late Preclassic period.

Bat Palace, is Complex N—most notable for its exquisite and well-preserved Late Classic Stela 16 and Altar 5. These two monuments have been moved to the Lithic Museum, but excellent copies have been erected in their places. The copies are easier to photograph because they are upright; the originals lay flat. Complex N dates to A.D. 711.

Still farther west is Temple IV, the largest of Tikal's pyramid-temples, built around A.D. 741. It soars 212 feet and is currently the tallest pre-Columbian structure in the Americas. The Pyramid of the Sun at Teotihuacán in central Mexico may originally have been a bit taller, but its temple is no longer in existence. Structure 1 at Mirador, in the northern Petén, has a substructure that is 20 percent higher than that of Temple IV, but its temple has also disappeared. It may have been taller than Temple IV originally. Its base is six times greater than that of Temple IV.

If you decide to climb Temple IV, you will probably feel that it is even taller than 212 feet. The temple on top has been consolidated and partly restored, although the pyramidal base has not been. The temple itself has three tandem rooms, with walls up to 40 feet thick. The two inner doorways were spanned by carved lintels that are now in the Museum für Völkerkunde in Basel. An epoxy resin cast of the innermost lintel is in the National Museum in Guatemala City. Access to the temple is up the slightly cleared northeast corner of the pyramidal base; ladders have been installed to make the climb easier. The best time of day for this climb is the afternoon, when the sun hits the beautifully decorated backs of Temples II and III and the front of Temple I in the distance. If you can manage it, take along a telephoto lens. You will find a lot of use for it. This is indeed the best spot for a comprehensive view of central Tikal. You can climb still higher to the roof of the temple (where it joins the base of the roof comb) via a metal ladder at the rear (west side) of the structure, near its south end. Be

Temple IV, the front (east side), Tikal. Late Classic period.

careful here. Stay close to the roof comb: the roof slants downward and there are no protective guard rails.

In addition to erecting the many buildings at Tikal, the Mayas also constructed causeways joining the more important groups. These *sacbeob* are, in a sense, still in use today, for some of the trails follow their routes. The original surface is not generally discernible, however.

From the base of Temple IV, the Maudslay Causeway heads northeast to Group H about 0.5 mile [0.8 kilometer] away. Group H includes a large plaza bordered by Late Classic temples, some of which have been excavated and partially restored. The most interesting is the massive Structure 3D-43, with its three large interior rooms and graffiti.

Complex P (A.D. 751), a part of Group H, had two interesting monuments, Stela 20 and Altar 8; both have been moved to the Guatemala City Museum.

From Group H, a trail follows the Maler Causeway south, joining the East Plaza near the rear of Temple I. There are two areas of interest along the causeway. One is a large bas-relief carved in limestone bedrock; it lies on the causeway just west of the trail, about 250 feet [75 meters] south of Group H. This somewhat eroded Late Classic sculpture shows two men with bound limbs. Its horizontal position, large size (12 by 20 feet), and covering of lichen make it difficult to photograph. You might try sitting on someone's shoulders to gain additional height, or use your monopod as described in "General Advice—Camera Gear." A wide-angle lens is really needed here.

East of the Maler Causeway, and about midway between Group H and the East Plaza, are two Twin-Pyramid Complexes, R and Q. Nine of these complexes have been recorded at Tikal, though one was demolished in ancient Maya times and others were partly dismantled. Although the complexes vary in size, certain features are found in all of them: two pyramids face each other on an east-west axis; the pyramids ave stairways on all four sides; the tops of the pyramids are flat and do not support a superstructure; and on the west side of the last pyramid is a row of plain stelae and altars. To the north of the pyramids, and more or less centered between them, is a roofless enclosure housing a single stela and altar that are generally carved. At the south end of the complex is a long, vaulted, single-room building with nine doorways. The four structures in each Twin-Pyramid Complex were built at the same time. These complexes were built at 20-year intervals during much of the Late Classic period at Tikal. This interval of 20 years is the Maya ka-un, one of several time intervals used by the Mayas. The function of Twin-Pyramid Complexes remains unknown. For a time these complexes were thought to be unique to Tikal, but after they were identified here, another complex was found at Yaxhá, with the same east-west orientation of the pyramids.

Complex R (A.D. 790) abuts the Maler Causeway and has been only partially excavated. Complex Q (A.D. 771), adjacent to the east and about the same size, has been largely restored and its monuments have been reerected. Carved Stela 22 and Altar 10 are in place in the northern enclosure and are additional examples of fine Late Classic sculpture, even though the figure on the stela has a mutilated face and both capves on the top of the altar are somewhat eroded. In addition to the trail that follows the Maler Causeway to the East Plaza, another goes from Complex Q southeast to the site entrance and the hotels.

Another trail follows the Méndez Causeway; it connects the East Plaza with the Temple of Inscriptions, where the causeway ends. The distance covered is about 0.8 mile [1.3 kilometers]. The trail passes near Group G, which is reached by a branch trail to the south that is marked with a sign. The structures of Group G are of the palace type and date to the Late Classic period. It is one of the largest clusters of this type of construction known at Tikal. Group G has 29 vaulted chambers basically on one level, and a few remains of two others that formed part of a second story. One entrance to Group G is through a vaulted passageway in the rear of one of the structures. The entrance to the passageway was surrounded by a huge fantastic mask, but little of this remains. Follow the passageway to the interior courtyard.

The other entrance to Group G is through a double range of rooms a few feet to the right of the passageway entrance. The rooms sit on a low platform; there a few steps up to the rooms and down again to the interior courtyard. The structures facing the courtyard are all worth a look, and there are graffiti in several of the rooms. One unusual feature in Group G is the use of vertical grooves as decorations on the exterior palace walls.

Last but not least is the Temple of Inscriptions, at the end of the Méndez Causeway. This temple is best visited in the morning when the sun hits the back of its roof comb, which is covered with hieroglyphs. Panels of glyphs also cover the sides of the roof comb. The central (and currently tallest) part of the roof comb is 40 feet high, and its inscription records the date A.D. 766. The building faces west onto a plaza and its front is somewhat in ruin, but at its base on this (west) side are the remains of two interesting monuments. Only the bottom fragment of Stela 21 is intact, however, the rest having been mutilated, probably in Late Classic times. The stela dates to 736, and the carving of the glyphs and the feet of the figure are superb examples of the sculptor's art. The stela is accompanied by Altar 9, the top of which depicts a bound captive—a motif found frequently at Tikal.

Recent History

Although the people living in the general area around Tikal were probably always aware of its existence, the first official expedition to the area took place in 1848. It was undertaken by Modesto Méndez, commissioner of the Petén, along with the governor of the Petén, Ambrosio Tut. They were accompanied by the artist Eusebio Lara, and their adventure was published in 1853 in Germany.

A list of later investigators at Tikal

Interior courtyard of Group G, Tikal. Late Classic period. Note the unusual grooves in the exterior wc on the right.

reads like a who's who of Maya archaeology and includes Gustav Bernoulli, Alfred P. Maudslay, Teobert Maler, Alfred M. Tozzer, Raymond E. Merwin, and Sylvanus G. Morley. Publication of data, maps, and beautiful photographs ensued through the years, thanks to their work.

In 1951 an airfield was built at Tikal, and five years later the University Museum of the University of Pennsylvania undertook an eleven-year program of excavation and restoration, with the cooperation of the Guatemalan government. This became known as the Tikal Project and was one of the largest of its kind ever attempted. It was originally directed by Edwin M. Shook and later by William R. Coe.

After the termination of the program by the University of Pennsylvania, Guatemala's Institute of Anthropology took over the work.

Restoration continued under the direction c C. Rudy Larios and Miguel Orrego Corzo.

From 1979 through 1984, the Tika National Project was undertaken. Durir this time the Lost World Pyramid an nearby structures were excavated and co solidated and Group 6C-XVI (an elite res dential area) was investigated. An interes ing and well-preserved ball court mark was discovered in this last group; it is no in the Guatemala City Museum (see tha section for details). Reports on all of th work were issued by Juan Pedro Laport Vilma Fialko, and Lilian Vega de Zea stal ing in 1984.

The ruins of Tikal are now centered i what has become Tikal National Park, whic encompasses 222 square miles [575 squa kilometers] of preserved area. The maint nance of roads, trails, and cleared areas is s

The back (east side) of the roof comb of the Temple of Inscriptions, Tikal. A.D. 766.

ervised by the director of parks under the
Institute of Anthropology of Guatemala.

Connections

, Tikal (*glorieta*) to Tikal ruins (Great
Plaza): 20 minutes on foot.

, El Remate to Tikal (*glorieta*): 20.9 miles
[33.6 kilometers] by paved road (:34).

, Flores to Tikal (*glorieta*): 39.7 miles [63.9
kilometers] by paved road (1:07).

, Guatemala City to Flores: 162.0 miles
[260.7 kilometers] by air (approximately
:00).

, Guatemala City to Tikal (*glorieta*): 236.4
miles [380.4 kilometers] by paved road

(5:53) and 103.7 miles [166.9 kilometers]
by rock road (4:55). Total 340.1 miles
[547.4 kilometers] (10:48).

6. Belize City to Tikal (*glorieta*). 101.2 miles
[162.9 kilometers] by paved road (2:39) and
39.7 miles [63.9 kilometers] by rough rock
road (3:00). Total 140.9 miles [226.8 kilo-
meters] (5:39).

Getting There

When you are driving north to Tikal, you
will enter the Tikal National Park 10.5
miles [16.9 kilometers] before reaching the
Tikal *glorieta* (traffic circle). There is a gate
at the park boundary where you stop, sign
a registration book, and buy a ticket. The
ticket is dated and is good for one day. Keep
the ticket to show at the ticket office at the

entrance to Tikal ruins if you are going to visit the ruins the same day that you enter the park. If you stay at Tikal for more than one day, you will have to buy another ticket for each extra day at the entrance to the site. To really see Tikal properly, a minimum of two days is recommended; three days would be better.

1. From the *glorieta* at Tikal, follow the rock road southwest to the entrance to the site (at the ticket office) and take a trail heading in a southerly direction to the Méndez Causeway. Then head northwest to the East Plaza and west to the Great Plaza.

2. From El Remate, head north to the Tikal *glorieta* and follow the directions just given.

3. From Flores, head east and then north to El Cruce and continue north to the Tikal *glorieta;* then follow the directions for Connection 1. Buses and shuttles run from Flores to Tikal.

4. Once you reach Flores by air from Guatemala City, follow the directions for Connections 3 and 1. *Note:* Direct flights from Guatemala City to Tikal were discontinued many years ago.

5. From Guatemala City, head northeast on Highway CA 9 to the junction with Highway CA 13 (the Petén Highway) 156.0 miles [251.0 kilometers] by paved road (3:57). Turn left (north) onto Highway CA 13 and continue to Modesto Méndez 43.8 miles [70.5 kilometers] by paved road (:59). Continue on Highway CA 13 for 103.7 miles [166.9 kilometers] by rock road (4:55) to the junction (near Flores) with the paved road to Tikal. Turn right (east), follow the road as it curves to the left (north) a bit later, and proceed to the Tikal *glorieta* 36.6 miles [58.9 kilometers] by paved road (:57).

6. From Belize City, take the Western Highway heading west to the Belize-Guatemala border. Continue west on Highway CA 13 to El Cruce. Turn right (north) and proceed to the Tikal *glorieta.* Then follow the directions for Connection 1. If you choose this route, expect to add 30 minutes to an hour to the time given under "Connections" to cross the international border. For close places to stay in Belize, see "General Information for Section 2, Central Belize."

At one time visitors were allowed to drive into the central area of Tikal, including the Great Plaza, as well as along the Méndez, Maudslay, and the southern part of the Maler causeways. This has not been permitted, however, for the last few years. *But* there are two dirt roads that go partly around the main part of the site, to areas some distance from the Great Plaza. Both begin at the entrance to the site at the ticket office. One road loops around to the north, passes the cutoff for Uaxactún, and loops back to the south; it ends in a parking area just south of the base of Temple IV. There is a restaurant at the parking area, as well as rest rooms. The other road goes southeast from the ticket office to a parking area in back (east) of the Temple of Inscriptions. These roads are a help in getting to certain areas of Tikal, and you should consider them if you have access to a vehicle.

Vendors with ice chests and cold drinks are found at the northeast corner of the base of Temple IV, and others are found near the Great Plaza area. When you walk from the hotel area to and around the site, you should carry a canteen or bottle of water. You can get a picnic lunch from one of the hotels and eat it in one of the shelters provided for visitors in the East or West Plaza. There are also rest rooms in both of these locations.

If you plan to climb only the restored structures, tennis shoes are adequate; if your plans include climbing Temple III and some of the other structures without restored bases, boots would be better.

The ruins of Tikal open at 6:00 A.M. and guards start clearing visitors out at 5:00 P.M.; the site closes at 6:00 P.M. If you want to see the Great Plaza on a moonlit night ask for a pass at the *Inspectoría.* This is a small building on the left side of the road that goes between the *glorieta* and the ticket office at the entrance to the site. It is almost directly across from the access road to the Jungle Lodge.

★ ★ ★
SYLVANUS G. MORLEY MUSEUM
(Tikal Museum)

The Tikal Museum, inaugurated in 1964, is named for the great Mayanist scholar Sylvanus G. Morley, who visited the site four times and devotedly recorded the inscriptions of Tikal, as well as those of other sites in the Petén.

The museum houses Stelae 23, 29, 31, and a fragment of 32. Dating to A.D. 292, Stela 29 is the earliest known monument from Tikal. Stela 31 dates to 445; it is beautifully carved and well preserved. This magnificent monument was ritually "killed" and buried in Structure 5D-33 in the North Acropolis about 300 years after it was originally carved and erected in front of the building. The stela was discovered in 1960 when archaeologists tunneled into the structure. Stela 23 is less well preserved; it has a panel of glyphs on its back and is believed to date to around 517. The fragment of Stela 32 depicts the Mexican deity Tlaloc; it is of Early Classic date. It was found in a trash pit cut into a stairway of Structure 5D-26 in the North Acropolis. Another very similar portrayal of Tlaloc is found on the right side of Stela 31, on a shield held by a standing figure.

A remarkable collection of ceramics is attractively displayed in cases, and photographs taken during excavation are hung on the walls. Other display cases contain Early Classic jade and shell from tombs, obsidian, eccentric flints, and an attractive small mosaic head made of jade, shell, and coral.

Perhaps the most spectacular display is the replica of a tomb known as Burial 116. This tomb was discovered beneath Temple I, and a rich assortment of grave goods accompanied the interred ruler. Among other items were 180 pieces of worked jade in the form of bracelets, anklets, necklaces, and ear ornaments—collectively weighing 16.5 pounds. Also in the burial were 96 bone artifacts, 37 of which were carved with hieroglyphs; some have incised mythologi-

cal scenes of deities paddling canoes. Some of the incised bones had cinnabar rubbed into the depressions, and this makes the motifs easier to see. There were also large polychrome plates and jars in the burial. Most of these items are in the replica tomb, although some of the incised bones are in display cases where visitors can better see and appreciate them.

The Tikal Museum is just a short dis-

Stela 31, Tikal. A.D. 445. On display in the Tikal Museum.

tance to the northwest of the Tikal *glorieta*; it is open from 9:00 A.M. to 5:00 P.M. on weekdays, and it closes an hour earlier on Saturday and Sunday. Photography is permitted, including the use of flash, which is helpful when photographing the stelae. Most of the items are labeled and the museum lighting is fair. Allow 45 minutes to view this excellent collection, or more if you plan to take a lot of pictures.

Note: Plans are under way to move the stelae from this museum to the Tikal Lithic Museum. The Tikal Museum will then be redesigned in order to make space for ceramics uncovered during excavations conducted in the early 1980s.

★ ★ ★

TIKAL LITHIC MUSEUM

The Tikal Lithic Museum is a relatively recent enterprise. It was inaugurated late in 1989 and is housed in the attractive new building that is the visitors' center (which also has a restaurant and rest rooms). The visitors' center is just southwest of the Tikal *glorieta*, and you will pass its entrance shortly before reaching the *glorieta* as you drive in from the south. Inside the visitors' center, at the entrance to the museum, is a large scale model of Tikal. A nearby stairway leads to an upper level, and from there you can get a comprehensive view of the model; this is also the best vantage point for photographing it.

As its name implies, the Lithic Museum houses some of Tikal's stone stelae and altars. In the museum's first phase, 24 monuments were installed; plans are to move more monuments there in the second phase, including those at the Tikal Museum and some others from the site. Additional plans call for placing copies of the originals at the site.

All of the displayed monuments are labeled, and for some, written information is provided (in Spanish) about the rulers depicted, giving their dates and histories. This is accompanied by drawings of their name glyphs. While all of the stelae and altars are interesting and worth some study, a couple of favorites come to mind: the Late Classic Stela 16 and Altar 5, originally found in Complex N (where copies have been placed), and the Early Classic Stela 39, the most recently discovered of Tikal's stelae, originally found in Structure 5D-86 in the Lost World Complex. It was discovered during excavation of the structure in the early 1980s.

One display is outstanding and unique. This is a statue of a seated figure, also discovered in the 1980s, in a tomb beneath Structure 3D-43 in Group H. The figure, called the Man of Tikal, is carved from a dense reddish stone; it is headless, and its current height is 24 inches (nearly life-size). Its back and shoulders are deeply incised with a hieroglyphic text, some of which is missing due to the decapitation (accidental or deliberate) of the figure. A circular hole in the center of the upper back was clearly made after the text was carved; it obliterated some portions of the glyphs. Nevertheless, a date of A.D. 406 has been deciphered from the text. A detailed drawing of the glyphs is displayed behind the figure.

The Lithic Museum is open from 9:00 A.M. to 5:00 P.M. on weekdays, and it closes an hour earlier on Saturday and Sunday. Photography is permitted, including the use of flash. This is fortunate because the collection consists almost exclusively of bas-relief carvings. The museum's lighting is adequate to view the monuments. Allow 45 minutes to see the collection, or more if you plan to photograph many or all of the monuments.

The "Man of Tikal," Tikal. A.D. 406. On display in the Tikal Lithic Museum.

★ ★ ★
UAXACTÚN
(wahsh-ahh-TOON)

Derivation:

Yucatec Maya for "Eight-stone." So named because of the Cycle 8 Stela 9 found at the site. This was the first Cycle 8 stela discovered.

Location:

Northern part of the Department of Petén, Guatemala.

Maps: 4 (p. 112) and 4C (p. 146)

The Site

There have been tremendous changes at Uaxactún in recent years, and it delights me to upgrade its rating from one to three stars. This change is due to a number of factors. Several structures have been cleared, consolidated, and partly restored. Shelters and rest rooms have been installed, and road signs erected. Areas around the buildings have been cleared, making photography easy, and the addition of tropical plants gives the site a delightful parklike ambience. Another important factor is that the road from Tikal to Uaxactún has been widened

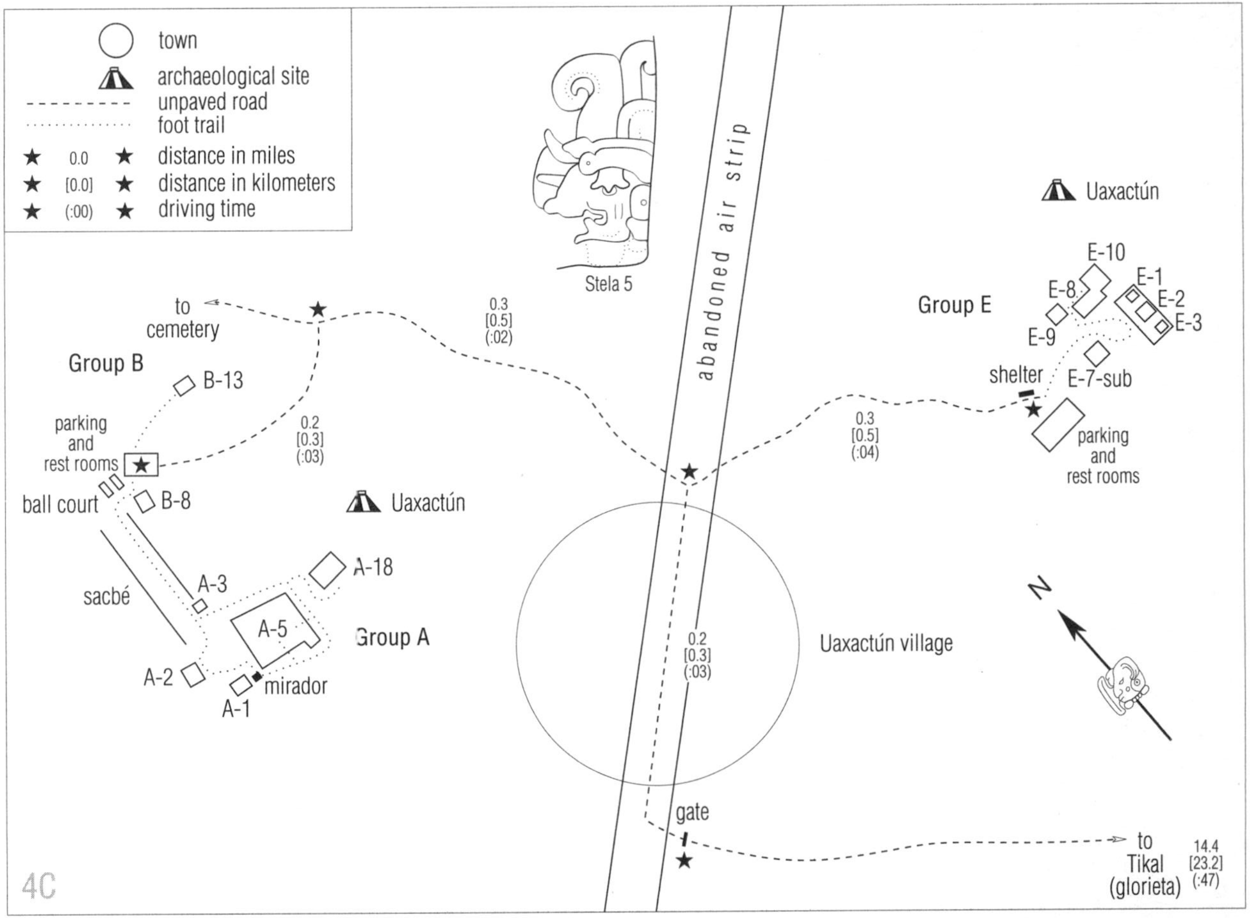

Legend

○	town
◮	archaeological site
– – –	unpaved road
······	foot trail
	distance in miles
★ 0.0	distance in miles
★★ [0.0]	distance in kilometers
★★ (:00)	driving time

Group B

parking and rest rooms

ball court

B-13

B-8

to cemetery

sacbé

A-3

A-2

◮ Uaxactún

A-5

A-18

Group A

mirador

A-1

0.2 [0.3] (:03)

0.3 [0.5] (:02)

Stela 5

abandoned air strip

Uaxactún village

0.2 [0.3] (:03)

gate

to Tikal (glorieta) 14.4 [23.2] (:47)

N

0.3 [0.5] (:04)

Group E

shelter

E-10

E-8

E-9

E-7-sub

E-1

E-2

E-3

◮ Uaxactún

parking and rest rooms

4C

Detail of the Uaxactún area

The front (west side) of Structure B-13, Uaxactún. Early Classic period.

and graded. This used to be an execrable road, making the trip difficult and hair-raising. When we last took this road it was a pleasant drive. Nevertheless, the road was reported to be in poor condition a few months later because of heavy rains. It is likely that the condition of the road will remain variable. Check at Tikal (at your hotel, at the ticket booth, or at the museums) for current conditions.

Uaxactún is formed of several groups of buildings atop low hills. The abandoned airstrip at Uaxactún—and the modern village that borders it—cuts through part of the archaeological zone. The groups of interest for the visitor are B and A on the west side of the airstrip and Group E on the east.

From the Group B parking area you will see, off to the right and a little behind you, Structure B-13. A short walk will get you to this consolidated building. The front rooms of the structure are gone except for

the lowermost parts of the walls, but the rear room is mostly intact. When first investigated, this room contained murals, which have not survived. Fortunately, the murals were copied by Antonio Tejada shortly after they were discovered. They dated to the end of the Early Classic period and depicted standing figures (one of whom held an atlatl) and others who were seated (some in an enclosure); there were also glyphs. It is believed that the scene depicted a meeting or ceremony between the local elite and a foreign representative, possibly from Kaminaljuyú or even Teotihuacán.

After visiting B-13, return to the parking area to continue your tour. Near a thatch shelter, where you will be asked to sign a registration book, is Stela 5. This monument dates to A.D. 378 and depicts a figure wearing non-Maya attire; he holds an atlatl and a club inset with obsidian blades. One interpretation has it that the figure rep-

Structure A-5, view from the southwest, Uaxactún. Early and Late Classic periods.

resents Smoking Frog, a lord of Tikal who conquered Uaxactún and became its ruler. His costume and weaponry are in the style of Teotihuacán, a style borrowed by the Mayas and one associated with war and sacrifice. A Tikal Emblem Glyph appears on the side of the stela following Smoking Frog's name glyph. Nearby is the middle portion of the eroded Stela 4 and other eroded monuments, all under thatch shelters—as are all the monuments at Uaxactún. A little to the north is a partly cleared but unrestored ball court. From here a broad *saché* heads south to Group A, 525 feet [160 meters] away, and enters it at the Main Plaza.

As you approach the plaza you pass the west side of Structure A-3, a pyramidal base rising in two tiers. The superstructure is gone, but the base has been cleared and consolidated. The structure faces south and has a stairway on that side.

The Main Plaza is bordered on three sides by major structures: A-5 on the east,

A-1 on the south, and A-2 on the west. There are a number of carved monuments in the plaza, mostly aligned in front of Structures A-1 and A-2. Some are fragmented and eroded, but they are worth a look. Two of the most interesting are Stelae 9 and 13. Stela 9 dates to A.D. 328 and is the earliest dated monument known from the site. Its Initial Series date is only moderately preserved; it is found on the back side of the stela. Stela 13 is all glyphic and its top part is in fairly good condition.

You come to Stela 9 first when you enter the plaza; Stela 13 is a short distance to the west, near the base of Structure A-2. This structure is a fair-sized pyramidal base with a broad stairway on the east, facing the plaza. It has been cleared and consolidated but practically nothing remains of the superstructure on top. To the southeast, at the base of Structure A-1, is Stela 7. It is badly fragmented, but you can see some clear carving on its top and a couple of well-preserved glyphs on the right side (as you face it).

The front (south side) of Structure A-18, view from the southwest, Uaxactún. Early Classic period.

To the west is the complex Structure A-5, which grew over time. It was greatly ruined when discovered but was thoroughly excavated. The remains have been cleared and consolidated. In one of its early stages (of Early Classic date), Structure A-5 consisted of three small temples facing a court, all atop a rather low platform with a stairway on the south. Over time, modifications were made and other temples were added. Later additions were of a different type, and the structure took on more of a residential character. The successive stages of development of Structure A-5 were beautifully drawn by Tatiana Proskouriakoff and were published in *An Album of Maya Architecture.*

For the benefit of visitors, a tall wooden tower (mirador) was constructed at the southwest corner of Structure A-5, and by climbing it you can look down into the building for a comprehensive view. This is, of course, a good place from which to photograph the structure.

The South Plaza abuts the south side of Structure A-5, and access to the interior of

the structure is on that side. After you roam around the area, exit the way you came and head east and then north; along the way you will pass another eroded stela. On the east side of Structure A-5 you can see one of the few intact vaults of the building. This long, low addition to the building was one of the last made; it is called the East Court. There were no superstructures above it, and it is possible that the structure was never finished. On the northeast exterior corner of Structure A-5 you can see the well-preserved remains of rounded corners and apron moldings.

A short distance to the east is the Early Classic Structure A-18; it has been cleared, consolidated, and partly restored. Although part of its front has fallen, it is one of the best preserved and most interesting buildings at Uaxactún. The two stories of the superstructure rest atop a fairly high pyramidal base that rises in tiers. The upper story is reached by an interior stairway from the first story. The structure faces south, and originally a stairway ascended the base on

The north side of Structure E-7-sub, Uaxactún. Late Preclassic period. Stela 20 is at the far left.

that side, but most of the lower part of the stair is now covered with earth and tropical plants.

The vaults in the superstructure are tall and bottle-shaped and are covered with plaster, much of which remains. The rear exterior (north side) of the structure once supported masks in stucco, a few fragments of which can still be seen. They are near the top of the building as it exists today.

From here head east to Structure A-3, turn right (north), and follow the *saché* back to the Group B parking area where you started your tour. You then drive to the Group E parking area, from which it is a short walk to Structure E-7-sub, perhaps the most famous building at Uaxactún. It is best known for its softly undulating lines and large masks that probably depict the celestial cycle of the sun and Venus.

Structure E-7-sub dates to the Late Pre-

classic period; it was discovered in excellent condition beneath a later structure that had protected it. The later structure (Pyramid E-7) was in a ruinous condition and its remains were removed to reveal the earlier pyramid. When first excavated, E-7-sub was brilliantly white, but with time and lack of maintenance it became overgrown. The reclearing has again revealed the structure, but its stucco surface is now a mottled dark blackish brown. For this reason, details of the mask panels are not as clear as they were when the pyramid was first excavated.

E-7-sub is roughly square in plan, with stairways on all four sides leading to a platform on top. The platform has a single stair on the east side. It is thought that a building of perishable materials originally crowned the top. The Early Classic Stela 20 is located at the base of the eastern stair of the building; it shows a figure in frontal view.

East of Structure E-7-sub is a platform that supports Structures E-1, E-2, and E-3 in a north-south line. The lower parts of the structures are standing and have been cleared and consolidated. At the base of the west side of the platform are remains of fragmented and eroded Early Classic stelae. The group of three temples atop the platform and Structure E-7-sub formed an astronomical observatory. From an observation point on the east stairway of E-7-sub, the sun could be seen rising behind Structure E-1, E-2, or E-3. Its relative position marked the summer and winter solstices (longest and shortest days of the year) and the vernal and autumnal equinoxes (when day and night are of the same length). Since the discovery of this group at Uaxactún, several similar assemblages have been identified at other Maya centers. These, however, are imitation E-Group complexes; that is, they were nonfunctional copies of the working-model solar observatory at Group E at Uaxactún. Though the architectural arrangement is similar, the buildings are not precisely oriented to the cardinal points as they are at Uaxactún. Imitation E-Group complexes are found at Cahal Pech, Pacbitun, and other sites.

To the north of this astronomical group is Structure E-8, with a stairway on the south and a smaller one on the north. The structure is a platform with rounded corners; there are no remains of a superstructure. An extension of this platform forms the base of the well-preserved Structure E-10, the only one at Uaxactún with a stepped vault. You can see the vault where some of the front of the building has fallen away. This Early Classic temple has the lower part of its roof comb intact. Structures E-8 and E-10 have been cleared and consolidated.

Near the entrance to Group E, there is a road to Group H, and a sign indicates that the distance is 500 meters (547 yards). Group H was studied in the mid-1980s by Guatemalan archaeologists who made some important discoveries. Among these were Late Preclassic vaulted structures adorned with large stucco masks on the exterior, some of which retained some of their original paint. The largest mask measures 25 feet long and 13 feet high.

The east (left) and north (right) sides of Stela 20, Uaxactún. Early Classic period.

We asked the caretaker at Group E about Group H and were told that only overgrown mounds could be seen there. I then specifically asked about the masks and was told that they had been re-covered; we did not attempt to reach Group H.

Recent History

The first archaeologist to see Uaxactún was Sylvanus G. Morley, when he headed an expedition for the Carnegie Institution of Washington in 1916. It is not clear how he first heard of the unnamed site, but he was

Structures E-1 (left), E-2 (center), and E-3 (right), Uaxactún. Late Preclassic period. View from the west, in front of Structure E-7-sub.

guided there by a trustworthy man named José. Although Morley and his staff were at the site for only six days, they examined, photographed, and made drawings of the glyphs on several carved stelae, took measurements for a site plan, and did sketch plans of the structures. It was Morley who gave the site its name.

In 1924, Frans Blom spent two months at Uaxactún, surveying the site and recording the architecture and sculpture. Blom was the first to suggest that Structures E-1, E-2, E-3, and E-7 might have functioned as a solar observatory.

From 1926 through 1937, the Carnegie Institution of Washington conducted studies at the site. The principal investigators were Oliver B. Ricketson and his wife, Edith B. Ricketson, the brothers A. Ledyard Smith and Robert E. Smith, and Edwin M. Shook. Ceramic analyses were undertaken by Robert E. Smith and James C. Gifford, and Alfred V. Kidder studied the artifacts.

A. Ledyard Smith and Shook returned in 1940 to resolve some points, and in 1974 Shook recleared and restored Structure E-7-sub. In 1978, archaeoastronomer Anthony Aveni took new measurements at the Group

E solar observatory, and in 1978 and 1979 Ian Graham recorded the carved monuments.

In 1982 a program of stabilization and restoration of some of the structures at Uaxactún was begun by Guatemala's Institute of Anthropology and History. In 1983 Guatemalan archaeologists began new investigations, and in 1985 the vaulted structures and stucco masks were discovered in Group H. An article by Juan Antonio Valdés, published in 1986 in *Mexicon*, reports on the work in Group H.

Uaxactún has been one of the most extensively investigated sites since the early years of Maya studies. The ceramic sequence that resulted from the early work there laid the foundation for the whole of lowland Maya chronology. This chronology was then linked to that of most of the rest of Mesoamerica. Uaxactún's ceramic sequence begins early in the Middle Preclassic period, at which time platforms were constructed. Structure E-7-sub and vaulted structures were built during the Late Preclassic. Uaxactún was an active center in the Early Classic period; then it was conquered by Tikal and ruled by the victorious Smoking Frog. Near the end of the Late Classic period, a stela dating to A.D. 889 was erected at Uaxactún. It is one of the latest dated monuments in the southern Maya lowlands.

Connections

1. Tikal to Uaxactún: 14.4 miles [23.2 kilometers] by rock road (:47) (see text), then 1.5 miles [2.4 kilometers] by poor rock road (:17). See "Getting There."

2. El Remate to Tikal: 20.9 miles [33.6 kilometers] by paved road (:34). Total El Remate to Uaxactún: 36.8 miles [52.9 kilometers] (1:38).

3. Flores to Tikal: 39.7 miles [63.9 kilometers] by paved road (1:07). Total Flores to Uaxactún: 56.5 miles [89.5 kilometers] (2:11).

Getting There

1. When you leave the Tikal *glorieta,* head southwest to the entrance for Tikal ruins and turn right (northwest). Follow the road for 1.4 miles [2.3 kilometers], where you will see a sign for Uaxactún. Turn right at the sign and proceed 12.8 miles [20.6 kilometers] to Uaxactún village. When you arrive at the village you will come to a guard post and gate. From the gate, the distance of 1.5 miles [2.4 kilometers] given under Connection 1 includes going to the Group B parking area, returning to the airstrip, and going on to Group E. After you go through the gate, turn right and drive along the airstrip to a sign (on the left) that indicates "ruins." This marks the cutoff for the Group B parking area. Turn left at the cutoff and go 0.3 mile [0.5 kilometer] to a fork in the road; take the left branch and continue to the Group B parking area. The road along the airstrip and the one to Group B are a bit rough but not too difficult to negotiate if you drive slowly.

After you have visited Groups B and A, return to the airstrip and cross it. On the other (east) side you will see another sign indicating "ruins." This is the cutoff for Group E. This road is very rutted and steep and you will probably need a high-clearance vehicle to drive there; otherwise you could walk in from the airstrip. Although you can tour Groups B and A on your own, you will cover the area faster by having the caretaker show you around. This is not necessary at Group E.

2 and 3. From El Remate, head north to Tikal; from Flores head east and then north to El Cruce and continue north to Tikal. Then follow the directions for Connection 1.

You do not need a guide to reach Uaxactún, but if you would prefer having one, check at the hotels at Tikal or at one of the travel agencies in Flores–Santa Elena. You can arrange a driver-vehicle package. You can also reach Uaxactún village by bus (two each day) from Tikal or Flores. The bus generally stops along the airstrip at the cutoff for Group B, and from there you can walk to that area. Then you would return, walk to Group E, and return again to the airstrip. This would entail a walk of 1.6 miles [2.6 kilometers].

Allow 2 hours for a tour of Groups B and A and another 30 minutes for Group E. There are rest rooms at Group B and Group E near the parking areas. There are no restaurants as such at Uaxactún village, but cold drinks are available at some stores along the airstrip. There are shelters at both parking areas for the ruins where you could eat a picnic lunch.

★ ★ ★
SEIBAL
(Ceibal)
(say-BAHL)

Derivation:
Spanish for "Place of the Ceiba Tree."
Earlier name:
Sastanquiqui.
Location:
South-central part of the Department of Petén, Guatemala.
Maps: 4 (p. 112) and 4D (p. 155)

The Site

Seibal is a very rewarding site visually and photographically, owing to the quality and quantity of its carved stelae. The monuments are sculpted from very hard limestone, which accounts for their excellent state of preservation.

The site, composed of three major groups (A, C, and D), is of medium size. Its central zone, which includes these groups, occupies 0.7 square mile [1.7 square kilometers]. Seibal was first occupied in the Middle Preclassic period around 800 B.C., and it grew steadily until around A.D. 1, when it was a major ceremonial center. It then declined until A.D. 500, was apparently abandoned until 690, and then was reoccupied. It grew again and became a major center for the second time in its history.

In A.D. 735, one of Seibal's rulers, Yich'ak Balam, was captured by Ruler 3 of Dos Pilas. Ruler 3 subsequently appears to have controlled Seibal for 10 years, after which another branch of the Dos Pilas dynasty may have controlled the site for an additional 50 years.

Around A.D. 830, a non–Classic Maya group arrived at Seibal, and non–Classic Maya traits appeared in the ceramics and sculpture. The site's peak period came during the next hundred years, when the population reached 10,000 people. In 930, Seibal was abandoned permanently.

Almost 200 structures have been recorded at Seibal and many of them excavated. Of these, only two have been restored, (Structures A-3 and C-79). The other architectural remains are now rubble and vegetation-covered mounds. For the visitor, it is really the stelae that are of greatest interest at the site. They date from A.D. 771 to 889 or 890.

The road to Seibal ends near a couple of neat thatch-roofed houses with plastered walls—used by archaeologists while working at the site. At one time, a few interesting fragments of Hieroglyphic Stairway 1 from Seibal were found around one of them. The hieroglyphic stairway records the earliest date known at Seibal (A.D. 744), and it is the only Initial Series date at the site. There is a nice picnic area nearby.

The trail to the ruins leaves from the picnic area, passes both restored structures, and returns. Begin your tour by taking the trail to the left; you will shortly come to Structure A-3, a three-tiered pyramidal base with stairs on all four sides, surmounted by a temple with the remains of a corbeled vault—the only one known at Seibal. Structure A-3 sits in the center of the South Plaza, which has been cleared. A number of stelae are visible at once when you enter the plaza, and this is the most interesting part of the site. There are five stelae directly associated with Structure A-3, one in front of each of the four stairways and another in the temple itself. All five stelae date to A.D. 849, and each depicts a principal figure accompanied by glyphs. These stelae and the others at Seibal are carved on only one side.

Stela 9 is on the west side of Structure A-3, and the personage it depicts wears an

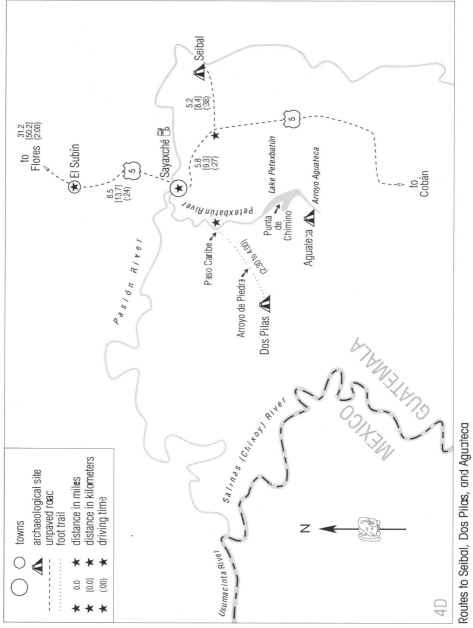

Routes to Seibal, Dos Pilas, and Aguateca

4D

Structure A-3, Seibal, view from the northwest. Stela 9 is at the base of the western stair. Late Classic period.

elaborate headdress and holds a ceremonial bar. The stelae is fragmented but has been restored; one section of the carving is missing.

On the north and east sides of Structure A-3 are Stelae 10 and 11, respectively. It is possible that the same Seibal lord is portrayed on both. Stela 10 is intact and is one of the best preserved at the site; both it and Stela 11 show the lord in elaborate attire. On Stela 10 he holds a ceremonial bar, and on Stela 11 he stands above a panel housing a captive. There are eroded remains of two other figures just above the panel. Stelae 11 is the only one in this group that has subsidiary figures.

Stela 8 is on the south side of Structure A-3, and the figure portrayed wears jaguar paw mittens and slippers; the monument is well preserved. It is possible that the same

lord is also depicted on Stelae 21, which is inside the central chamber atop Structure A-3.

Stela 21 was discovered in the mid-1960s when extensive work at Seibal was undertaken and when Structure A-3 was excavated. Stela 21 was fragmented when the vault of the structure collapsed upon it, and erosion has also taken its toll. The stela was restored and the lord portrayed holds a manikin scepter.

On the periphery of the South Plaza are three more stelae. On the north is Stela 1 (A.D. 869); it portrays a figure holding a lance in his right hand and a bag in his left hand. On the east side of the plaza is Stela 2, where the single figure, wearing a mask, is portrayed in frontal view. This is the only frontal portrayal at Seibal. There are no glyphs on this monument, but it is believed to date to around 870. At one time the three-paneled Stela 3 stood next to Stela 2. Stela 3 is now in the Guatemala City Museum; it is believed to date to the same time as Stela 2. To the southwest (and a short distance to the east of Structure A-3) is Stela 19. Its figure wears a mask of Éhecatl (the wind god aspect of Quetzalcóatl, the central Mexican deity), and there is a speech scroll in front of the figure's mouth; he stands on a panel of glyphs.

To the west (and somewhat outside the South Plaza) stands Stela 13. Its figure also has a speech scroll in front of his mouth, and he wears a necklace of large beads and a large ear flare. Realistic-looking serpents emanate from his loincloth apron, and another is tied in a sort of bow around his waist. There is a panel of glyphs at the top of the stela, the first of which has a squared cartouche; the monument dates to around A.D. 870. Farther west is Stela 20, which dates to 889; it is one of the latest monuments at Seibal. The figure holds a staff in his right hand and darts in his left hand.

Now return to the South Plaza, go to Stela 1, and head north a short distance. There are three stelae in a north-south row in this area, of which Stela 5 is the southernmost. Only the large middle fragment of Stela 5 remains, but it is known to date to around A.D. 780. The principal figure is dressed as a ball player, and a subsidiary figure faces him (on the left as you view the stela).

A few feet to the north is the all-glyphic Stela 6, dating to A.D. 771. Later in the history of Seibal, an upper fragment of the monument was broken off and reerected before a small altar, a short distance away from the original placement of Stela 6.

A little to the north of Stela 6 is Stela 7, the companion piece of Stela 5. Stela 7 is

Stela 10, Seibal. A.D. 849.

whole and better preserved than Stela 5, and like the latter, it portrays a ruler clad as a ball player. The hieroglyphic text records the accession of the ruler in A.D. 771, though the stela was probably erected in 780.

About 65 feet [20 meters] to the west of the line of stelae just described is Stela 18, one of the latest at Seibal. On it, a figure is seated, with one knee raised; he sits upon an elaborate network of serpentine scrolls.

Return again to the South Plaza and take a trail that begins just south of Stela 2; the trail heads east following the route of an ancient sacbé. After a while you will come

Stela 13, Seibal. Dates to around A.D. 870. The use of Mexican speech scrolls and a non–Classic Maya figure implies foreign influence.

(which overlies a Late Preclassic structure) has a jaguar altar in front of it; the altar is supported by three pedestals, two of which are representations of crouching figures. The altar itself is circular and is crudely carved with a jaguar head on its edge. Structure C-79 and the altar probably date to around A.D. 870.

From here, follow the trail south, then west and north, and return to the picnic area where you started.

Some of the non–Classic Maya sculptural traits you will have noticed during your tour are speech scrolls, a representation of Éhecatl, squared cartouches, darts, unusually long hair on some of the figures, very large beads in necklaces, foot slippers, and a physiognomy that seems different from Classic Maya types.

Some of the non-Classic sculptural traits seem to be derived from the northern lowlands of the Yucatán Peninsula, and architectural studies show that some of Seibal's structures exhibit Puuc and Chenes influence. (The Puuc and Chenes sites are also in the northern lowlands of Yucatán.) Other sculptural traits on Seibal's stelae have Gulf Coast affinities (emanating from somewhere between western Yucatán and southern Veracruz). At Seibal, foreign traits are often combined with others that are typically Classic Maya.

Ceramic studies at Seibal support the hypothesis that the site was taken over by a non–Classic Maya group in the ninth century A.D.—and certainly by 830—according to Jeremy A. Sabloff. Some authorities favor the idea of two incursions into the area, one by the Chontal, or Putun, Maya of the Gulf Coast and another by people from farther north. Before Seibal was taken over by outsiders, it had been a typical Petén-type Maya ceremonial center. The most impressive stelae, however, date from after the arrival of foreigners.

to another *saché*, joining the first on the south; Stela 14 is at the junction. This well-preserved monument depicts a figure that is almost obliterated by detail. His feet are shod in slippers similar to those found on ball player carvings at Chichén Itzá in Yucatán, although at the latter site only one foot wears a slipper. The figure stands on a panel carved with a brief hieroglyphic inscription, and the monument dates to around A.D. 870.

From Stela 14, follow the trail (again over a *saché*) heading south to Structure C-79. This structure is a three-tiered, circular platform with a major stairway on the west and a smaller one on the east. The platform was probably topped originally by a building of perishable materials. Structure C-79

Recent History

Seibal was discovered around 1890 and was first reported in 1893 in an article by Federico Arthes in a Guatemala City newspaper. In 1895, Teobert Maler was in Flores and was advised to visit Seibal to see some fine sculptures that had been uncovered some time before, during the establishment of a woodcutters' camp. Maler visited Seibal for four days in July 1895. He photographed the stelae (including one he personally discovered) and made a rough site plan. In August 1905 he revisited Seibal and corrected some details on his plan, but he discovered no new monuments, "so thorough had been my research at that time [1895]." He was working for the Peabody Museum of Harvard University on both of these visits, and the museum published his work in 1908; it included superb photographs of many of the stelae.

Sylvanus G. Morley visited Seibal in 1914 for the Carnegie Institution of Washington, to study the glyphs for his work on Maya inscriptions.

In 1964, the Peabody Museum reentered the field and conducted extensive research at the site through 1968. Publication of data began in the 1970s and continued into the 1980s. One especially interesting find during this work was that of a jade Olmec bloodletting tool from a cache dating to the Middle Preclassic period.

Ian Graham mapped the site. Other archaeologists involved in the project were Gordon R. Willey, A. Ledyard Smith, Gair Tourtellot, John A. Graham, and Jeremy A. Sabloff.

Stela 7, depicting a ruler dressed as a ball player, Seibal. A.D. 780.

Connections

1. Sayaxché to Seibal: 11.0 miles [17.7 kilometers] by rock and dirt road (1:05).

2. Flores to Sayaxché: 39.7 miles [63.9 kilometers] by rough rock road (2:24). Total Flores to Seibal: 50.7 miles [81.6 kilometers] (3:29).

3. El Remate to Sayaxché: 18.8 miles [30.3 kilometers] by paved road (:33), then 39.7 miles [63.9 kilometers] by rough rock road (2:24). Total El Remate to Seibal: 69.5 miles [111.9 kilometers] (4:02).

4. Tikal to Sayaxché: 39.7 miles [63.9 kilometers] by paved road (1:07), then 39.7

Detail of the upper portion of Stela 14, beside the trail between Structures A-3 and C-79, Seibal. Dates to around A.D. 870.

miles [63.9 kilometers] by rough rock road (2:24). Total Tikal to Seibal: 90.4 miles [145.5 kilometers] (4:36).

Getting There

1. As you are leaving Sayaxché, there is a cutoff to the right, followed by a curve to the left. Ask directions locally to be sure you are on the right road out of town—there are a couple. From Sayaxché, follow the rock road (Highway 5) for 5.8 miles [9.3 kilometers] to a junction. At the junction the highway curves to the right; you take a branch to the left, which is the road to Seibal. There is a piece of metal sculpture (made from machine parts) at the junction. Locally it is called a *muñeca* (doll) or *muñeco* (puppet), and residents of the area use it as a landmark when giving directions to visitors. There is also a small sign for Seibal at the junction, but the last time we passed, it was facing the wrong way.

Highway 5 is a rather poor rock road, and after you take the

Structure C-79 and the jaguar altar, Seibal. Both date to around A.D. 870.

cutoff to Seibal, conditions worsen. This part is not being maintained and it gets progressively narrower and more rutted. You will need a high-clearance vehicle to reach the site; in wet weather you will need four-wheel drive as well.

You can also reach Seibal by boat from Sayaxché in 2 to 2.5 hours. From the landing place it is reportedly an uphill climb of about 330 feet [100 meters] to the site, which will take about 40 minutes.

2. From Flores, take Highway 5 heading southwest and then south to Sayaxché. On the outskirts of Flores the road branches three ways; the center branch is the road to Sayaxché.

3. From El Remate, head south to El Cruce and then continue south and then west to Flores; from there follow the directions just given.

4. From Tikal, head south to El Remate, then follow the directions just given.

Allow 2.5 hours to see and photograph Seibal. Bring your own food and drink—neither is available at the site. Wear boots if you are going to Seibal by boat and will have to climb to the site.

Note: The Late Classic Panel 2 (formerly called Stela 2) from La Amelia is on display in Sayaxché in front of the municipal building, facing the river. It is fragmented but has been restored. It retains some clear carving and is worth a few minutes to see and a few frames of film.

Panel 2 (formerly Stela 2) from La Amelia. Late Classic period. On display in front of the municipal building in Sayaxché.

★
DOS PILAS
(dohs PEE-lahs)

Derivation:
Spanish for "Two Springs."
Named for two nearby springs
(only one of which is
perennial).

Location:
Southwestern part of the
Department of Petén,
Guatemala.

Maps: 4 (p. 112) and 4D (p. 155)

The Site

The distribution of structures at Dos Pilas is unusual for a Classic Maya site. The buildings are arranged in a linear pattern along an east-west axis, with the most important structures near the east and west edges. The mapped portion of the site covers 178 acres [0.7 square kilometers], and the entire site covers two or three times that area. All together, 492 mounds of various types, from large pyramidal structures to small residential buildings, have been recorded. The population of Dos Pilas and the surrounding area during its heyday is estimated at 10,000.

The main part of Dos Pilas that visitors see today is composed of a number of structures around a plaza and others a short distance away. The group called El Duende lies to the east.

Some of the structures at Dos Pilas were dismantled in ancient times in order to build a defensive wall when the city was under siege, so there is little to see architecturally. The site's glory is its carved monuments, which abound. There are stelae, altars, panels, and hieroglyphic stairways, all protected by thatch shelters. Some monuments have been removed from the site and are preserved by the Guatemalan authorities.

Note: In 1993, a new enumeration of the Dos Pilas structures and many of its monuments was introduced by Stephen D Houston; this was published—in a concordance with the old numbers—in his *Hieroglyphs and History at Dos Pilas*. Here I have followed the new enumeration, which in the case of some monuments is the same as the old numbering.

In the center of the plaza and aligned along its east side are a number of carved stelae, some of which are fragmented but most of which retain some well-preserved carving. Structure L5-1 is on the east side of the plaza, and in front of it is Stela 8, dedicated to Ruler 2 of Dos Pilas; it was erected by Ruler 3. The inscription on the back of the stela tells of the birth, accession, conquests, death, and burial of Ruler 2. It also indicates that Ruler 2 was buried at Dos Pilas. Archaeologists, thinking that Ruler 2 might have been buried in the nearby Structure L5-1, dug a 30-foot shaft into the structure and hit bedrock. They then tunneled to the side and found the expected tomb, believed, but not proven, to be that of Ruler 2. The front of Stela 8 is completely eroded, because it fell with that side up. After it was turned and the back side recorded, it was again placed face up to protect the glyphs on the back.

Stelae 2 and 1, in the center of the plaza, are worth some study. Stela 2 is fragmented but retains some clear carving; it depicts Ruler 3 of Dos Pilas, who subdued Yich'ak Balam, the ruler of Seibal, in A.D. 735. Seibal's lord is depicted as a crouching captive in a panel below the feet of Ruler 3. This panel is now in three separate fragments. Stela 1 is whole except for an upper corner; it dates to 706 and portrays Ruler 2, who is elaborately attired. The inscription on Stela 1 records the defeat of someone from Tikal and is the last mention of Tikal in the Dos Pilas texts.

A short distance to the west is Structure L4-35, which borders the west side of the plaza; at its base is Hieroglyphic Stair-

Detail of Stela 2, depicting an owl as part of a pectoral worn by Ruler 3 of Dos Pilas. A.D. 735.

way 1. It, like Hieroglyphic Stairway 2 (at the base of Structure L5-49) on the south side of the plaza, is composed of a series of steps that are carved on the risers. The middle of the bottom step of Hieroglyphic Stairway 1 shows a group of figures in regal attire; they are moderately well preserved. There are figures on the two upper steps as well, but they are more eroded. There are glyphs on all three steps, but some of those on the upper step are unfinished. Several dates inscribed on Hieroglyphic Stairway 1 (A.D. 716 to 724) record events in the life of Ruler 2 of Dos Pilas.

Hieroglyphic Stairway 2 is all glyphic, although the middle sections of the steps are formed of uncarved blocks. This stairway shows signs of disturbance in ancient times, and parts of the inscription are missing. It is believed that the uncarved blocks were used

to replace the originals, which were carved. This stairway and the large Structure L5-49 behind it were built during the reign of Ruler 1 of Dos Pilas, who is believed to have founded the site's dynasty. The inscriptions on Hieroglyphic Stairway 2 record war-related activities. Panels 6 and 7 are found at the west and east ends of the stairway; they are all glyphic and record additional information.

Partway up the east side of Structure L5-49 is the beautifully preserved Panel 10. Once thought to portray a woman, it is now believed to be a representation of Ruler 1 attired for a particular ritual. Structure L5-49 is the largest in this part of Dos Pilas, rising 60 feet above the plaza.

Four hundred feet [120 meters] south of the southeast corner of the plaza is Hieroglyphic Stairway 3; it is somewhat

Hieroglyphic Stairway 1, with unfinished glyphs on the third step, Dos Pilas. Events in the life of Ruler 2 of Dos Pilas, from A.D. 716 to 724, are recorded.

eroded, but reclining captive figures can be discerned. The figures represent foreign lords captured by Ruler 4 of Dos Pilas, who in turn was possibly captured and killed by warriors from Tamarindito in A.D. 761.

Hieroglyphic Stairway 4—another very important monument—was discovered in 1990 on the east side of the royal palace of Ruler 1. The glyphs give the history of Ruler 1 and the origin of the Dos Pilas dynasty. During the siege of Dos Pilas in A.D. 761, the stone palace was torn down by the people of Dos Pilas, and the material was used to erect a defensive wall that went right across Hieroglyphic Stairway 4. It was during the excavation of the wall that the stairway was discovered; it was then excavated, studied, and re-covered for protection.

You now return to the plaza and head

to its northeast corner. In a ball court (Structures L4-17 and L4-16) are the mostly whole but eroded Panels 11 and 12. Each depicts a standing lord holding a spear.

A little over 0.5 mile [0.8 kilometer] away is El Duende pyramid. At 125 feet tall, it is the tallest and largest structure at Dos Pilas. I have not seen this structure, but reportedly there is a well-preserved megalithic stairway on the north side. Stelae 14 and 15, also reportedly well preserved, are nearby. A trail from the main group to El Duende passes an excavated elite residential complex where some architecture is visible.

Recent History

Two residents of Sayaxché, José and Lisandro Flores, made the first reported discov-

Hieroglyphic Stairway 2, recording events in the life of Ruler 1, Dos Pilas. Dates from A.D. 625 to 6̶ are recorded. The all-glyphic panel 7 is on the left. A.D. 686.

ery of Dos Pilas in 1953 or 1954, although the ruins were likely known to local residents previously. In 1954, a brief report appeared in a Guatemalan newspaper. (For a comprehensive review of early visitors to the site, see *Hieroglyphs and History at Dos Pilas,* mentioned earlier.)

In 1960, Pierre Ivanoff led an expedition to Dos Pilas and in 1973 he published a book, *Monuments of Civilization: Maya,* in which Dos Pilas (which he called Dos Pozos) was described along with other Maya centers. In this work (which included color photographs) he claimed to have discovered the site.

Later, Ian Graham photographed the monuments, and in 1977 he discovered a couple of well-preserved and previously unreported stelae in El Duende group. Merle

Greene Robertson did rubbings of some of the stelae and carved steps in the main group. Over the years, a number of scholars have worked to decipher the Dos Pilas inscriptions, including Houston, Peter Mathews, and David Stuart.

Excavations at Dos Pilas (and the study of some other Petexbatún sites) began in 1989 under the direction of Arthur A. Demarest of Vanderbilt University and Juan Antonio Valdés of the University of San Carlos in Guatemala. During the first field season a research center was built at the site. In 1990, Hieroglyphic Stairway 4 was discovered, and in 1991 the tomb of Ruler 2 was excavated.

Support for the project came from the National Geographic Society, the Institute of Anthropology and History of Guatemala,

Panel 10, possibly a representation of Ruler 1, Dos Pilas. Late Classic period.

to Dos Pilas), then abo
miles [12.1 kilometers] o
(2:30 to 4:00).

2. Punta de Chimino to
Caribe: about 15 minute
boat.

3. Flores to Sayaxché:
miles [63.9 kilometers]
rough rock road (2:24).

4. El Remate to Sayaxché: 1
miles [30.3 kilometers] by pav
road (:33), then 39.7 miles [6:
kilometers] by rough rock ro
(2:24).

5. Tikal to Sayaxché: 39.7 mil
[63.9 kilometers] by paved roa
(1:07), then 39.7 miles [63.9
kilometers] by rough rock road
(2:24).

Getting There

Getting to Dos Pilas is a bit difficult; indeed, the site is the
most difficult to reach of all
those rated in this guide, which
accounts for its rating of only
one star.

One plan is to spend the
night before you go to Dos Pilas
in Sayaxché. Ask at the Hotel
Guayacán about a boat and
guide to the site, and someone
will come to talk to you to make arrangements. Or you can check with Pedro Méndez, who has an office on the waterfront in
Sayaxché and rents both large and small
boats. If you work through the Hotel Guayacán, you will be assured of a reliable boatman and guide, and the hotel will provide
sandwiches and water for the trip.

Another possibility is to spend the
night before you go to Dos Pilas at the Posada de Mateo on Punta de Chimino. This is
closer to Paso Caribe.

Travel time by boat varies tremendously. A fast launch (*launcha rapida*) can
make the trip from Sayaxché to Paso Caribe

Vanderbilt University, and several other or-
ganizations; the project continued through
1994.

In February 1993, an article by Demarest about Dos Pilas and other Petexbatún
sites was published in *National Geographic*.
In it the history of the site is recounted. The
graphics accompanying the text clearly show
what happened at Dos Pilas when it was
under siege in A.D. 761.

Connections

1. Sayaxché to Dos Pilas: 30 minutes to 3
hours by boat to Paso Caribe (the trail head

in about 30 minutes, whereas a boat with lots of cargo and passengers (and a small motor) will take two to three hours for the same trip.

You must leave early in the morning to go to Dos Pilas, from wherever you start, in order to have even a chance of returning before dark. Since you should allow 2 hours for a visit and an hour to eat and rest, it means the trip can take from 9 to 17 hours if you start from Sayaxché, and half an hour less if you start from Punta de Chimino.

The condition of the trail will determine how long it takes you to reach Dos Pilas on foot. The trail can vary from being a muddy stream—which tends to pull your boots off—to being fairly solid ground; it is gently but persistently uphill all the way from the river to the site.

1. When you leave Sayaxché, you head west a short distance on the Pasión River, then you turn left (south) into the Petexbatún River and continue to Paso Caribe. From there you walk in a westerly direction to the site.

2. From Punta de Chimino, you head northwest on Lake Petexbatún to the Petexbatún River and go on to Paso Caribe.

3, 4, and 5. See "Getting There" under "Seibal."

Visitors are not encouraged to stay overnight at Dos Pilas. The archaeological research center is occupied by staff and workers during the field season and is boarded up the rest of the time. Guards at the site might allow you to sling a hammock somewhere or to camp near their huts, but you will have to provide your own equipment. Another possibility would be to check with specialty tour groups that provide camping equipment and arrange tours to remote sites. Look for their ads in *Archaeology* magazine. This way you would not have to walk in *and* out in one day.

When you walk to Dos Pilas you should wear boots and travel as light as possible. Your guide will carry the food and water, but you should strip down your camera gear to essentials. You do not need a tele-

photo lens at Dos Pilas, but you should have a wide-angle lens and plastic bags or sheeting to protect your camera gear should you get rained on. You will also find a windbreaker or light-weight rain gear useful for the boat trip back to Sayaxché or Punta de Chimino, especially if you are on the river in the cool of evening, or if it rains.

It is sometimes possible to hire mules or horses at Paso Caribe to reach Dos Pilas. Reportedly, it will take about the same amount of time as walking to the site over the same trail.

If you plan to visit Seibal and/or Aguateca while you are in the area, see them first. I guarantee that after a trip to Dos Pilas you will be too exhausted for a trip to either of the others on the following day.

Postscript

Along the trail to Dos Pilas, somewhat after midway, you will pass the site of Arroyo de Piedra, reportedly a small but nice site with a plaza and structures that are kept cleared. I have not visited the site, but apparently one well-preserved and two moderately well-preserved stelae can be seen there. If you stop for a visit, add some time to the figures given earlier for the trip to Dos Pilas.

★
AGUATECA
(ah-gwah-TEH-kah)

Derivation:
   Named after Arroyo Aguateca,
   above which the site lies.
Location:
   Southwestern part of the
   Department of Petén,
   Guatemala.
Maps: 4 (p. 112) and 4D (p. 155)

The Site

Aguateca lies on a north-south ridge that
runs along the west side of Lake Petexbatún; the site covers 175 acres [0.7 square
kilometers]. There are a number of walls,
probably defensive, at Aguateca; when the
site was remapped in 1984, the combined
length of the walls was 2.3 miles [3.7 kilo-
meters]. Since then more walls have been
discovered and mapped, some in outlying
hilltop areas. At least 157 structures have
been recorded at Aguateca, but the architectural remains have not been restored—
though stairs can be seen in front of a couple
of the structures. A via (a street delineated
by structures rather than by walls or para-
pets) was also found recently at Aguateca;
before this, the only known vias in the
Petén were at Yaxhá. Vias are known, however, at Chacchoben and Chichmuul (both
in Quintana Roo, Mexico) and at Caracol,
Belize.

The main areas of the site are kept
cleared, and the view from the edge of the
escarpment is spectacular.

The main reason to visit Aguateca is to
see the carved stelae—though over the
years, some parts of some of them have been
looted. The stelae were cleaned recently
and are protected with thatch shelters. The
carved stelae are in the Main Plaza, in front
of buildings that border the east and south
sides. There are two plain stelae in front of

the structure on the west side of the plaza,
and another fragmented one on the north
side of the plaza. Unhappily, the carved stelae are also fragmented. It is difficult to get
overall photos of the monuments, but some
detail shots are possible. The most interesting are Stelae 1 and 2 on the east side and
Stela 7 on the south side of the plaza.

Stela 1 shows a single figure who is
richly attired and almost completely surrounded by panels of glyphs; the figure has
been identified as Ruler 4 of Dos Pilas. By
the time of his accession in A.D. 741, recorded on the stela, Aguateca was a twin
capital with Dos Pilas, and Ruler 4 lived
mostly at Aguateca. Sadly, some of the text
on the stela was sawn off and illicitly removed from the site in 1993.

Stela 2 was erected by and portrays
Ruler 3 of Dos Pilas, and it commemorated
a victory over Seibal in A.D. 735. Stela 2 of
Dos Pilas, bearing the same date, also commemorates this event; there are many simi-
larities between the two stelae. The regalia
worn by Ruler 3 on both monuments exhibits some influence from central Mexico.
There is a trapezoidal element—generally
called the Mexican Yearsign—in the headdresses, along with depictions of Tlaloc on
the loincloth aprons. There are other points
of similarity as well. The major upper fragments of Stela 2 are lying on the ground; a
bottom fragment, depicting the crouching
captive lord Yich'ak Balam of Seibal, stands
upright nearby.

Stela 7 is badly fragmented, and some
major portions are missing. It dates to A.D.
790, the latest date known from Aguateca.
The stela portrays a late ruler of Dos Pilas
conducting a period ending ceremony. One
fragment, forming the lower section of the
stela, is lying on its side. This part has the
clearest carving. A realistic fish and a mask
that decorate the ankle of the figure are especially well preserved.

It appears that about two-thirds of the

Stela 7, Aguateca. Detail of the lower section showing the left leg and foot of the principal figure with a grotesque mask at the ankle. A fish nibbling at vegetation is seen at right center. A.D. 790.

very bottom of the stela—portraying the head and torso of a prone, bound captive when it was originally carved—has been neatly cut away. The remaining third, with the captive's legs, is still attached to the rest of the fragment. The other parts of Stela 7 lie nearby.

Carved stelae 8, 9, and 10, on the south side of the plaza, lie on their backs and are badly eroded, and Stela 5, on the east side, is in many small fragments; some fragments have not yet been located.

Photographs and drawings of stelae 3 and 6 (as well as the other carved stelae from Aguateca) were published by Ian Graham in 1967. Both appear well preserved in the photos. Some time later, we saw only a minuscule portion of the bottom

of Stela 3—bound in the roots of a tree—and only one top fragment of Stela 6.

An additional feature of interest at Aguateca is a sheer-sided ravine that runs through part of the site. It is crossed by several natural bridges, and one of these serves as the present access to the site. If you want to explore the ravine, bring along a flashlight and be careful, for it can be wet and slippery. It is about 200 feet to the bottom in some places.

Recent History

Aguateca was discovered in 1957 by Jesús Segura of Sayaxché, and the first published description of the site was by G. L Vinson, a geologist with Standard Oil Company, in 1960. Ian Graham—one of the early principal investigators of the site—visited Aguateca briefly in 1959, for a longer period in 1960, and again in 1962. His work resulted in a site plan and descriptions, photographs, and drawings of the carved monuments. These were published by the Middle American Research Institute of Tulane University in 1967. Merle Greene Robertson did rubbings of several of the carved stelae, and these were published in 1972.

Aguateca is one of the sites being studied as part of the Petexbatún Regional Archaeological Project under the direction of Arthur A. Demarest of Vanderbilt University. During this work, a previously unrecorded stela was found buried in the Main Plaza at Aguateca, several outlying sites west and south of the main part of Aguateca were mapped, and buildings along the via were studied by Takeshi Inomata, who is in charge of Vanderbilt research at the site. In one of the small palaces that he excavated, Inomata found evidence that the structure had burned; it collapsed atop all of its contents, which formed a rich assortment of artifacts. See "Dos Pilas" for more information on the Petexbatún project.

Connections

1. Sayaxché to Aguateca: 1.25 to 4 hours by boat, then 20 minutes on foot. See "Getting There" under "Dos Pilas" for information on renting boats.

2. Punta de Chimino to Aguateca: about 30 minutes by boat, then 20 minutes on foot.

3. Flores to Sayaxché: 39.7 miles [63.9 kilometers] by rough rock road (2:24).

4. El Remate to Sayaxché: 18.8 miles [30.3 kilometers] by paved road (:33), then 39.7 miles [63.9 kilometers] by rough rock road (2:24).

5. Tikal to Sayaxché: 39.7 miles [63.9 kilometers] by paved road (1:07), then 39.7 miles [63.9 kilometers] by rough rock road (2:24).

Getting There

1. From Sayaxché, you head west a short distance along the Pasión River, then south onto the Petexbatún River. This river later opens up into the lovely Lake Petexbatún. Near the south end of the lake, you turn right, going through the Arroyo Aguateca, a narrow stream that eventually enters a small pool. The pool lies at the foot of the ridge on which Aguateca stands. From the landing at the pool it is a steep but not-too-difficult climb to the site.

2. From Punta de Chimino, you head to the south end of Lake Petexbatún, then proceed as just described.

3, 4, and 5. See "Getting There" under "Seibal."

The caretaker of Aguateca will act as your guide at the site. There are no facilities there; bring your own food and drink. You could leave a small ice chest in the boat while you visit the site—you will enjoy a cold drink afterward. If you start early from Sayaxché and have a fast boat, you will get back in time for a late lunch. On the other hand, since the boat ride is rather long, eating along the way gives you something to do. If you are starting from and returning to Punta de Chimino, you can easily make it back for lunch.

You will need fast film at Aguateca, for tall trees shade the area. Allow 1.5 hours to visit the site once you reach it; wear boots.

If you are also a fisherman, you can combine a trip to Aguateca with fishing along the Petexbatún. The river has rinco, bass, and, in September, tarpon. Ask about this at the Hotel Guayacán.

SECTION 5

• • • •

SOUTHERN GUATEMALA

Monument 26, a composite reptilian monster, El Baúl. Classic period. On display at Finca El Ba
headquarters.

GENERAL INFORMATION FOR SECTION 5, SOUTHERN GUATEMALA

Guatemala City is the starting point for most visitors to the country. It offers hotels and restaurants in various price ranges. Other popular stopovers in the highlands are Antigua, Panajachel (on Lake Atitlán), and Chichicastenango, all of which also have accommodations at various prices. Good accommodations can be found in other areas as well.

Car rentals are available in Guatemala City from agencies in town and at the international airport and from some of the larger hotels. Some of the larger towns in the country also have car rental agencies. A standard vehicle is adequate to reach many of the sites covered in this section. Where a high-clearance vehicle is needed, it is mentioned in the text. Also mentioned are cases in which a guide is needed to reach a particular archaeological site.

Driving (or busing) from Guatemala City to the Petén is possible but not recommended. It is a long and difficult trip over many miles of poor roads. It is better to fly from Guatemala City to Flores and then travel by car from there.

The highways in southern Guatemala are paved, though some stretches are potholed, and invariably you will encounter areas where the road is under reconstruction. Both conditions will dictate slow driving. Where there are unpaved final stretches to the archaeological sites, they are mentioned in the text.

Although highway numbers are shown on the maps included here, and on regular road maps as well, you will rarely see a highway number posted *on* a highway. Road signs at junctions are relatively rare as well, and sometimes when there is a sign, the actual junction is some distance farther along.

The points of reference for southern Guatemala are as follows: (1) in Guatemala City, El Trebol interchange at the junction of Highways CA 1 and CA 9; (2) in Santa Lucía Cotzumalguapa, the intersection of Highway CA 2 and 3a Avenida (3rd Avenue); (3) in Retalhuleu, the plaza in town; (4) in Huehuetenango, the plaza in town; (5) in Chichicastenango, the Texaco gasoline station at the south entrance to town; (6) in Tecpán, the junction of Highway CA 1 and the entrance to town; (7) in Antigua, the town plaza; (8) in Panajachel, the junction of Highway 15 and Calle Principal; and (9) in Teculután, the Longarone Hotel on Highway CA 9, at the east end of town.

There are an adequate number of gasoline stations in southern Guatemala, so gas pump symbols are not included on the maps of this area.

Among the travel agencies in Guatemala City, some specialize in tours to the archaeological sites. There are also travel agencies in Antigua.

Buses run on all the major roads and many of the minor ones as well.

Southern Guatemala is a good place for shopping. You will find a wide array of handwoven textiles made into blouses, shirts, blankets, place mats, sashes, and so forth. Other handcrafted items are wooden masks, baskets, and ceramics; silver and jade jewelry is also sold, much of it in Antigua. Jades S. A. at 4 Calle Oriente No. 34 has an especially wide selection. The other items can be found in artisans shops and markets in the more touristed cities and towns.

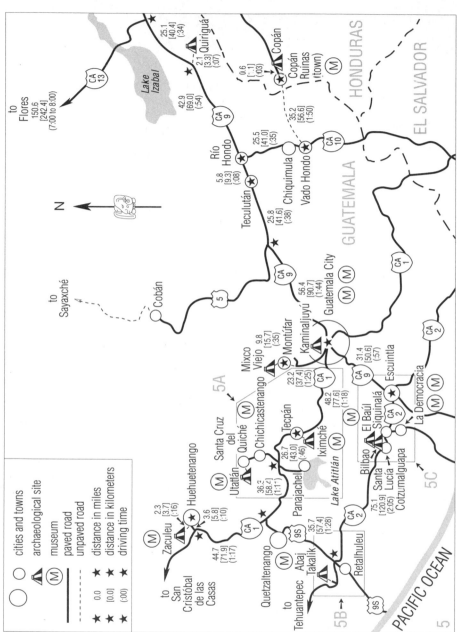

Southern Guatemala

Legend:

cities and towns ○
archaeological site ▲
museum Ⓜ

paved road ——
unpaved road - - -

distance in miles 0.0 ★
distance in kilometers [0.0] ★★
driving time (:00) ★★★

Map labels:

to Flores 150.6 [242.4] (7:00 to 8:00)

CA 13

Lake Izabal

to Sayaxché

Cobán

N

Quiriguá 25.1 [40.4] (:34)
2.1 [3.3] (:07)
Copán
0.6 [1.] (:03)
Copán Ruinas (town) Ⓜ

HONDURAS

EL SALVADOR

42.9 [69.0] (:54)
CA 9
Río Hondo
25.5 [41.0] (:35)
35.2 [56.6] (1:50)
CA 10
5.8 [9.3] (:08)
Teculután
Chiquimula
Vado Hondo

25.8 [41.6] (:38)

5

GUATEMALA

CA 9
56.4 [90.7] (1:44)
Guatemala City Ⓜ Ⓜ
CA 1

Kaminaljuyú
Montúfar 9.8 [15.7] (:35)
Mixco Viejo

Santa Cruz del Quiché Ⓜ
Chichicastenango
23.2 [37.4] (1:25)
Tecpán
Iximché Ⓜ
CA 1
48.2 [77.6] (1:18)

31.4 [50.6] (:57)
CA 9
Escuintla
La Democracia Ⓜ Ⓜ
El Baúl
Siquinalá
CA 2
Santa Lucía Cotzumalguapa
Bilbao
75.1 [120.9] (2:05)

CA 2

5C

Huehuetenango
2.3 [3.7] (:16)
Zaculeu ▲ Ⓜ
3.6 [5.8] (:10)
44.7 [71.9] (1:17)
to San Cristóbal de las Casas
CA 1

Utatlán
36.3 [58.4] (1:11)
Panajachel
Lake Atitlán

26.7 [43.0] (:46)

Quetzaltenango Ⓜ
9S
35.7 [57.4] (1:28)
Abaj Takalik ▲
Retalhuleu
CA 2

to Tehuantepec
5B
9S

PACIFIC OCEAN

5

The front (south side) of Structure 7-3rd, Santa Rita. Early Classic period.

Structure 350, Cuello, view from the south. Late Preclassic period.

Structure N10-9, Lamanai, showing the mask on the lower east side of the building. Early Classic period.

The front (west side) of Structure B-4 (Temple of the Masonry Altars), Altun Ha. Dates to early in the Late Classic period.

Stucco mask on the east side of Structure A-6 (El Castillo), Xunantunich. Late Classic period.

The east side of Structure A-2, Cahal Pech. Dates to early in the Late Classic period.

The front (south side) of Caana, Caracol. Late Classic period.

Stela 2, Nim Li Punit. Late Classic period.

Structure 12, Lubaantun, view from the northwest. Late Classic period.

The front (south side) of Structure 1, Uxbenka, with a row of stelae in front. Late Classic period.

The front (west side) of Structure 216 (undergoing consolidation), Yaxhá. Late Classic period.

The front (west side) of Structure 5C-54 (Lost World Pyramid), Tikal, view from the southwest. Late Preclassic period.

The front (south side) of Structure A-18, Uaxactún. Early Classic period.

Monument 7 from Monte Alto, now on the plaza in La Democracia. Middle Preclassic period.

Stela 1, Seibal, showing non–Classic Maya traits. A.D. 869.

Monument 18, Bilbao. Classic period.

Stela 5, Abaj Takalik. A.D. 126.

The front (northwest side) of Structure 4, Zaculeu, view from the north. Postclassic period.

The front (west side) of Structure C-1, Mixco Viejo. Late Postclassic period.

Structure 2, Iximché, view from the east. Late Postclassic period.

The front (south side) of Monument 2 (Zoomorph B), Quiriguá. A.D. 780.

The back (west side) of Stela 4, Copán. A.D. 726.

The major structure bordering the south side of the plaza, San Andrés, view from the northeast. Classic-Postclassic period.

The front (west side) of Structure 1, Tazumal. Classic period.

★ ★ ★ ★
NATIONAL MUSEUM OF
ARCHAEOLOGY AND ETHNOLOGY
(Guatemala City Museum)

The Guatemala City Museum has the finest archaeological collection in the country—as you would expect—and is a must for all visitors. The exhibition rooms of the museum are laid out around a central rotunda, and from the entrance you proceed counterclockwise. This takes you from the earliest time period covered to the latest. Half-way around is the main access for the rotunda proper; after seeing the monuments there, you continue counterclockwise and return to the entrance.

The first room deals with comparative cultures and early human migrations. A map shows prehistoric sites in Guatemala, and another shows all of Mesoamerica. Technology and instruments come next, with displays of bone tools and ornaments, a huge core of obsidian, and some large obsidian blades. An interesting display is a human skull carved with designs; it was found at Kaminaljuyú. The skull is somewhat crushed, but the designs are visible. A drawing of the skull and its designs has been placed above it.

The next room is devoted to the Preclassic period in the lowlands. There is a full-size replica of one of the masks from Structure E-7-sub at Uaxactún, and a model of the structure itself. Ceramics are displayed, and at the junction with the next room are two columnar stone heads from Kaminaljuyú and the Preclassic Stela 5 from the same site. This adjoining room contains objects from the highlands dating to the Preclassic period. One large carved stone is unusual in showing a number of small seated figures that are widely spaced, with large plain areas in between. This is unlike most monuments, on which almost all areas are covered with designs. The monument is unlabeled, but when we asked, the guard said it came from Kaminaljuyú and was discovered fairly recently.

Other stone carvings from Kaminaljuyú are a potbellied figure and a part of Stela 10 with some beautifully preserved carving. It dates to the Miraflores phase at Kaminaljuyú (100 B.C. to A.D. 200). It is nicely lighted and can be fully appreciated.

The next room is devoted to the Preclassic period on the south coast, although some monuments from Kaminaljuyú are placed here as well; they are Monument 2 and Stela 4. Another interesting display is the bottom of Stela 3 from Abaj Takalik; it is similar to Stela 12, which is still at the site. Well-lighted glass cases contain ceramics. Unfortunately, most of the stone monuments are not so well lighted.

The Classic period in the lowlands is covered in the next room. There is a model of Quiriguá and a reconstruction of a burial from Tikal. Ceramics are displayed in cases along the walls. There are models and displays of religious and agricultural life.

The next room covers the Classic period in the highlands and on the south coast. The displays are mostly ceramics and a few carved stone monuments.

You next come to one of the truly outstanding monuments—a ball court marker that was discovered at Tikal in the early 1980s. This limestone marker has a composite silhouette shape, with an upper oval section, a spherical part below, a truncated cone below that, and, at the bottom, a tall cylindrical base. A variety of motifs are carved on the monument, including (in the upper parts) a stylized Tlaloc head, an owl holding an atlatl, two human heads with foreign headdresses and butterfly-shaped nose plugs, and a Mexican Yearsign. The cylindrical base has two panels of glyphs with a total of 72 glyph blocks. The date A.D. 378 is recorded, and the text apparently deals with the death of Jaguar Paw III of Tikal and the inauguration

Green stone, jade, pyrite, and shell mask from burial 160, Tikal. Dates to around A.D. 527. On display in the Jade Salon in the Guatemala City Museum.

site's reconstruction, and some beautiful polychrome ceramics.

You next come to the Jade Salon in a separate side room; it is open on Tuesday through Friday. The Jade Salon has some truly spectacular displays, two of which have been widely published. One is a carved jade plaque, drilled horizontally to be used as a pectoral. It portrays a seated Maya lord who leans toward, and is apparently conversing with, a dwarf. Although the plaque was found at Nebaj, a Postclassic site in the highlands, it is believed to have been carved in the lowlands during the Late Classic period, perhaps near Piedras Negras in the Usumacinta valley.

The other well-published object is a realistic mosaic funeral mask made of jade and other green stones, pyrite, and shell; it comes from Burial 160 at Tikal, an interment that took place around A.D. 527. Originally it was believed that all of the green stones in the mask were jade, but spectrometer testing proved that only the lower section of the ear flares were jade. See the September 1987 issue of *National Geographic* for more interesting details. This magnificent mask was discovered in 1963 in 174 pieces; it has since been beautifully restored.

Three other mosaic masks that are less well known come from Abaj Takalik. Made of jade and dating to the Classic period, they are somewhat less realistic than the Tikal mask but are equally splendid. Their reconstruction is listed as hypothetical.

Other items in the Jade Salon include necklaces, ear spools, and a carved *hacha,* all made of jade. There is a display on the technology of jade working and a map showing where jade is found in Guatemala; another map shows the sources of serpentine. There is also a reconstruction of Burial 116 from Temple I at Tikal, which includes the skeleton and jade and ceramic offerings.

Outside of the Jade Salon is Stela 33

of the new ruler, Smoking Frog. While the designs on the upper part of the marker have affinities with the art of Teotihuacán, the glyphs on the lower part are purely Maya, and they are in pristine condition. The marker was found in Group 6C-XVI, an elite residential area south of the Lost World Pyramid at Tikal. The marker was of dynastic significance and presumably was displayed publicly from 378 onward. The Tikal marker, with its four distinct parts, is quite similar to a marker found in La Ventilla section of Teotihuacán, though the designs carved on the markers are different.

Nearby, against a wall, is an epoxy resin cast of the innermost lintel from Temple IV at Tikal. It would be hard to tell that it isn't the original. In a side room there is a large model of Tikal, photographs showing the from Naranjo, dating to A.D. 780. Unfortunately, it is hard to appreciate because of the lack of lighting. Next comes an open area that faces the rotunda; along the walls of one side are a couple of lintels from Piedras Negras. Within the open area are a number of monuments, including a huge ceramic pot and one of the three supports of Altar 4 from Piedras Negras; it is in the form of a grotesque head and dates to 790. Along the back wall of this area is the well-published Throne I from Piedras Negras, dating to 785. The fronts of the two legs and the edge of the seat are covered with hieroglyphs. The back shows the heads of two humans and one hand of each person. They appear to be gesturing toward each other. They occupy an open space that also represents the eyes of a grotesque mask that surrounds the humans. Also against the back wall is the all-glyphic and well-preserved Stela 36 from Piedras Negras; it dates to 667.

Along another wall in this area are some magnificent but poorly lighted stone monuments, including a Late Classic three-dimensional skull wearing a plume; it comes from the Cotzumalhuapa region. Next are three stela (numbers 7, 3, and 4) from Machaquilá, in the Petén, that date to the ninth century A.D.

You now go to the rotunda proper, which is encircled with more than two dozen major stone monuments, most of which date to the Late Classic period and come from sites in the Petén. All are worth some time to study. These monuments get some natural illumination and can be fully appreciated; this is one of the most interesting displays in the museum. A few highlights are Stela 20 from Tikal (A.D. 751) and its accompanying Altar 8, depicting a bound captive; Stela 26 from Uaxactún (445), the glyphic side of which is very well preserved (the other side is greatly eroded); Stela 6

Stela 20, Tikal. A.D. 751. On display in the rotunda of the Guatemala City Museum.

from Piedras Negras (687), with a figure in a niche in the upper part; Stela 1 from La Amelia (810), showing a figure in a dancing pose; Stela 3 from Seibal (810), with an unusual three-panel format; Stela 4 from Ucanal (849), with a warrior ancestor in the upper part; and the all-glyphic Stela 4 from Ixtutz (586), the upper part of which is in pristine condition.

In addition to the Maya monuments just listed, there are five monuments from the south coast carved in Cotzumalhuapa style. They are Stelae 1, 2, and 3 from Palo Verde, each portraying a standing figure with upraised arms, and Monuments 88 and 89 from

The glyphic side of Stela 26, Uaxactún. A.D. 445. On display in the rotunda of the Guatemala City Museum.

Following this is the ethnological section, where typical costumes are displayed. There are also a dugout canoe, examples of basketry, hats, ceremonial painted pottery from various parts of the country, and modern jewelry. On an upper wall in this section is an interesting mural.

From this room you reenter the main entrance area, where, off to the right, a special section exhibits materials from Río Azul, a site in the far north of the Petén. It features a reconstruction of Tomb 19 and a display of ceramics, the most interesting of which is a unique Early Classic vessel from Tomb 19 that has a screw top with a handle. The painted glyphs on the pot have been deciphered by David Stuart, who understood the text to mean that the pot was intended to hold two kinds of chocolate drink. His reading was confirmed when Hershey Food Laboratories analyzed some residues in the pot and found them to be cacao. The exhibit also includes a map of Río Azul, photographs taken during excavation, and paintings of the Tomb 19 burial and the structure where it was found. The Río Azul section is open on Tuesday through Friday.

The National Museum is located in Aurora Park at Number 5 La Aurora in Zona 13, at the south end of the Guatemala City. It can be reached by private vehicle, bus, or taxi, although it is sometimes hard to hail a taxi when you want to return to the main part of town.

The museum is open from 9:00 A.M. to 4:00 P.M. on Tuesday through Friday and from 9:00 A.M. to noon and 2:00 to 4:00 P.M. on Saturday and Sunday (except for the Jade Salon and the Río Azul section, which are closed on the weekend). The whole museum is closed on Monday. Photography is permitted, but flash and tripods are not allowed. Rest rooms are available. Allow 2.5 hours to see this splendid collection.

Las Ilusiones, with circular cartouches typical of the area. All the south coast monuments date to the Late Classic period.

On the floor of the rotunda, bordering the garden area that lies below, is an array of tenoned heads, in various forms, and a potbellied figure. The figure comes from Kaminaljuyú and the heads are mostly from the south coast.

Return now to the open area off the rotunda and continue your counterclockwise tour. You next come to a room devoted to the Postclassic period, with a scale model of Zaculeu in the center and cases displaying ceramics along the walls. There are also a few unlighted stone monuments.

Stela 4, Ucanal. A.D. 849. On display in the rotunda of the Guatemala City Museum.

★ ★ ★ ★
POPOL VUH MUSEUM
(poh-POHL VOOH)
(Guatemala City)

The Popol Vuh Museum is named for the sacred book of the Quiché Maya that relates their ancient creation myths. It is one of the best archaeological museums in Guatemala, its collection surpassed only by the Guatemala City Museum.

Entrance to the museum is through the ticket counter in the museum store, where publications (including a guidebook for the museum in Spanish or English), postcards, and gift items are sold. The museum has five exhibition rooms and an outside corri-

Display of funerary urns from the Ixil region of the Guatemala highlands. Late Classic period. On display in the Popol Vuh Museum.

dor with archaeological specimens from various parts of the country. One room is devoted to folklore, and another to the colonial period.

Room 1, the largest, contains an incredible display of 61 ceramic funerary urns from the Ixil region in the highlands of the Department of Quiché. This is the most extensive collection of its kind in the world. Some of the urns are more than three feet tall and were used to hold human remains, with the deceased placed inside in a fetal position. Other, smaller urns were used to hold possessions of the deceased. The urns, which date to the Late Classic period, were decorated after firing with various painted motifs, but jaguar images predominate. The vessels line both long walls of the room, and at the far end of the room are a couple of bas-relief stone carvings from Kaminaljuyú that date to the Late Preclassic period.

Room 2 is devoted to the southern Maya lowlands, with displays of ceramics dating from Late Preclassic through Late Classic times. There are well-preserved figurines and polychrome pots, along with a display of eccentric flints. Stone monuments include a fragment of a Late Classic stela carved with glyphs and an Early Classic incised altar that comes from somewhere north of Tikal. There is also a model of the North Acropolis at Tikal showing its construction sequence.

The displays in Room 3 are from the highlands and are mostly of ceramics dating from the Late Preclassic through the Late Classic period. One unusual vessel takes the form of a human head; its lid forms the upper part of the head, which shows the eyebrows. The nose is short, wide at the nostrils, and has wrinkles across the bridge. The mouth is very wide and the lower lip is unusually thick. The physiognomy is distinctly non–Classic Maya. The vessel dates to the Late Classic period and comes from the highlands, though no specific site is listed. This is perhaps the one flaw in an otherwise top-notch museum; all of the objects bear some labeling in Spanish, but only a few are attributed to a particular site. This results, unfortunately, when artifacts are not excavated in an archaeological context by professionals; when they are properly excavated, abundant contextual information is available.

Room 4 contains items from the central highlands and the south coast of Guatemala. Among them are several Late Preclassic carved stones from Kaminaljuyú and some nice carved stone *hachas* from the south coast that date to the Classic period. One outstanding ceramic display is a group of *incensarios*, including some in tubular form. The *incensarios* were recovered from Lake Amatitlán (a little south of Guatemala City) by divers between 1950 and 1960; they date to around A.D. 400 to 600. There also are Middle and Late Preclassic ceramics from Kaminaljuyú and Late Preclassic and Early Classic ceramics from the south coast.

Room 5 is devoted to items from the southeast Maya lowlands, a peripheral region that includes southeastern Guatemala, western Honduras, and northwestern El Salvador. Highlights in this room are Ulúa-style alabaster vases, Copador ceramics (made principally at Copán), and tops of two Late Classic *incensarios* with seated figures who wear headpieces. Parts of the figures are brightly painted.

Next is the room with folkloric materials. One of its outstanding displays is a collection of masks used in traditional dances—one of the finest collections in Guatemala. There are also manikins dressed in traditional dance costumes and a figure representing Maximón, a pagan deity considered "miraculous."

Last in the row is the room devoted to objects from the colonial period, which are mostly of a religious nature. You will see part of a highly decorative altarpiece, covered with gold leaf, that dates to the eighteenth century; it is a good example of the Guatemalan Baroque style. There also are silver candlesticks, images and oil paintings of saints, and small religious images that were displayed in homes. One nonreligious display has silver imperial crowns and ducal coronets.

You leave this room by a side door that brings you to an open corridor bordered by an atrium on the right and the outside wall of the museum on the left; there is a walkway in between. Against the long wall of the museum is a collection of pedestal sculptures, most of which are from the south coast and date to the Late Preclassic period. Farther along the wall is a selection of plain yokes.

On the right, in and between beds of vegetation, are other carved stones. An important one is a stela from the Department of Quiché with a square face in its lower section. There are also mushroom stones and carved serpent heads, one of which has a human head emerging from its mouth; it is Late Classic and comes from the south coast. A corner fragment of a Late Preclassic monument from Kaminaljuyú is nicely carved and well preserved. Nearby are tenoned animal heads, some naturalistic and some stylized. They are Late Classic and come from the south coast.

Near the end of the corridor is a group of three kneeling stone figures, all of them headless. They come from the site of Sin Cabezas on the south coast and date to the Late Classic period.

Lighting in the museum is well above average. There is natural light along the outside corridor and some in the first room that is supplemented by spotlights. The interior rooms and display cases are well illuminated artificially. Nevertheless, there are still some objects that will benefit photographically from the use of flash. There is a small extra charge to use flash; pay it at the ticket counter when you enter the museum.

The Popol Vuh Museum began as a department of Francisco Marroquín University in 1977, when the private collection of Jorge and Ella Castillo was donated to the university along with other bequests.

The museum is located in an office building (Edificio Galerías Reforma), and a curbside sign identifies it. The building is at Avenida La Reforma 8-60 in Zona 9 in Guatemala City. The museum is on the sixth floor, with access by elevator; it is open from 9:00 A.M. to 5:00 P.M. on Monday

Stylized stone jaguar head with a tenon on the back, from the south coast of Guatemala. Late Classic period. On display in the Popol Vuh Museum.

through Saturday. There are rest rooms in Room 4 of the museum.

The museum is easy to reach by taxi or bus as well as by private vehicle. Allow 1.5 hours to see and photograph this exceptional collection. You may want to add another few minutes to see some pre-Columbian stone sculptures at the entrance to the underground parking garage of the building.

★ ★
KAMINALJUYÚ
(kah-mee-nahl-hoo-YOO)

Derivation:
  Quiché Maya for "Hills of the Dead."
Location:
  Central part of the Department of Guatemala. On the outskirts of Guatemala City.
Map: 5 (p. 174)

The Site

Kaminaljuyú is one of the largest sites in the Guatemala highlands, and it was an important port of trade for 800 years. The site is extremely important archaeologically, but for the visitor there are few visual rewards. More than 200 mounds have been recorded at Kaminaljuyú—the remains of temples, residences, shrines, ball courts, and tombs. Most, however, have been destroyed by encroaching residential and commercial development. Part of the archaeological zone has been declared a park, and it sits like an island in a sea of residences. The areas of interest are excavations, covered with tin roofs, that can be seen below ground level and behind chain-link fences. None of the excavations is visible when you enter the site, but easily followed trails lead to them.

The trail to the left goes to the Acropolis, where remains of stairways and temple bases can be seen. Some of the early build-

View of some unrestored mounds and a covered excavation in the Acropolis, Kaminaljuyú. The suburbs of Guatemala City are in the background.

A standing stela in front of an excavation in the Palangana section, Kaminaljuyú. Possibly Late Preclassic period.

seum. The stela just mentioned is the only carved stone monument we saw at the site. In the excavation, various construction stages can be seen. The rest of the remains at Kaminaljuyú are grass-covered mounds that have not been excavated.

At one time the guard at the site would take visitors down into the excavated areas (he provided the candles needed), and skeletal and architectural remains could be seen close up. It seems that this is no longer allowed, so there is less for visitors to see today than in years gone by.

Kaminaljuyú was first occupied around 2500 B.C., when it was a simple farming community. It continued to grow through the Middle Preclassic period, and in the Late Preclassic it reached a peak in sculptural art. A prime example is the beautifully carved Stela 10, which bears an early form of Maya hieroglyphs; the stela is now displayed in the Guatemala City Museum.

Around A.D. 400, strong influence from Teotihuacán appeared at Kaminaljuyú in both architecture (*talud-tablero* temple bases) and ceramics; this influence lasted 200 years, after which there was a return to earlier Maya styles. The site continued to flourish until around 800, a time of unsettled conditions in the highlands, when a more defensible setting became imperative. During the Postclassic period, many Late Preclassic sculptures (most of which were already broken) were brought to the Palangana and erected, making it a sort of shrine.

Recent History

Kaminaljuyú has been known for a long time and was visited by Alfred P. Maudslay near the turn of the century. He later published a plan of the site and a photograph of the mounds. Extensive excavations were undertaken at Kaminaljuyú by the Carnegie

ings at Kaminaljuyú are adobe substructures that supported temples of perishable materials. Later buildings were faced with volcanic pumice blocks, covered with clay, and plastered. Rich burials have also been discovered at the site.

The trail to the right from the entrance leads to the Palangana (Basin) section. This area was given its name because it has a plaza surrounded by high mounds, forming a sort of basin. In front of this excavation is a standing stela. The top and bottom of the monument are plain, but in the middle there is a panel with a dragon-head motif. The design seems Izapan, and the stela probably dates to the Late Preclassic period. A number of carved stone monuments have been excavated in the Palangana, and some are displayed in the Guatemala City Mu-

Excavation in the Palangana section, Kaminaljuyú.

Institution of Washington in 1936, and the work continued for several years. Publications by Alfred V. Kidder, Jesse D. Jennings, and Edwin M. Shook in 1946 and by Shook and Kidder in 1952 reported on this work.

In the late 1960s, Pennsylvania State University sponsored work at the site, directed by William T. Sanders and Joseph W. Michels, who in 1969 reported on work done the previous year. In the 1970s, Charles D. Cheek studied the Teotihuacán-style structures at Kaminaljuyú. A series of monographs on the site was published by Pennsylvania State University beginning in the 1970s.

In 1994 Kaminaljuyú was made an archaeological park, and Guatemala's Institute of Anthropology and History began a project that is concentrating on one of the few structures still standing. As this work progresses, perhaps there will be more for visitors to see.

Connection

Guatemala City to Kaminaljuyú: 1.9 miles [3.1 kilometers] by paved road (:10).

Getting There

From El Trebol interchange in Guatemala City, head northwest for a few blocks, then bear right onto Calle (Street) de San Juan Sacatepéquez. Proceed to 23 Avenida (Avenue) and turn right; then go straight ahead to the site. This street reaches Kaminaljuyú near the entrance gate.

The site can be reached by taxi or bus from Guatemala City, as well as by private vehicle. If you take a taxi to the site, you might want to ask the driver to wait for you or to return later; taxis are hard to find in this area. Allow one hour to visit the site. There is no food or drink available, and when we last visited, the rest rooms were nonoperational. Kaminaljuyú is reportedly open from 8:00 A.M. to 6:00 P.M. daily, but it was still unopened when we arrived at 9:15 A.M. Our taxi driver eventually honked his horn, and shortly afterward someone arrived to open the gate.

★ ★ ★
MIXCO VIEJO
(MEESH-koh vee-EH-hoh)

Derivation:
Mixco means "Place of Clouds" in Pokomam Maya. Viejo means "Old" in Spanish.

Location:
Extreme northeastern part of the Department of Chimaltenango, Guatemala.

Map: 5 (p. 174)

The Site

Mixco Viejo is delightfully situated, its structures grouped in clusters atop flattened areas of a steep hill bordered by ravines that made the site easily defensible. Mixco Viejo is surrounded by mountains, and views from the site are superb.

The more than 120 structures at Mixco Viejo include temple bases, altars, ball courts, and platforms. The remains visible today date to the Late Postclassic period. Multiple layers of construction are visible in certain buildings, and some are built with

Structure B-3 (double pyramid), Mixco Viejo. Late Postclassic period.

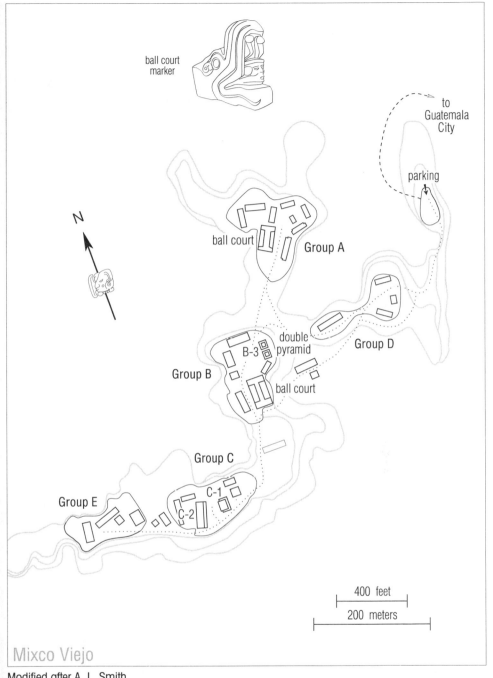

ball court
marker

to
Guatemala
City

parking

N

ball court
Group A

double
pyramid
B-3
Group B
ball court
Group D

Group C

Group E
C-1
C-2

400 feet
200 meters

Mixco Viejo

Modified after A. L. Smith.

Ball court in Group B, with copies of sculptured markers on each wall, Mixco Viejo. Late Postclassic period.

slate-thin layers of stone. The groups of buildings are designated by letters; the most interesting are Groups A, B, and C.

At the entrance to Mixco Viejo there is a large scale model of the site. Take a look at the model to become oriented before you start your tour. From the model, follow the trail south (you will pass a building where you sign a registration book) and then west to Group D, where there are remains of a temple base and platforms. From there you can see Group A (to the north) and Group B (to the west); foot trails lead to both. Follow the trail that heads north to Group A. One of Mixco Viejo's two ball courts is on the west side of the group; both courts are sunken and l-shaped, and the court in Group A is somewhat smaller than that in Group B. A temple base and platforms are also found in Group A. From there, head south to Group B, which features a double pyramid (Structure B-3). The twin pyramids share a common base; each rises in

five tiers and has a stairway on the west bordered by wide *alfardas*.

There are also platforms and another temple base in Group B, but even more interesting is the ball court at the southeast edge of the group. When this court was excavated, a carved stone marker was discovered intact; it depicts a human head in the open jaws of a serpent. The marker has been removed and two cement replicas placed in the upper walls of the court. The marker is the only known sculpture from Mixco Viejo.

To the south and southwest of Group B lies Group C. Its most important structure is C-1, which had three construction stages, the earlier ones serving as fill for the later. It also has a western stairway. After excavation, the structure was nicely restored, but unfortunately it was damaged in the 1976 earthquake, and the upper part of the structure is now rubble. The two photographs of the structure shown here, one taken before

Structure C-1, Mixco Viejo, before the 1976 earthquake. Late Postclassic period.

the earthquake and one afterward, show the damage clearly. Facing Structure C-1 is C-2, a long, two-tiered platform. A single stairway in the center of the east side ascends the first tier, and four stairways ascend the second. Structure C-2 was also restored and later damaged by the earthquake. It was undergoing reconstruction when we last visited Mixco Viejo.

A trail leads to Group E, where there are remains of platforms and a temple base. When you retrace your steps to Group B, you can take a side trail (beginning just south of the ball court) down to a lower level of the group, which has a temple base and a platform. From there another trail leads back to the entrance of the site.

Recent History

The exact date of the founding of Mixco Viejo, the capital of the Pokomams, is unknown, but the oldest structures at the site date to no earlier than the thirteenth century A.D., according to Henri Lehmann. The site was a flourishing city at the time of the Spanish conquest in 1525. Its residents were confident of their defensive position and fought ferociously against Pedro de Alvarado and his forces for a month before succumbing.

After Alvarado defeated Mixco Viejo, he ordered the city burned and deported the survivors. They were sent to a place about 17 miles [27.4 kilometers] to the south (near the western outskirts of modern Guatemala City), where a new town called Mixco was formed under the tutelage of the Spaniards.

Structure C-1, Mixco Viejo, after the 1976 earthquake. Late Postclassic period.

Francisco Antonio Fuentes y Guzmán mentioned Mixco Viejo in 1690 in his history of Guatemala. After that, there is little to be said about the site until 1896, when the German geographer Karl Sapper visited, mapped, and recorded it. His work was published in 1898, and for 50 years it formed the only basis for study of the site.

A. Ledyard Smith conducted a reconnaissance in central Guatemala that included Mixco Viejo for the Carnegie Institution of Washington, which published his work in 1955. In 1958, Jorge F. Guillemín published a study of one of the structures at the site. Major excavations and restoration were undertaken by the French-Guatemalan Archaeological Mission, directed by Lehmann, who was then subdirector of the Museum of Man in Paris. Four field seasons, each of five to six months' duration, were conducted, beginning in 1954 and ending in 1967.

Connection

Guatemala City to Mixco Viejo: 19.9 miles [32.0 kilometers] by paved road (1:11), then 13.2 miles [21.1 kilometers] by rock and dirt roads (:49).

Getting There

From El Trebol interchange in Guatemala City, head northwest for a few blocks, then bear to the right onto Calle (Street) de San Juan Sacatapéquez (Highway 5). Continue northwest to the western outskirts of the city, where you will cross a small bridge, 4.8 miles [7.7 kilometers] from El Trebol. Immediately past the bridge the road curves to the right, and another road comes in on the left. This junction is unmarked, but the road you want is the one on the left that goes to San Pedro Sacatepéquez and later to San Juan Sacatepéquez (Highway 5). Watch

Temple base and platform on a lower level between Group B and Group D, Mixco Viejo. Late Postclassic period.

carefully here, because it is easy to miss the correct cutoff. (The road that curves to the right enters a subdivision.) Highway 5 curves and climbs and offers some nice views of Guatemala City below and off to the right. The highway is paved as far as the cutoff for San Raimundo, 15.1 miles [24.3 kilometers] past the bridge. There is a sign for Mixco Viejo at this junction; take the road on the left and go to Montúfar. At the far end of Montúfar is another sign for Mixco Viejo at which you turn left and continue to the site. This part of the road is very steep and has many tight curves. Shortly before you reach Mixco Viejo you can get a view of some of the structures off to the left.

At the time of our last visit to Mixco Viejo, road repairs were going on near the bridge and in another section farther along.

This accounts for the rather long driving time on the "paved" road part of the trip. When the work is finished, you will be able to drive that part in less time, as we did on an earlier trip.

There is no food available at Mixco Viejo, but soft drinks (unchilled) are sold at the building where you sign the registration book. A shelter with a picnic table stands nearby. Allow 2.5 hours for a visit.

Buses from Guatemala City pass within 0.5 mile [0.8 kilometer] of Mixco Viejo on their way to Pachalum, but reportedly there is only one a day each way, and the interval between their stopping at the junction and returning to it is only a couple of hours. This would scarcely allow enough time to hike up to the site, visit it, and return to catch the bus back to Guatemala City.

IXIMCHÉ

(eesh-eem-CHEH)

Derivation:
The Cakchiquel Maya name for the breadnut tree, which grows in the area and bears an edible fruit.

Original name:
Iximché.

Another name:
Patinamit, meaning "the city" in Cakchiquel Maya.

Location:
Northwestern part of the Department of Chimaltenango, Guatemala.

Maps: 5 (p. 174) and 5A (p. 193)

The Site

Iximché, the capital of the Cakchiquels, lies on a ridge almost completely surrounded by deep ravines. It is connected to outside areas only by a thin tongue of land; this is the access to the site today, as it was in ancient times. The structures are laid out around four large ceremonial plazas (A, B, C, and D), and some of the plazas and buildings are identified with small signs. The buildings at Iximché are constructed of stone, and originally they were plastered and painted, sometimes with murals in Mixtec-Puebla style, though little of this remains today. The architectural style is called Epi-Toltec, and Mexican influence is quite evident. Several structures and platforms have been restored or partly restored; Plazas A, B, and C and the structures around them are kept nicely cleared.

As you walk to the site you will pass a few platforms before you reach Plaza A. When you enter the plaza you will see a large restored ball court (Structure 8) on the right (south). It is an l-shaped enclosed court with stairways on the two ends.

Structure 2 is on the west side of the plaza. It rises in tiers and has a stairway on the east side. Originally it had a two-room temple with a beam and mortar roof on top, but that has not survived, nor has any of the other superstructures of temples or residential units at Iximché. None of the structures at the site supported vaulted masonry roofs.

Along the north side of the plaza are some platforms that were the bases for long rooms that may have been residences. You will see the remains of the lower parts of pillars on Structure 22; they formed five doorways that entered the single room of the structure.

On the east side of the plaza is Structure 3; it is similar to Structure 2, and both were pyramidal bases for temples. The stairway of Structure 3 faces west, and in front of it at plaza level is a small rectangular platform. Other larger but lower platforms are found near the center of the plaza. A little to the southeast of these platforms is one of the entrances to Plaza B; it passes along the side of Structure 1.

Structure 1, another pyramidal temple base, has a single stairway facing onto Plaza B. The other structures around this plaza are restored platforms of various heights believed to have supported residential buildings. A large compound on the northeast side of the plaza is called the Palace; it was definitely residential. Three distinct levels of construction were discovered during excavation of the Palace (and in other areas of the site as well), the earliest of which corresponds to the founding of Iximché. All that remains of the Palace today are a sunken patio and the low platforms on which the houses stood. There is a small circular platform in Plaza B.

From the southeast corner of Plaza B head east for a look at Structure 7, an unrestored ball court. Beyond the court is Struc-

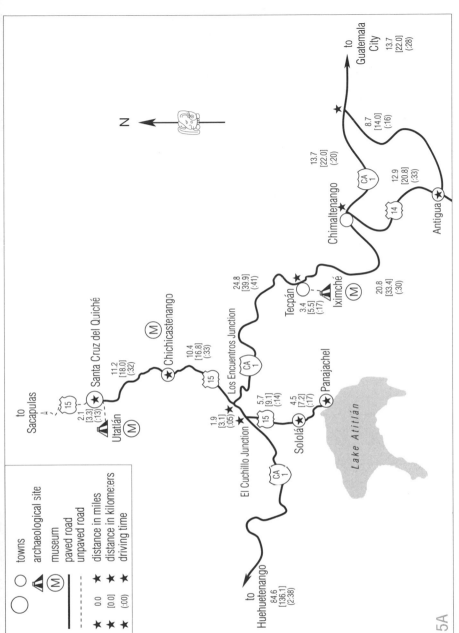

Legend

○	towns
○	archaeological site
▲ M	museum
	paved road
- - -	unpaved road
	distance in miles
	distance in kilometers
	driving time
★ 0.0	distance in miles
★ [0.0]	distance in kilometers
★ (:00)	driving time

N →

to Sacapulas

Santa Cruz del Quiché

15

2.1
[3.3]
(:13)

▲ M
Utatlán

11.2
[18.0]
(:32)

M
Chichicastenango

15

10.4
[16.8]
(:33)

Los Encuentros Junction

CA 1

1.9
[3.1]
(:05)

El Cuchillo Junction

5.7
[9.1]
(:14)

15

Sololá

4.5
[7.2]
(:17)

Panajachel

CA 1

to Huehuetenango

84.6
[136.1]
(2:38)

Lake Atitlán

24.8
[39.9]
(:41)

Tecpán

3.4
[5.5]
(:17)

▲ M
Iximché

20.8
[33.4]
(:30)

13.7
[22.0]
(:20)

CA 1
Chimaltenango

8.7
[14.0]
(:16)

★

to Guatemala City

13.7
[22.0]
(:28)

12.9
[20.8]
(:33)

14

Antigua

5A

Routes to Iximché and Utatlán

Structure 8 (ball court), view from the east, Iximché. Late Postclassic period.

The front (east side) of Structure 2, Iximché. Late Postclassic period.

The front (west side) of Structure 3, with remains of platforms in front, Iximché. Late Postclassic period.

ture 6, a pyramidal temple base that is also unrestored. From the ball court, head left (northwest) and enter Plaza C; there has been some restoration in this plaza, but less than in the first two. The most interesting building in Plaza C is Structure 4 (another pyramidal temple base) on the west side of the plaza. Beyond Plaza C is Plaza D; it is not as well cleared as the others and there are few remains to be seen.

At one time the Cakchiquels were allied with but subordinate to the Quichés. Around 1470, two Cakchiquel lords founded their own capital at Iximché. Although there were a number of construction phases at the site, the city's history was short. In 1524, Pedro de Alvarado arrived with his forces at Iximché, where he was initially welcomed. He took peaceful possession of the city, intending it to be the first Spanish capital of Guatemala. But Alvarado placed heavy tribute burdens on the Cakchiquels, and they rebelled. The Spaniards abandoned Iximché later in 1524 but returned in 1526 and burned the city.

Recent History

One of the men accompanying Alvarado in 1526 was Bernal Díaz del Castillo, who described Iximché in his chronicle *True History of the Conquest of New Spain,* written in his old age.

Iximché and other sites in the highlands were described by Francisco Antonio Fuentes y Guzmán in 1690, in his *History of Guatemala.*

John Lloyd Stephens and Frederick Catherwood visited Iximché in 1840, and Stephens used the name Patinamit. He described the site, but Catherwood apparently did no drawings of the structures—at least

The front (east side) of Structure 1, Iximché. Late Postclassic period.

none was published. Stephens commented that for many years Indians carried stones from the site to build the modern town of Tecpán. In 1887, Alfred P. Maudslay visited Iximché (which he called by that name and Patinamit); he surveyed the site and produced a site plan, which was published in 1889–1902.

The ceramics of the site were studied by Robert Wauchope for the Middle American Research Institute of Tulane University in the 1940s. His work was published in 1948 and 1949. In 1959, Jorge F. Guillemín began excavation and restoration at Iximché, and the work continued into 1961. It was conducted under the auspices of an agency of the Guatemalan government, and Guillemín published reports in 1959, 1967, and 1969.

Connections

1. Chichicastenango to Iximché: 35.2 miles [56.7 kilometers] by paved road (1:14), then 3.4 miles [5.5 kilometers] by dirt road (:17).

2. Guatemala City to Tecpán: 48.2 miles [77.6 kilometers] by paved road (1:18).

3. Antigua to Tecpán: 33.7 miles [54.2 kilometers] by paved road (1:03).

Getting There

1. From Chichicastenango, head south on Highway 15 to Los Encuentros Junction and turn left onto Highway CA 1. Follow CA 1 to the edge of Tecpán (marked with a sign). Turn right at the sign, right again at a pyramid sign a little farther along (in town), and

finally left at another pyramid sign. Continue ahead as the road leaves the town and follow it to a gate, a short distance beyond which is the parking area near the Iximché Museum. From there it is a short walk to the site.

2. From Guatemala City, head west on Highway CA 1 to the sign at the edge of Tecpán and turn left; then follow the directions just given.

3. From Antigua, head northwest on Highway 14 to Highway CA 1 and turn left; this junction is on the eastern outskirts of Chimaltenango. Follow CA 1 to the sign for Tecpán and turn left; then follow the directions for Connection 1.

After you turn off Highway CA 1 and enter Tecpán, the first part of the road is laid stone; later you will be driving over rutted dirt streets and roads. Buses go to Tecpán, but there is no public transportation to Iximché.

No food or drink is available at Iximché, but there are picnic tables and rest rooms near the museum. Along Highway CA 1, 0.5 mile [0.8 kilometer] south of the sign for Tecpán, is the popular restaurant Katok; it is on the east side of the highway. Allow 1.5 hours to visit Iximché; it is open from 9:00 A.M. to 4:00 P.M. daily.

Stone objects recovered from Iximché. Late Postclassic period. On display in the Iximché Museum.

★ ★
IXIMCHÉ MUSEUM

The Iximché Museum opened in 1988, housing its collection in one large room. It is definitely worth a look while you are at the site; I recommend that you visit the museum first, for orientation, before you tour the ruins. Guatemala's Institute of Anthropology and History has prepared a leaflet about Iximché that includes a site plan, and this is sometimes available at the museum. You will find it a help in getting around.

Along the walls of the museum are pedestals supporting small stone carvings, including tenoned heads. There are also manos and metates, diagrams, photographs of the restoration of the site by Jorge F.

Guillemín, who excavated Iximché, and a map of the site. There is a large scale model of the site, and some drawings show details of the murals found on Structure 2.

The museum is open from 8:00 A.M. to noon and from 1:00 to 4:00 P.M. daily. Photography, including the use of flash, is generously permitted; the ambient light is only fair, though it is adequate for viewing. All of the items in the museum come from Iximché, and there is some labeling in Spanish. Allow 30 minutes to see the collection.

★ ★ ★

REGIONAL MUSEUM
(Chichicastenango Museum)

The Chichicastenango Museum is in a building on the south side of the town's main plaza. Sometimes the museum is almost hidden by temporary market stalls.

As you enter the first room of the museum you come to a carved stone roof slab in the center of the room. It is unlabeled but is quite similar to a roof slab from Chuitinamit, a Late Postclassic site in the Guatemala highlands.

The main room of the museum is off to the right, with a double row of display cases down the center that contain ceramics and other artifacts. Some of the ceramic pots and *incensarios* are in mint condition, but none of the items in the collection is labeled with the name of the site from which it comes. Nevertheless, there are some attractive pieces, and visiting the museum is definitely worthwhile.

There are also displays of obsidian blades and lance heads, stone bark beaters, copper axes, and a hammered gold disc depicting the stylized head of an animal. The museum also houses the Rossbach collection, which includes some carved jades, among other items. Ildefonso Rossbach was a priest who worked in Chichicastenango from 1894 until his death in 1944. During that time he collected pre-Columbian artifacts. Nearby are large jade beads, jade necklaces, ear flares, and collars.

In niches in the wall and in the corners of the room are stone carvings, including a seated figure in the round, a decorative box with a lid, and a rectangular receptacle with a face on the front.

The museum is open every day except Tuesday from 8:00 A.M. to noon and from 2:00 to 5:00 P.M. Lighting in the museum is fair and photography is permitted, but flash is not. Allow 45 minutes to see the collection.

Chichicastenango is renowned for its market, held on Thursdays and Sundays. The market is conducted primarily for local people, who carry their wares into town from miles away, but it is also a major tourist attraction. A visit to Chichicastenango would hardly be complete without attending a market, but be forewarned that it will be packed with people.

A variety of items that will appeal to visitors is sold: jackets, shawls, blankets, napkins, place mats, and other textiles, interesting and inexpensive jewelry, and other items. Bargaining is expected.

While you are in Chichicastenango you might want to see the Idol of Pascual Abaj on top of a hill south of town. It is a steep climb and you will have to ask directions a few times along the way to find it—unless you hire a guide. You will pass the house of a mask maker along the way. Pascual Abaj is a crude stone carving of a figure. Its age is undetermined, but it is possibly pre-Columbian; it is still venerated by the people of the area, who bring offerings of incense, flowers, and thin white candles to burn before it.

From the top of the hill there is a good view of the town below, and so there are two reasons to make the climb if you don't mind puffing a bit.

Carved stone roof slab, similar to one from Chuitinamit, a Late Postclassic site in the highlands of Guatemala. On display in the Chichicastenango Museum.

★ ★
UTATLÁN
(oo-taht-LAHN)

Derivation:
Nahua for "Place of Reeds." Name by which the site was known in Mexico. A close translation of K'umarcaaj.

Original name:
K'umarcaaj. Quiché Maya for "Place of Old Reeds."

Location:
Southwestern part of the Department of Quiché, Guatemala.

Maps: 5 (p. 174) and 5A (p. 193)

The Site

Utatlán, capital of the Quichés, was built in a defensive position on a hilltop surrounded by ravines, as were many other Postclassic sites in the Guatemala highlands. The architecture at all of these sites shows strong influence from central Mexico.

Some early Spanish reports on Utatlán described the site in glowing terms; unfortunately, there is little to see there today. The site was razed in 1524 by the Spaniard Pedro de Alvarado, and later the facing stones of the buildings were removed for construction of the nearby town of Santa Cruz del Quiché.

Access to Utatlán is over part of an ancient causeway that heads east from the entrance to the site; a modern trail follows the causeway's path. The trail makes a couple of turns before reaching the Central Plaza, the most interesting part of the site. On the west side of the plaza is the Tojil Temple, the most important structure at Utatlán; it was a temple of human sacrifice. All that remains today is the rubble and mud core of the structure, with an opening in the lower section where offerings are still made. Originally this structure was formed of a steep pyramidal base with balustraded stairways on three sides and a temple and sacrificial stone on top. Just to the south of the Tojil Temple, and also on the west side of the plaza, is a large, grass-covered ball court.

The most interesting building on the east side of the plaza is the Awilix Temple; its irregular shape hints at its original design. It had a large—and rather high—rectangular platform as a base, which supported another smaller platform and temple toward the east side of the base. Indications of a stairway on the west side of the base can still be discerned.

On the south side of the plaza is the Jakawitz Temple, which is simply a mound today, as are most of the structures at Utatlán. The plaster floor of the Central Plaza is visible, and square and circular impressions in it are the remains of small constructions, one of which was the K'ucumatz Temple.

North of the Central Plaza, and accessible by a marked trail, is the opening to a small cave and a tunnel. From the trail, steps lead down and around to the cave entrance; the tunnel starts just inside the cave. It reportedly heads south to an area under the Central Plaza; there is also a side branch that loops around from the main tunnel. The tunnel is tall and narrow and its walls are covered with soot, no doubt deposited by torches and candles for hundreds of years. The cave at the entrance to the tunnel is used by the Quichés of today as a place of sacrificial offerings. You will probably see remains of chicken feathers, candles, or other offerings in the area.

Recent History

The Quichés claimed to be descended from the Toltecs of Mexico and to have migrated to what we now know as the Guatemala

The front (east side) of the Tohil Temple, Utatlán. Late Postclassic period.

highlands. They first lived in an area east of Utatlán and subjugated the local populace. They later moved toward the west, and around A.D. 1400, K´ucumatz, a Quiché ruler, founded Utatlán. The Quichés became the most powerful highland nation.

For a detailed account of Alvarado's conquest of Utatlán, see *The Quiché Maya of Utatlán,* by Robert M. Carmack; this comprehensive study was published by the University of Oklahoma Press in 1981. It also presents much new information on the archaeology of Utatlán, the origin of the Quichés, their social structure, the reigns of their rulers, and the symbolism of their buildings.

A number of visitors reported on Utatlán, beginning in the seventeenth century. In 1834, Miguel Rivera y Maestre explored the site under a commission from the Guatemalan government, and in 1840 he kindly gave a copy of his manuscript report to John Lloyd Stephens, who was visiting the region. Stephens considered the report "full and elaborate" and therefore felt it unnecessary to devote much of his own time to the site. Frederick Catherwood, who accompanied Stephens, produced a map of the site and a drawing of the Tojil Temple. Alfred P. Maudslay visited Utatlán in 1887, made a survey of the site, and published a plan in 1889–1902.

In the twentieth century, the ceramics of the site were studied by Samuel K. Lothrop and Robert Wauchope. Though some date to the Preclassic period, the bulk shows that Utatlán's most active era was during the Late Postclassic. Wauchope also did some excavating at the site; he discovered three periods of construction and remains of a mural on a clay wall. In 1956, Jorge F. Guillemín cleared the site and mapped the structures.

In the early 1970s, the State University of New York at Albany carried out excavations during three field seasons, and some data were summarized in a monograph by Dwight T. Wallace and Carmack in 1977.

Connections

1. Chichicastenango to Utatlán: 11.2 miles [18.0 kilometers] by paved road (:32), then 2.1 miles [3.3 kilometers] by dirt road.

2. Panajachel to Chichicastenango: 22.5 miles [36.2 kilometers] by paved road (1:09).

3. Antigua to Chichicastenango: 67.6 miles [108.7 kilometers] by paved road (2:13).

Getting There

1. From Chichicastenango, head north on Highway 15 to Santa Cruz del Quiché, go straight ahead to Calle (Street) 9, and turn left. Stay on this street until you are near the edge of town, then turn left for a block to Calle 10, and turn right onto it. (Calle 10 is a one-way street in the center of town, until it reaches the edge of town, so you cannot turn left on that street when you first enter Santa Cruz del Quiché.) Follow the extension of Calle 10 to a junction (marked with a sign). Turn right at the sign and go a short distance to the parking area for Utatlán, near the museum. From there it is a short walk to the site. The streets in Santa Cruz del Quiché and the road to the site are very rutted; expect to drive slowly.

2. From Panajachel, take Highway 15 north to Highway CA 1, turn right onto the highway, and continue to Los Encuentros Junction. Turn left at the junction onto another part of Highway 15 and continue to Chichicastenango. From there follow the directions for Connection 1.

3. From Antigua, head northwest on Highway 14 to Highway CA 1 and turn left; this junction is on the eastern outskirts of Chimaltenango. Follow CA 1 to Los Encuentros Junction, turn right onto Highway 15 and continue to Chichicastenango, then follow the directions for Connection 1.

There is no food or drink available at Utatlán. The site is open from 8:00 A.M. to 5:00 P.M. daily, and there are rest rooms near the museum. Allow an hour to visit the site; this will give you enough time to take a short look at the cave and tunnel. Once you enter the tunnel, there is really little to see, but if you want to have a look, you should bring a flashlight. The guardian at Utatlán has a flashlight available to visitors, but when we rented it, we found that the batteries were weak. It would be better to have your own light.

Buses go to Santa Cruz del Quiché, but there is no regular transportation from there to Utatlán.

Although a guide is not necessary to reach Utatlán, if you would prefer having one, ask around in Santa Cruz del Quiché, or in Chichicastenango if you will be returning there.

★
UTATLÁN MUSEUM

The most interesting feature at the Utatlán Museum is a scale model of the site. I recommend seeing it to get an idea of the site's layout before visiting the ruins. There are maps, drawings, and a burial from the site in the museum, as well as modern ceramics and baskets.

The museum is open from 8:00 A.M. to 5:00 P.M. daily; allow 10 minutes for a visit.

★ ★ ★
ZACULEU
(sah-koo-LEH-oo)

Derivation:
Quiché Maya for "White Earth."
Original name: Zaculeu.
Location:
Southwestern part of the Department of Huehuetenango, Guatemala.
Map: 5 (p. 174)

The Site

Zaculeu is in the western highlands of Guatemala, on a defensive plateau surrounded by deep ravines. Mountain ranges ring the area, providing a lovely setting. It was occupied continuously from Early Classic times to the Spanish conquest, and several superimpositions of construction are found there.

Zaculeu is a relatively small site, with simple architecture and no monumental stone sculpture, but it is certainly one of the most interesting sites in the Guatemala highlands, partly because of its restoration.

The architectural remains seen at the site today are of stone, covered either with lime plaster or with adobe and a thin lime

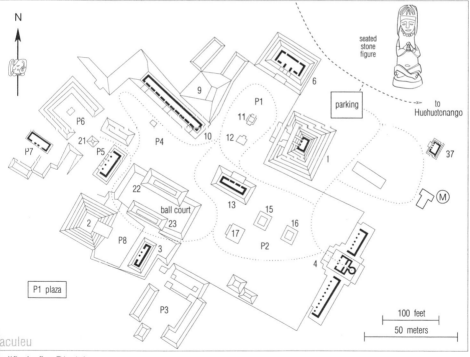

Zaculeu

Modified after Dimick.

Structure 4, Zaculeu, view from the west. Postclassic period.

coating. Some remains of polychrome painting were found during excavation, but today the structures are white—painted during reconstruction. It is probable that stucco decorations were originally used on the exteriors of the buildings.

Many of Zaculeu's architectural features show influences from central Mexico, such as beam and mortar roofs, divided stairways, dance platforms, and *alfardas* with vertical upper zones. Luxury trade items from Mexico, including alabaster vases, were discovered during excavation. Other important items uncovered were objects of copper, silver, gold, and their alloys. These show influence from, or were imported from, Mexico and lower Central America. Pyrite-encrusted mosaic plaques were discovered that may have been used as symbols of wealth and power on state occa-

sions. The pyrite plaques and others c nicely worked jade date to the Early Classi period, whereas the metal objects date to later time.

There are more than 40 structures a Zaculeu, some of which are simply grass covered mounds today. The buildings ar mostly arranged around several plazas, an most of the restored structures borde Plazas 1 and 2. The site is well cleared, an getting around is easy. The following se quence for visiting the structures is but on of the possibilities.

When you enter the site, go straigh ahead (southwest) and enter Plaza 2. Off t the left is Structure 4, which borders th southeast side of the plaza; this is a rathe complex building for Zaculeu. In its cente is a pyramidal base with a three-room tem ple on top; the rearmost room is circula

Structures 23 (left) and 22 (right) (ball court), Zaculeu, view from the southeast. Postclassic period.

The front facade of the temple is intact, but the roof is gone. The temple is approached by a main stairway bordered by *alfardas* with vertical upper zones; this stairway faces the plaza, and there are two smaller stairways on the sides of the pyramidal base that are also bordered by *alfardas* with vertical upper zones. This part of Structure 4 is flanked by two wings, each containing one long room set atop a low platform. Along the front of each room is a row of large columns, only the lower parts of which remain today.

There are a couple of small platforms (Structures 16 and 15) in front of Structure 4, on a center line with the pyramidal base and temple. To the southwest is Structure 17, a two-room structure with two columns at the entrance to the first room and a double stairway that ascends the pyramidal base on the northwest side. The lower walls of the rooms and the lower parts of the columns are in place.

Now head west to the ball court and circle around its south side. This brings you to the small, sunken Plaza 8, with the mostly unrestored pyramidal Structure 2 on the northwest. Across the plaza stands Structure 3, a platform with a double stairway. Circle now to the northwest end of the ball court (Structures 22 and 23). The court is sunken and I-shaped with sloping walls in the playing area. Above the two walls of this area are the remains of low walls of buildings.

To the northwest of the ball court is Plaza 5; the only partly restored building there is the small Structure 21, a low rectangular platform with a stair on the northwest side. The buildings around Plazas 6

Structure 1, the northwest side, Zaculeu. Early Postclassic period.

and 7 are simply mounds today. You now head to Plaza 4, bounded on the northeast by the long Structure 10. This building was investigated and found to have multiple doorways entering one long room and three stairways ascending the platform base as access to the rooms. A little of the original stonework can be seen, but the structure has not been restored.

You now head southeast, then northeast, and enter Plaza 1, the most interesting part of Zaculeu. Structure 1, on the southeast side of the plaza, at 39 feet high is the tallest building at the site. It rises in eight terraces, and the temple on top is entered through three doorways. The beam-and-mortar roof was reconstructed when the temple was restored, but it collapsed during the 1976 earthquake; the temple walls remain standing. The temple is approached by a double stairway up the pyramidal base. There were seven construction stages in Structure 1; the one visible today dates to

the Early Postclassic period.

Bordering the northeast side of the plaza is Structure 6, which rises in tiers. A stairway facing the plaza that is split in its upper section gives access to the one-room temple on top. The lower walls and piers of the temple are standing. On the northwest side of the plaza is Structure 9, a pyramidal construction of which only the lower part of the base has been restored.

Structure 13 borders the plaza on the southwest; it has a double stair up to the first platform and a wider single stair up to the level of the temple, where the lower walls and piers remain. In the middle of Plaza 1 are two restored small platforms (Structures 11 and 12).

The last building of interest is Structure 37, which does not seem to be associated with a plaza. It lies just north of the Zaculeu Museum and is worth a look on your way out of the site. Though unrestored, the structure has been investigated; some of the

Structure 1 (left) and Structure 13 (right) facing Plaza B, Zaculeu, with Structures 11 (left) and 12 (right) in the plaza. Structure 4 is in the center background. Postclassic period.

original stonework and remains of its plaster coating can still be seen.

During the Postclassic period, when militarism increased, many sites in the Guatemala highlands were built on easily defensible hilltops or plateaus, but Zaculeu had been in such a location from an earlier time. The sites of the Postclassic period took on the dual role of administrative and commercial capitals; they also served as places of refuge and of festive gatherings.

Recent History

Zaculeu was a living city at the time of the Spanish conquest. The Mam valiantly attempted to defend their capital, but they were ultimately defeated by Gonzalo de Alvarado—brother of the more famous Pedro—in 1525, after a bloody campaign and siege.

Knowledge of the site was never lost, and it was visited by John Lloyd Stephens and Frederick Catherwood in 1840. The ruins were in such a poor state that Catherwood did not produce a drawing of them, though he did depict some vases that the two uncovered while excavating one of the mounds. Stephens gave a description of the remains and a diagram indicating a stepped pyramid shape for the main structure.

Major excavation and restoration were undertaken by Aubrey Trik, Richard Woodbury, and John M. Dimick for the United Fruit Company in the mid-1940s. Woodbury and Trik's 1953 publication is the major source of information on the site.

Connections

1. Huehuetenango to Zaculeu: 2.3 miles [3.7 kilometers] by dirt roads (:16).

2. Guatemala City to Huehuetenango: 159.5 miles [256.7 kilometers] by paved road (some poor) (4:42).

Getting There

1. From the northwest corner of the Huehuetenango town plaza (called Parque Central), head north on 5a Avenida (5th Avenue) for one block and turn left onto 1 Calle (1st Street). Go one block to 6a Avenida and turn right onto it. Shortly after this there is a fork in the road. We took the right branch because the left was under repair. We curved around and later joined the road that we would have been on had we been able to take the left branch at the fork. At this junction we turned right (it would have been straight ahead in the other case). From there it is 0.9 mile [1.4 kilometers] to another junction that is marked with a pyramid sign. Turn left at the sign and proceed 0.5 mile [0.8 kilometer] to the parking area for Zaculeu. You may have to ask directions along the way, depending on which part of the road is closed for repairs.

2. From Guatemala City, head west on Highway CA 1, follow it to the cutoff for Huehuetenango (marked with a sign), and turn right. Follow the road to the outskirts of town and you will start to see signs for "Ciudad Centro." When you follow these signs you will be coming into the center of town on 7 Calle. When you reach 5a Avenida, turn left; it is then five blocks to the northwest corner of the plaza. From there follow the directions for Connection 1.

There is no food at Zaculeu, but vendors sell cold drinks near the entrance. The site is open from 8:00 A.M. to 6:00 P.M. daily; allow 1.75 hours for a visit.

Zaculeu can be reached by taxi from Huehuetenango as well as by private vehicle. Some jitney vans pass within 0.5 mile [0.8 kilometer] of the site (at the last junction with the pyramid sign). Ask to make sure before you board. Buses run between Guatemala City and Huehuetenango.

★ ★
ZACULEU MUSEUM

The small Zaculeu Museum is well kept and is worth a look while you are at the site. All of the items in the collection come from the site, and displays include a map of the site and, nearby, an interesting urn burial. There are cases with ceramics, including a ladle censer. Another case has, among other items, a vessel in the shape of a stylized human head, a seated stone figure, and ceramic bowls. There are paintings of two of the structures at Zaculeu showing ceremonies; they are at the back of the case. Other paintings on a wall depict daily life.

The lighting in the museum is better than average, and with fast film it is not too difficult to get photographs. Since everything is behind glass, flash is not useful. There is some labeling in Spanish.

The museum is open from 8:00 A.M. to noon and from 1:00 to 5:00 P.M., although sometimes it closes early if there are no visitors around. Allow 15 minutes to see the displays.

Seated stone figure, Zaculeu. Probably Postclassic period. On display in the Zaculeu Museum.

★ ★ ★
ABAJ TAKALIK
(ah-BAH tah-kah-LEEK)

Derivation:
Quiché Maya for the Spanish "Piedra Parada." In English, "Standing Stones."

Location:
Far northern part of the Department of Retalhuleu, Guatemala.

Maps: 5 (p. 174) and 5B (p. 211)

The Site

Abaj Takalik is a large site covering 3.5 square miles [9.0 square kilometers] on the southwest part of Guatemala's Pacific slope. The site, which covers parts of several coffee fincas, is noted for its abundance of carved monuments in both Olmec and early Maya styles. Ceramic studies show that Abaj Takalik was first occupied in the Early Preclassic period, and the Olmec-style monuments also may have been carved then. The population was probably sparse, and afterward the site was apparently abandoned for a time. In the Middle Preclassic period the site was reoccupied, and during that time and the following Late Preclassic period there was a great deal of architectural activity. It was also during the Late Preclassic that the early Maya-style monuments were carved.

The earliest structures were made of clay, sometimes partially burned for solidification. In Late Preclassic times, natural volcanic stones were used, held together with clay. In the Early Classic period, some of the earlier sculptures were repositioned in front of some of the major structures built at that time. The excavated Structures 11 and 12 were covered with rounded boulders held together with clay. Also during the Early Classic period, some of the already existing monuments were deliberately destroyed.

For the Late Classic and Postclassic periods, there is little evidence of occupation at Abaj Takalik. What is found lies on the surface of the plaza in the south part of the Central Group and on top of already collapsed structures.

According to Miguel Orrego Corzo, this scant late occupation seems to be related to people from the highlands, who perhaps made sporadic visits to the already abandoned site.

Abaj Takalik occupies a ridge that runs north-south, with a slope toward the south; it is laid out in a series of terraces with steep fronts that were partly altered in ancient times. The site is formed of four groups; the Central, North, and West groups are adjacent to each other and comprise the major part of the site, while the South Group is 3.0 miles [5.0 kilometers] to the south. In the main part of the site, 70 major mounds have been recorded, exclusive of habitational units and minor mounds. Most of the excavation at the site so far has taken place in the south part of the Central Group, and this is the area visitors see today.

The first major excavation at Abaj Takalik was undertaken in the southwest part of this area so that it could be investigated before the archaeological camp was built over it. It was here that the Middle Preclassic clay structures were discovered. The south part of the Central Group has the greatest quantity of sculptured monuments of any of the groups; it also has a high percentage of the known plain monuments. Nevertheless, this area is thought to have more an elite residential character than a ceremonial one. The ancient ceremonial part of the site is believed to lie just to the north, where the tallest mound at Abaj Takalik is found. The south part of the Central Group provided the best access to the ceremonial area.

The stone carvings at Abaj Takalik are classified into three categories: monuments,

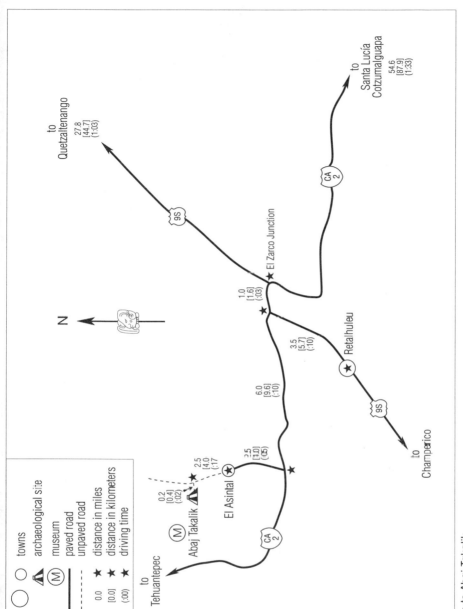

Legend

- ○ ○ towns
- ★ archaeological site
- ⛨ museum
- Ⓜ museum
- —— paved road
- - - - unpaved road
- distance in miles
- distance in kilometers
- driving time

★	0.0
★	[0.0]
★	(:00)

to Quetzaltenango
27.8
[44.7]
(1:03)

to Santa Lucía Cotzumalguapa
54.6
[87.9]
(1:33)

N

9S

El Zarco Junction

CA 2

1.0
[1.6]
(:03)

3.5
[5.7]
(:10)

Retalhuleu

6.0
[9.6]
(:10)

9S

to Champerico

2.5
[1.0]
(:05)

2.5
[4.0]
(:17)

El Asintal

0.2
[0.4]
(:02)

Abaj Takalik

to Tehuantepec

CA 2

5B

Route to Abaj Takalik

The early Maya Stela 5, Abaj Takalik, showing two figures facing each other with a panel of glyphs in between. A.D. 126.

stelae, and altars. The order in which the structures and sculptures are covered here follows the tour of the site as we did it. Since work is continuing, this route may change. We began at Structure 12, which lies on the east side of the plaza in the south part of the Central Group; the plaza is bordered on the west by Structure 11. Structure 12 is a basal platform of three tiers, with stairways on the east and west sides. What is seen today is the last construction phase, which dates to the early part of the Early Classic period. This phase is being consolidated; it overlies Late Preclassic constructions. (The architectural dating is based on excavations and ceramic studies.) Even more interesting than the structure is a row of sculptures arranged in a north-south line along the west facade. It includes six monuments, one stela, and an altar. All the monuments around Structures 11 and 12 are under tin roofs. Starting at the south end of Structure 12, you come first to Monument 9, a partly destroyed depiction of a human head. It has eyes in the shape of coffee beans and wears a helmet; its style is considered Olmec.

Next is Monument 65, a badly mutilated head that also wears a helmet and is considered Olmec. Monument 66 is the head of an alligator in an unidentified

Monument 8, Abaj Takalik, an Olmec-style carving showing a zoomorphic monster with feline characteristics and an anthropomorphic figure emerging from its mouth. Preclassic period.

style; it may date to the Middle Preclassic period.

The next sculpture is the magnificent Stela 5, discovered in 1976. It portrays two standing figures facing each other; in between them is a panel with a hieroglyphic inscription recording two dates, the later of which is A.D. 126. This is 166 years earlier than the earliest known dated monument at Tikal. The top of this early Maya stela has scaled off (or was perhaps destroyed) and the lower section is somewhat eroded, but

the two figures and the bar-and-dot numerals are discernable. On each of the narrow sides of the stela is a small seated figure and a short glyphic inscription that is very eroded. According to John A. Graham, these figures "bear a very close resemblance to similarly placed figures on Izapa Stela 18 and perhaps represent Izapan visitors to the site although the figures are rendered in Maya fashion." The plain Altar 8 is found in front of the stela.

Monument 68 is a carving of a toad. Al-

Monument 11, Abaj Takalik, a Preclassic Maya carving on a natural pear-shaped boulder, with a column of five glyphs down the center and the bar-and-dot numeral 11 on the left, above another glyph.

the center of the boulder's broadest face. Off to the left (as you view this face) are a single glyph and the numeral 11 in a bar-and-dot notation, both recessed from the main face of the boulder. Although the glyphs are somewhat eroded, the magnificent quality of the carving can still be discerned. The glyphs are personifications shown in profile; the three middle glyphs in the main column are human representations, and the others are anthropomorphic.

You now return to Structure 12 for a look at its other sides. On the east side there are some monuments, one of which appears to be another alligator head; the others appeared plain. On the south side of the structure is Monument 69; it represents a seated human figure, though this is hard to make out because the monument is poorly preserved.

To the west of Structure 12 is Structure 11, which has the same construction phases as the former. Of interest here are the two remaining fragments of Stela 12. The larger fragment is the lower part of the stela, and it shows the legs and feet of a figure, both feet pointing in the same direction. The figure stands on a panel divided into five trapezoidal sections, each containing a design. In front of the figure's legs are a single glyph and part of a bar-and-dot numeral that appears to be the number 10. The style of the monument is typical of early Maya art. A smaller fragment of the side of the stela is nearby, as are some plain monuments.

To the south of Structure 11 is a covered excavation. A nice feature is that skylights have been installed in the roof, so there is enough light for photography. The remains seem to be of clay—and therefore probably early—and you will pass right by them on your way to the museum.

though its style is undefined, it is believed to date to the Middle Preclassic period. The toad is a motif found at Kaminaljuyú, Izapa, and other sites. Monument 67 represents a figure emerging from the mouth of a jaguar, a theme seen in Olmec and Izapan art. The figure is poorly preserved. The last sculpture in the row is Monument 8, which represents a zoomorphic monster with feline characteristics. From its mouth emerges a small anthropomorphic figure.

From here you turn north to Terrace 3, passing along the way a large circular altar that is plain on top but has a head carved in low relief on its rim. On the southwest part of Terrace 3 stands the intriguing Monument 11, a natural pear-shaped boulder with a vertical band of five glyphs carved in

Recent History

Abaj Takalik has been known under different names since before the twentieth century. The first important report on the site was a brief account by Gustav Bruhl published in 1888. A few years later, Karl Sapper saw Stela 1 along the road he was traveling, and in 1894 he described it. He did not see any of the other monuments. German artist Max Vollmberg sketched Stela 1 and made note of other monuments; this motivated Walter Lehmann to visit the site, which he did in 1925, and in 1926 he issued a brief report. He was the first to recognize the great antiquity of the monuments.

In 1942, Sir J. Eric S. Thompson visited Abaj Takalik, and he published comments on the monuments in 1942 and 1943. Later the site was visited by other archaeologists, among them Suzanna W. Miles and Lee A. Parsons. Up until this time the site was known by various names, including Santa Margarita and San Isidro Piedra Parada (names of fincas on which the site lies) and Colomba (a village to the north). In 1965, Miles gave the site its current name, the one generally accepted today. Parsons studied and reviewed the iconography of one of the monuments in 1972.

The first real excavation at the site was begun in 1976 by Graham, Robert F. Heizer, and Edwin M. Shook, under the auspices of the University of California at Berkeley, which partially funded the project. Until that time a few more than a dozen sculptures were known from Abaj Takalik; by the end of the exploratory season in 1976, 40 new monuments had been uncovered, including the important Stela 5. The project continued through 1981, and during the later seasons more monuments were found and test pits were dug.

In 1987, the Abaj Takalik National Project was begun under the auspices of Guatemala's Institute of Anthropology and History. The project was directed by Orrego Corzo, who was assisted by a number of other scholars and graduate students. Excavations uncovered the first Middle Preclassic architecture at Abaj Takalik, and additional sculptures came to light. A report by Orrego Corzo and others on the work accomplished through 1988 appeared in 1990. The project continues and it will be interesting to follow its progress. No doubt a great deal of new information will be presented about this important and unusual site.

Connections

1. Retalhuleu to Abaj Takalik: 12.0 miles [19.3 kilometers] by paved road (:25), then 2.7 miles [4.4 kilometers] by dirt road (:19).

2. Quetzaltenango to Abaj Takalik: 37.3 miles [60.0 kilometers] by paved road (1:21), then 2.7 miles [4.4 kilometers] by dirt road (:19).

3. Santa Lucía Cotzumalguapa to Abaj Takalik: 64.1 miles [103.1 kilometers] by paved road (some poor) (1:51), then 2.7 miles [4.4 kilometers] by dirt road (:19).

Getting There

1. From Retalhuleu, head northeast on Highway 9S and turn left onto Highway CA 2; then go to the cutoff for El Asintal (marked with a sign). Turn right at the cutoff and continue straight to and through El Asintal to the end of the paved road. Then continue straight ahead on the dirt road to the cutoff for Abaj Takalik (marked with a sign). Turn left at the sign and follow the road as it makes a couple of turns before arriving at the parking area for the site.

2. From Quetzaltenango, take Highway 9S heading southeast to Zunil and then southwest to Highway CA 2. Turn right onto this highway and continue to the cutoff for El Asintal, then follow the directions just given.

3. From Santa Lucía Cotzumalguapa, head west on Highway CA 2 to the cutoff for El Asintal, then follow the directions for Connection 1.

Along the dirt road between El Asintal and the cutoff for Abaj Takalik, you will pass the entrance to the headquarters of Finca Santa Margarita. At this junction there is a three-dimensional stone portraying a seated figure; it is under a shelter. It comes from Abaj Takalik and is worth a couple of minutes to see and photograph on your way to or from the site. The figure faces the road and is on the west side. It is 1.8 miles [2.9 kilometers] north of the north end of El Asintal, where you pick up the dirt road.

When you arrive at the entrance to the site and park, you will see a stand that sells soft drinks (unchilled) and some publications; a bit farther along is a building where you sign a registration book. Ask here to have someone show you around; this will allow you to tour the site more efficiently and will ensure that you don't miss anything of interest. There is no food available at Abaj Takalik. Allow 1.25 hours to visit the site. Fortunately, the use of flash is permitted; you will especially need it to photograph Stela 5, which, when viewed under ambient light, almost looks like a plain monument.

You can taxi to the site from Retalhuleu, but this might be a bit expensive. Buses run along Highway CA 2 but do not go to El Asintal or Abaj Takalik.

★ ★
ABAJ TAKALIK MUSEUM

The Abaj Takalik Museum is in a small building bearing a sign saying "Archaeological Exposition." On the porch of the building is a scale model of the main part of the site showing the North, Central, and West groups, which are labeled. On the wall above the model is a map of the same area.

Inside the museum are some carved stones, one of which has a bas-relief. Another is the remains of a three-dimensional, headless figure with hands placed on the knees; yet another is an eroded head, perhaps that of a monkey.

There are displays of ceramic vessels, both inside and outside of glass cases, as well as small clay heads and parts of figurines. One display has small stone implements and obsidian blades.

Although the collection is not extensive, there are some interesting pieces, and happily, most of the items are well labeled. The museum is definitely worth a look when you visit Abaj Takalik. Allow 20 minutes to see the collection.

★ ★
BILBAO
(beel-BAH-oh)

Derivation:
   At one time this was the name of
   the finca on which the site lies.
Location:
   North-central part of the
   Department of Escuintla,
   Guatemala.
Maps: 5 (p. 174), 5C (p. 218),
   and 5C1 (p. 219)

The Site

The ruins of Bilbao are in the midst of a sugarcane plantation, and the mounds that remain are covered with cane. There are no
observable architectural features. There are,
however, impressive large stone carvings
that are well preserved, and this is the reason to visit the site. A short walk from the
dirt access road, through part of a cane field,
gets you to Monument 21.

This monument is an in situ basalt
boulder with a bas-relief carving on the top
of its artificially flattened surface. It measures 11 feet from top to bottom and 13 feet
from side to side; the surface is on a slope of
about 35 degrees from the horizontal. This
is the largest of the Cotzumalhuapa-style
narrative compositions, about which more
later. The carving is spectacular and shows
an elaborate scene with three principal figures; the largest is the central standing figure whose head faces a figure seated on a
throne. On the other side of the standing figure is a smaller standing one who holds a
hand puppet. Vines twine around the scene,
and cacao pods with simplified human faces
sprout from them. (Cacao was a highly
prized commodity in pre-Columbian Mesoamerica, and the Pacific coastal slope was
one of the richest growing areas.) Birds,
snakes, and a butterfly with a human head
are also depicted on Monument 21.

According to Lee A. Parsons, "this complex composition is fraught with symbolism." There have been a number of interpretations of the meaning of this scene;
Parsons believes the iconography has ball-
player associations. Marion P. Hatch studied the Cotzumalhuapa-style monuments
and made a preliminary attempt to "arrange
the sculptures in a meaningful order [chron-
ologically]." She proposed that three rulers
were identifiable, and that the central figure
on Monument 21 was Ruler 1.

Monument 18 lies about 150 feet [45
meters] southeast of Monument 21, but to
reach it you must walk back to the road and
head south along it to a wide trail; then follow the trail west a short distance to the
monument.

Monument 18 is a large stela portraying three standing individuals. The top of
the roughly rectangular stone is irregular,
and there is a raised border around the edge
of the stela. A figure on the viewer's left has
outstretched hands and faces the two others
on the right. Between the left and central
figures is a tall rectangular object with crab
claws at the bottom; they are joined by a lat-
ticework pattern. (The bottom of the stela is
partly buried and hidden by weeds, so the
crab claws are not generally visible.) Hatch
interprets this object as a staff of office
being passed from Ruler 1 (the central figure) to Ruler 2 (the left figure). At the top of
the stela, near the center, is a circular cartouche enclosing a monkey head. Both
Monument 21 and Monument 18 date to
the Classic period.

Recent History

Bilbao is one of several sites in the vicinity
of Santa Lucía Cotzumalguapa that have
sculpture in the Cotzumalhuapa style. Some
of the hallmarks of this style include bas-relief carvings of figures in angular poses,
with hands and feet depicted in plan view

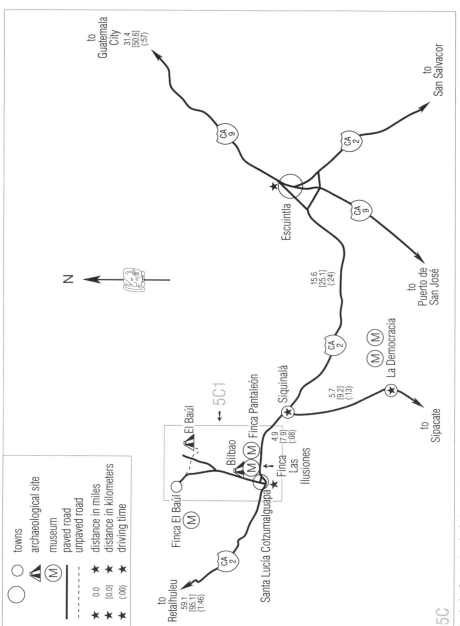

Legend:

- ◯ towns
- ◯ towns
- ▲ archaeological site
- Ⓜ museum
- —— paved road
- - - - unpaved road

	distance in miles	0.0
	distance in kilometers	[0.0]
	driving time	(:00)

- ★ 0.0
- ★★ [0.0]
- ★★★ (:00)

N ←

to Guatemala
City
31.4
[50.6]
(:57)

CA
9

Escuintla
★

CA
2
to San Salvacor

CA
9
to Puerto de
San José

15.6
[25.1]
(:24)

CA
2

Ⓜ Ⓜ
La Democracia

Siquinalá
★

5.7
[9.2]
(:13)

to Sipacate
★

Finca Pantaleón
Ⓜ

Bilbao
▲ Ⓜ

El Baúl
▲

5C1
↓

4.9
[7.9]
(:08)

Finca
Las
Ilusiones
←
★

Santa Lucía Cotzumalguapa

Finca El Baúl
◯ Ⓜ

CA
2

to
Retalhuleu
59.1
[95.1]
(1:46)

5C

Route to Santa Lucía Cotzumalguapa

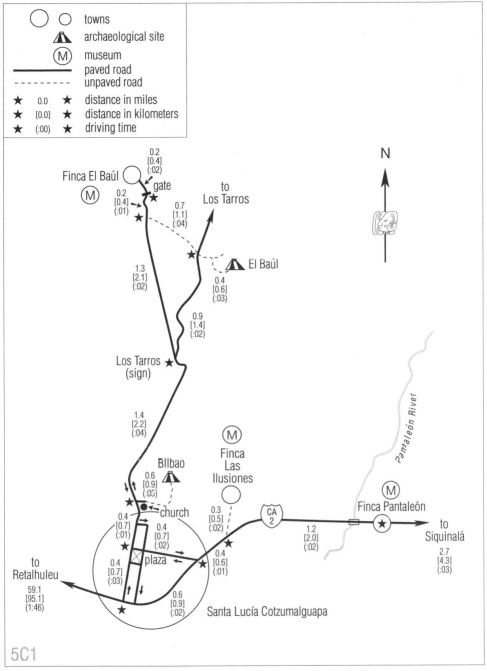

Legend:
- ○ ○ towns
- ▲ archaeological site
- Ⓜ museum
- —— paved road
- - - - - unpaved road
- ★ 0.0 ★ distance in miles
- ★ [0.0] ★ distance in kilometers
- ★ (:00) ★ driving time

N

Finca El Baúl Ⓜ

0.2
[0.4]
(:02)

gate

0.2
[0.4]
(:01)

to
Los Tarros

0.7
[1.1]
(:04)

▲ El Baúl

0.4
[0.6]
(:03)

1.3
[2.1]
(:02)

0.9
[1.4]
(:02)

Los Tarros
(sign)

Pantaleón River

1.4
[2.2]
(:04)

Ⓜ
Finca
Las
Ilusiones

Bilbao
▲

0.6
[0.9]
(:05)

church

Ⓜ
Finca Pantaleón ★

to
Siquinalá

2.7
[4.3]
(:03)

0.4
[0.7]
(:01)

0.4
[0.7]
(:02)

0.3
[0.5]
(:02)

CA 2

1.2
[2.0]
(:02)

to
Retalhuleu

59.1
[95.1]
(1:46)

0.4
[0.7]
(:03)

plaza

0.4
[0.6]
(:01)

0.6
[0.9]
(:02)

Santa Lucía Cotzumalguapa

5C1

Detail of the Cotzumalhuapa area

Monument 21, in a cane field at Bilbao. Classic period.

(as though seen from above), eyes rendered with a double outline, faces with straight noses and thin lips, and ears in the shape of question marks. There is emphasis on ball players and a good deal of death symbolism, including death's heads and skeletal figures. Some of the monuments display elaborate scenes with two or more individuals interacting. These scenes are called narrative style. There is also a great deal of three-dimensional sculpture, including colossal heads, seated figures, and human busts.

Many Teotihuacán motifs are incorporated into the Cotzumalhuapa style, including, among other things, tabbed speech scrolls, depictions of Mexican deities such as Tlaloc, horizontally tenoned heads (including death's heads, serpents, and jaguars), and stepped fret motifs.

The majority of Cotzumalhuapa-style monuments are found in a limited nuclear area around Santa Lucía Cotzumalguapa and nearby, though some are found at coastal sites and in the Antigua basin. Of the 127 monuments listed by Parsons in the nuclear area, 58 are from Bilbao and 28 from El Baúl. Bilbao and its recent history are tied in with the histories of other sites, including El Baúl; what follows includes the latter as well.

French Count Jean Frédéric Waldeck visited Guatemala in 1819 and recorded (in a very stylized ink and wash drawing) one of the two nearly identical sculptures (Monument 12 at Finca El Baúl or Monument 1 at Finca Pantaleón) but never published it. This drawing was finally published by Parsons 150 years later, after he discovered it in the Ayer collection of the Newberry Library in Chicago.

In 1860, Pedro de Anda, a local civil of-

The top part of Monument 18, a stela with three figures, in a cane field at Bilbao. Classic period.

ficial, was clearing his finca (Peor es Nada) in order to establish a coffee plantation; during the clearing he came across some ruins and monuments. Later, under other ownership, another plot of land was added to Finca Peor es Nada, and around 1890 the two plots were renamed Bilbao. Although other additions to the property were made, and the name of the whole changed to Finca Las Ilusiones in 1957, Bilbao has remained the name for the archaeological site.

In 1863, Siméon Habel, an Austrian physician, made drawings of some of Bilbao's sculptures, which were published in 1878 by the Smithsonian Institution. In 1876, Adolph Bastian, of the Royal Museum in Berlin, also visited the site; he contracted with Anda to explore it and to remove some of its monuments to the Royal Museum. For this purpose Bastian hired Carl H. Berendt,

who arrived at Bilbao in 1877. After many problems and delays, the monuments were taken to Puerto San José on the Pacific coast of Guatemala for shipping; one monument was lost when it fell overboard at the port. The monuments finally reached Germany in early 1883. Of the 31 monuments taken to Berlin, eight were well-preserved ball-player stelae, some of the finest carvings produced at Bilbao.

In 1882, Eduard Seler published a description of the Bilbao sculptures that were in the Royal Museum, and from 1895 to 1897, Seler and his wife, Caecilie Seler-Sachs, visited Bilbao. During this time she made molds and took photographs of some of the monuments.

There were many other visitors to the Cotzumalhuapa area in the early to mid-twentieth century, and there was speculation about the non-Maya style of the sculptures and questions about what its source might be. Not until 1941, however, did the first excavation in the area take place. This was a limited excavation at El Baúl, by Sir J. Eric S. Thompson of the Carnegie Institution of Washington (CIW). His work also included a thorough reconnaissance of sites in the area and a survey of the many sculptures found in them; the results were published by CIW in 1948. Edwin M. Shook, also with CIW, undertook investigations in the area, though not at Bilbao. In 1962 and 1963, the Milwaukee Public Museum and the Saint Paul Science Museum sponsored excavations at Bilbao; the work was directed by Parsons, whose report was issued in two volumes (1967 and 1969) published by the Milwaukee Public Museum.

During the 1970s and 1980s, a number of projects were undertaken on the Pacific coastal slope of Guatemala and Chiapas, Mexico, and the results of some were published in 1989 by Arizona State University in a volume edited by Frederick Bove and Lynette Heller.

What is now known about the Cotzumalhuapa area is that it was occupied in the late Middle Preclassic period (around 600 to 400 B.C.), and that the region a little to the south was occupied even earlier (around 800 to 600). Bilbao and other sites proceeded to a peak during Late Classic times, after which there was a sudden decline.

When the Spaniards first entered Guatemala in 1524, they encountered colonies occupied by Pipil—a Nahua-speaking people from central Mexico. Historians sought to learn when these people had migrated to the area. That there were several migrations is undisputed, but when the first one occurred was the question.

In the recent past it was proposed that the Pipil migrated to the Pacific coastal slope around A.D. 400 to 500; this group was called the Teotihuacán-Pipil. It was further suggested that this group was responsible for the Teotihuacán or Mexican motifs found in Cotzumalhuapa-style art, which appeared around this time and somewhat later.

In a 1989 study of the Pipil-Nicarao people of Central America, William R.

Fowler, Jr., makes some interesting points. He states that there is almost no archaeological or linguistic evidence to support a Pipil migration as early as A.D. 400 or 500, and that it is misleading at best to link the Pipil with Teotihuacán. He says that present evidence indicates that there were no Nahua migrations to Central America before the Early Postclassic period, although other groups from the Mexican Gulf Coast may have entered the Pacific coastal areas of Central America during the Late Classic period.

If the Pipil were not responsible for the Teotihuacán influence, who was? Did this influence arrive through trade connections, or was there a takeover of the area? Did the Teotihuacán symbols arrive via Kaminaljuyú?

The exact ethnic identity of the people who carved the Cotzumalhuapa-style monuments is still uncertain. A great deal is yet to be learned about the archaeology of this area, and future projects, some under way, should help to fill in the gaps.

Connections

1. Santa Lucía Cotzumalguapa to Bilbao: 0.9 mile [1.4 kilometers] by paved road (:05), then 0.5 mile [0.8 kilometer] by rough dirt road (:04).

2. Guatemala City to Santa Lucía Cotzumalguapa: 51.9 miles [83.5 kilometers] by paved road (1:29).

Getting There

1. From Santa Lucía Cotzumalguapa, head north on 3a Avenida to the north end of town and continue along the road as it curves and climbs. You will soon pass a church (on your right), and the cutoff for Bilbao (unmarked and also on the right) is just past the church. The cutoff is paved for a short distance and then continues as a dirt road. It curves to the right and then to the left before it reaches the stopping place for Monument 21; you walk to the west from the road.

The monuments in the cane fields are

totally obscured, and you must have a guide to find them. Locally, the monuments are called *las piedras* (the stones). You might ask around in the town, at the cane fields (if anyone is around), or at the headquarters at Finca Las Ilusiones. See that section for how to get there. You can also taxi from town to Bilbao, but unless your driver knows where the stones are, you will still need a guide. The dirt cane-field road is rough and rutted, so a high-clearance vehicle would be best. If the road is very wet, you will need four-wheel drive as well. Otherwise you could walk in from where the paved road ends.

2. From Guatemala City, take Highway CA 9 to the northern outskirts of Escuintla, then take a branch road to the right at a fork. This road bypasses central Escuintla and leads to Highway CA 2 a short distance ahead, where there is a sign for Siquinalá. Bear to the right at this junction and continue west on Highway CA 2 to Santa Lucía Cotzumalguapa. Then follow the directions for Connection 1 to reach Bilbao. If you start from Guatemala City, you could take a guide along with you. Some travel agencies there have guides who know where the monuments in the cane fields are located.

Note: Other sculptures are reported to be in situ at Bilbao, including the impressive Monument 19, some distance to the southwest of those described earlier, but Monuments 21 and 18 are the only ones we saw.

Allow half an hour to see, study, and photograph the monuments. There is no food or drink at the site, but you are just on the outskirts of town where both are available.

In a day trip from Guatemala City you can visit all the sites and fincas around Santa Lucía Cotzumalguapa, as well as the Monte Alto heads and the town museum in La Democracia. This trip would take over 7.5 hours, including the time recommended to visit each spot and an hour for a lunch break. This does not include the time to locate a guide if you haven't brought one along. If you prefer a more leisurely pace—or if you will be continuing west on Highway CA 2 the

next day—you could stay over in Santa Lucía Cotzumalguapa. The Caminotel Santiaquito is a pleasant place with air-conditioned rooms, a restaurant and bar, nicely landscaped grounds, and a swimming pool. It is on the north side of Highway CA 2, 0.4 mile [0.6 kilometer] west of the 3a Avenida junction with CA 2. Across the highway is the more modest Hotel El Camino.

★ ★
EL BAÚL
(ehl bah-OOL)

Derivation:
Spanish for "The Trunk (Chest)," the name of the finca on which the site lies.

Location:
North-central part of the Department of Escuintla, Guatemala.

Maps: 5 (p. 174), 5C (p. 218), and 5C1 (p. 219)

The Site

There are two interesting sculptures atop the acropolis at El Baúl, Monuments 2 and 3. Both are revered today by the area's inhabitants, who come to make offerings of candles and flowers, the remains of which you will see on and around the monuments.

Monument 2 is a stela depicting a single standing figure wearing a skirt; locally it is called "La Reina" (the queen), but it more likely represents a male in special attire. A Tlaloc glyph adorns the front of the skirt, and the figure wears a Xiuhcóatl headdress formed of a band of overlapping plates with a serpent or other effigy head at the front. Xiuhcóatl is the alter ego of Xuihtecuhtli (also called Huehuetéotl), the old fire god of ancient Mexico. In Aztec mythology, Xiuhcóatl carried the sun through the sky from dawn to zenith. To the right of the figure as you view the stela are six ringed dots; to the left of the figure are two more, plus a larger cartouche enclosing an animal head, probably that of a deer. The date "8 deer" seems to be indicated. Marion P. Hatch believes that the monument is probably related to Ruler 3 in her series. See "Bilbao" for more on this series.

Monument 3 has been widely pub-lished; it is a well-preserved, three-dimensional, large stone head depicting an old man who also wears a Xiuhcóatl headdress and is thought to represent Huehuetéotl. Hatch believes that the monument relates to Ruler 3. Monuments 2 and 3 both date to the Classic period.

Recent History

See "Bilbao" for the recent history of the area, including El Baúl.

Connections

1. Santa Lucía Cotzumalguapa to El Baúl: 3.1 miles [5.0 kilometers] by paved road (:10), then 0.4 mile [0.6 kilometer] by dirt road (:03).

2. Guatemala City to Santa Lucía Cotzumalguapa: see "Bilbao."

Getting There

1. From Santa Lucía Cotzumalguapa, head north on 3a Avenida to the north end of town and follow the road as it climbs and curves around until you come to a fork in the road with a sign for Los Tarros. Take the right branch (the road to Los Tarros) for 0.9 mile [1.4 kilometers]. Then turn right onto an unmarked dirt road and follow it for 0.2 mile [0.3 kilometer] to a junction with another unmarked dirt road on the right. Take the road on the right and follow it as it curves around and climbs to near the top of the acropolis, where it ends (and where you can park). Follow a foot trail on the left; it goes a little higher and then turns to the left to reach the monuments.

The dirt road to El Baúl can be negotiated in a standard vehicle when it is dry—if you take it slowly. When it is wet, a high-clearance vehicle with four-wheel drive will

Monument 2, a stela depicting a single figure wearing a skirt, El Baúl. Classic period.

Monument 3, depicting an old man believed to be Huehueteotl, El Baúl. Classic period.

be needed. Allow 20 minutes to see and photograph the monuments and a couple more to walk to them from where you parked. You should have a guide to reach El Baúl.

2. See "Bilbao" for this connection and for more information about the area, including where to find a guide.

★ ★ ★
FINCA EL BAÚL
(FEEN-kah ehl bah-OOL)

Monument 27, a ball-player stela, El Baúl. Late Classic period. On display at Finca El Baúl headquarters.

At Finca El Baúl headquarters, several dozen stone monuments have been assembled on a cement platform under a thatch shelter, and a few other monuments are found in front of the shelter. There are bas-relief and deep-relief sculptures and three-dimensional monuments, with dates ranging from the Preclassic period through Classic times. Most of the carvings come from the site of El Baúl. Four of the major monuments stand near the center of the front of the shelter. They are described here from right to left as you face them.

Monument 12 of El Baúl is a twin of Monument 1 at Finca Pantaleón. Both monuments came from the acropolis at El Baúl (or nearby) and were probably placed close together originally. See "Finca Pantaleón" for a description. The next monument, Stela 1 (the Herrera Stela), was discovered in 1923 by T. T. Waterman, who believed the monument might pertain to Aztec culture; further study showed that the style of the stela was related to early Maya and Izapan art. An unusual version of a Maya-style Long Count date indicates that the stela was dedicated in A.D. 37.

Next to this stela is a beautifully preserved, Late Classic, three-dimensional representation of a squatting jaguar. Next to that is Monument 27, a ball-player stela with a raised border, discovered in 1964 in almost perfect condition. This Late Classic monument is almost 8.5 feet tall and is carved in deep relief from a gray basalt. It depicts a principal standing figure and a secondary figure who is seen falling backward. Both figures hold balls in their mited or gloved hands. Below these two figures is a panel portraying six small seated figures

Monument 26, a composite reptilian monster, El Baúl. Classic period. On display at Finca El Baúl headquarters.

Monument 30, heads of two confronting figures, El Baúl. Classic period. On display at Finca El Baúl headquarters.

with arms crossed over their chests—a common motif in Cotzumalhuapan art.

As you circle the platform you will see other monuments, somewhat more modest but still quite interesting. In front of the platform are horizontally tenoned depictions of human heads and a three-dimensional seated figure with arms crossed over the chest. Allow 45 minutes to see and photograph the monuments. See "Bilbao" for more information on the archaeology of the region and the recent history of the area.

Finca El Baúl is 3.9 miles [6.3 kilometers] by paved road (:13) from Santa Lucía Cotzumalguapa (highway junction with 3a Avenida). Take 3a Avenida heading north through Santa Lucía Cotzumalguapa and follow its extension as it curves around a bit past the northern outskirts of town. Shortly thereafter you will come to a fork in the road marked with a sign saying Los Tarros; take the left branch and continue to the gate at Finca El Baúl. There will be a guard at the gate; ask permission to enter the finca grounds to see the sculptures, which are be-

hind a fence with a locked gate. You may have to ask to have the gate opened to get a closer look and to photograph the monuments.

★ ★
FINCA LAS ILUSIONES
(FEEN-kah lahs ee-loo-SEEOHN-ehs)

Finca Las Ilusiones has a number of interesting stone sculptures from Bilbao at its headquarters. The first one you come to is on the right, along the access road to the finca headquarters. It is Monument 42, the bottom part of a stela believed to date to around A.D. 1; the top part of the stela has never been located. The well-preserved remaining part depicts a figure (from the waist down) with both feet facing in the same direction. The figure stands on a panel containing a dragon head in profile. Monument 42 is carved from a pink granite, which is unusual because most of the sculptures in the area are carved from basalt. It was discovered in 1963 in a ceremonial dump under a stairway (along with some plain monuments) when Bilbao was being excavated by Lee A. Parsons. The dragon profile panel is similar to some found in Izapan art; the

The bottom portion of Monument 42, Bilbao. Dates to around A.D. 1. On display at the entrance to Finca Las Ilusiones headquarters.

Monument 58, a potbelly figure, Bilbao. Probably Middle Pre-classic period. On display at Finca Las Ilusiones headquarters.

other motifs on the monument are charac-teristic of early Maya art from the Petén.

From the stela, continue ahead to the finca headquarters and park. Then walk around to the left where the other stone carvings are displayed against the wall of the building and nearby. There are half a dozen bas-relief carvings dating to the Clas-sic period, as well as Monument 58, a three-dimensional figure of potbelly style and Preclassic date. See "Bilbao" for more infor-mation on the archaeology of the region and the recent history of the area.

The cutoff to Finca Las Ilusiones is 1.0 mile [1.6 kilometers] by paved road (:03) northeast of Santa Lucía Cotzumalguapa on Highway CA 2. Turn left (north) at the cut-off (unmarked) and go 0.3 mile [0.5 kilo-meter] by cobblestone road (:02) to the finca headquarters.

★
FINCA PANTALEÓN
(FEEN-kah pahn-tah-leh-OHN)

At one time there were over a dozen stone sculptures displayed at Finca Pantaleón; now only Monument 1 remains, but it is the most interesting of the former group. The other sculptures have been moved to an office building in Guatemala City. Monument 1 is almost six feet tall and depicts a human head in frontal view, topped by an elaborate headdress that goes up and curls forward. A nearly identical sculpture is found at Finca El Baúl headquarters; both date to the Classic period. See "Finca El Baúl" for more details on the monuments and "Bilbao" for more information on the archaeology of the region and the recent history of the area.

Monument 1 of Pantaleón is now behind a fence, on top of a mound at the old entrance to the finca, near the bridge over the Pantaleón River.

The finca is adjacent to Highway CA 2 (on the north side), and you can pull off the road right in front of the monument. A telephoto lens is useful to photograph it.

Finca Pantaleón is 2.2 miles [3.5 kilometers] east of Santa Lucía Cotzumalguapa by paved road (:05). If you are driving by, it is worth a few minutes to see and photograph the monument.

Monument 1, Pantaleón. Classic period. On display on a mound at Finca Pantaleón headquarters.

★ ★ ★
LA DEMOCRACIA PLAZA
(THE MONTE ALTO SCULPTURES)
(lah deh-moh-KRAH-see-ah)

Arranged around La Democracia's pleasant plaza, with its benches and bandstand, are 10 monumental boulder sculptures from the nearby site of Monte Alto. Another sculpture is found in front of the museum, across the street diagonally from the plaza. There are potbellied figures with arms and legs wrapped around their bodies, and colossal heads. One head is different from the rest in that it represents a stylized jaguar; the other heads and potbellied figures represent humans. The human representations have puffy baby faces and closed eyes (except in one case), indicating that they are dead.

Monument 9, Monte Alto. Late Preclassic period. On display in La Democracia Plaza.

232 • *THE SITES AND MUSEUMS*

Monument 8, Monte Alto. Late Preclassic period. On display in La Democracia Plaza.

Their limbs are carved in low relief, and the carving tends to follow the natural contours of the boulders.

These sculptures were brought to La Democracia Plaza by the townspeople during the Monte Alto project, which was undertaken in 1968 and continued through 1971. Monte Alto was excavated by Lee A. Parsons and Edwin M. Shook under the auspices of the Milwaukee Public Museum and the Peabody Museum of Harvard University, with funding from the National Geographic Society.

Ceramics recovered from Monte Alto date from 800 B.C. to A.D. 300, and the site's greatest architectural activity took place in Late Preclassic times. Parsons believes the jaguar head is Olmecoid and the other sculptures are post-Olmec, which he dates to 500 to 200 B.C.

Allow an hour to see these splendid sculptures and the nearby indoor museum.

To reach La Democracia from Guatemala City, take Highway CA 9 to Escuintla, then CA 2 to Siquinalá. (There is a sign on CA 2 in Siquinalá indicating a left turn to get to the La Democracia Museum, but the actual cutoff is way beyond the sign.) Turn left at the cutoff and continue to La Democracia. As you enter the outskirts of town you will see a sign for the museum that indicates you should take the left branch of the road at a fork. Take this branch and go 0.4 mile [0.6 kilometer] to a small sign saying INGUAT (Guatemala's tourism department) and turn left for a block. This will get you to the plaza. From Guatemala City to La Democracia Plaza it is 52.7 miles [84.4 kilometers] by paved road (1:34).

From Santa Lucía Cotzumalguapa, take Highway CA 2 to Siquinalá, turn right, then follow the directions just given. From Santa Lucía Cotzumalguapa to La Democracia Plaza it is 10.6 miles [17.1 kilometers] by paved road (:21). See "Bilbao" for accommodations in Santa Lucía Cotzumalguapa. There are also a couple of modest hotels in Escuintla, 21.3 miles [34.3 kilometers] by paved road from La Democracia.

★ ★

RUBÉN CHÉVEZ VAN DORNE MUSEUM
(La Democracia Museum)

The museum in La Democracia is named for a local citizen who was concerned with preserving the pre-Columbian heritage of the region. The museum houses a collection of archaeological items that come from the area. In the main room of the museum there are low, glass-covered cases along the walls and larger, standing cases down the center of the room. They contain mostly ceramic specimens, some of which are well preserved. Only a few of the cases are labeled with the name of the finca or area from which the items inside come. There are hollow figurines as well as vessels. Stone carvings of various sizes are found on the floor of this room, and nearby, on a wall, is a jade mask. It is unlabeled, but when we questioned the museum guard, he said it came from Monte Alto.

Potbelly figure, similar to those found on the Pacific slope of Guatemala and elsewhere. Probably Preclassic period. On display in La Democracia Museum.

A corridor goes from the main room to an open area in the back where there are some plain stone discs and rectangular slabs. Off to the side of the corridor is a patio area and another room. Near the patio is a slab set on upright stones, on the top of which is a design in very low relief with the depiction of a head in the center. The slab is unlabeled but the style of the carving seems similar to Cotzumalhuapa-style art. See "Bilbao" for information on this style. In the patio behind the slab is a three-dimensional stone carving also unlabeled) of a figure with puffy cheeks and arms wrapped around its chest. It seems related to some of the potbelly figures found along the Pacific slope and elsewhere.

In the room off the corridor are more cases with ceramic figurines, potsherds, and obsidian cores. On the floor are plain stone implements, including manos and metates.

La Democracia Museum is open from 8:00 A.M. to noon and from 2:00 to 5:00 P.M. Photography is permitted but flash is not. Over the years the museum has been upgraded, and while you are in La Democracia to see the plaza monuments, you should visit the museum as well. See "La Democracia Plaza" for getting to La Democracia and for information about accommodations.

★ ★ ★
QUIRIGUÁ
(kee-rhee-GWAH)

Derivation:
Unknown to me.
Location:
South-central part of the Department of Izabal, Guatemala.
Map: 5 (p. 174)

The Site

Quiriguá is a major Maya lowland site, located in the floodplain of the lower Motagua Valley. It is a relatively small site, but its glory is an abundance of massive sculptured monuments. Excavation and partial restoration of some structures in the Acropolis have made the site even more interesting than before. The entrance to the core area (formerly called the Main Group, and the part of the site visitors see today) is at its north end; from there a stone walkway leads south to the Acropolis, passing the Great Plaza and the Ball Court Plaza along the way. The grassy plazas are kept neatly cut, and it is easy to walk around to see the fantastic sculptured monuments in them, all of which are covered with protective thatch shelters. No special sequence is recommended in visiting the site. Both new and old monument designations are shown on the accompanying site plan and are used in the text that follows.

As you enter the site you can see many of the monuments in the Great Plaza at a glance. Most are on the left (east) side of the walkway, but Monument 8 (Stela H) is on the right (west). Some of the stelae in the site core are carved with figures on the front and back and with glyphs on the sides, while others have a figure on the front and glyphs on the back. The heads of the figures are mostly carved in frontal view and in high relief. The rulers of Quiriguá erected carved and dated monuments every five years from A.D. 751 to 805, and in 810, a building with a glyphic inscription was dedicated. In some cases, two monuments were erected on the same date. There are also a few monuments that predate 751. Some highlights of the monuments are as follows.

In the northern part of the Great Plaza, Monument 3 (Stela C) was erected in A.D. 775; interestingly, it is also inscribed with an Initial Series date of 455, believed to be a historical reference to the first ruler of Quiriguá, who was perhaps the founder of the Quiriguá dynasty. The nearby Monument 1 (Stela A) was erected at the same time. Monument 4 (Stela D) has well-preserved and relatively rare full-figure glyphs on the upper part of its sides; the monument dates to 766. A little to the south is Monument 5 (Stela E), the largest carved Maya stela. It is 35 feet tall—about eight feet of it are underground—and weighs 65 tons; it dates to 771. Monument 8 (Stela H) has glyphs arranged in the rare mat pattern

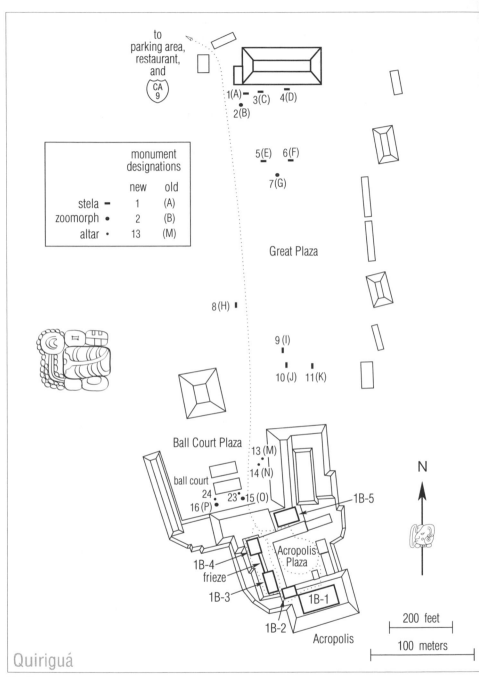

to parking area, restaurant, and CA 9

1(A) 3(C) 4(D)
2(B)

5(E) 6(F)
7(G)

monument designations
	new	old
stela	1	(A)
zoomorph	2	(B)
altar	13	(M)

Great Plaza

8(H)

9(I)
10(J) 11(K)

Ball Court Plaza

13(M)
14(N)

ball court
24 23 15(O)
16(P)

1B-5

N

Acropolis Plaza

1B-4
frieze
1B-3
1B-2
1B-1

Acropolis

200 feet
100 meters

Quiriguá

Modified after Morley.

The upper section of the east side of Monument 4 (Stela D), Quiriguá, showing full-figure glyphs. A.D. 766.

has glyphs arranged in the rare mat pattern on its back (west) side; it dates to 751.

In the Ball Court Plaza (formerly called the Ceremonial Plaza) there are monuments along the east and south sides, all of which are worth some study. Those on the south are Monument 15 (Zoomorph O) and Monument 16 (Zoomorph P) and their accompanying altars—Monuments 23 and 24, respectively. Monument 15 and its altar date to A.D. 790; Monument 16 and its altar date to 795. The intricate carvings on these monuments are truly astonishing.

A nice feature at Quiriguá is the use of small plaques to label the monuments. Another plus is that all the monuments have been cleaned and preserved. So although they are sheltered and cannot be photographed in full sunlight, the removal of moss and lichens makes the details of the carvings clearer. The Quiriguá sculptors were fortunate to have excellent sandstone nearby; this material has a close and even grain, making carving results predictable. This no doubt accounts, at least in part, for the intricacy of the sculptures.

Detail of one of the full-figure glyphs on the east side of Monument 4 (Stela D), Quiriguá. A.D. 766.

Monument 7 (Zoomorph G), one of the great mythological monsters, Quiriguá. A.D. 785.

Monument 5 (Stela E), the tallest carved Maya stela, Quiriguá. A.D. 771.

Quiriguá's Acropolis is the largest and most complex architectural assemblage at the site, and it is the only area with partly restored architectural remains. The Acropolis grew over time as new buildings and features were added; its construction began during the period from A.D. 550 to 720 and continued through 810.

Access to the Acropolis is via the restored stairway just south of Monument 15. There are several structures of interest in the Acropolis, surrounding the sunken Acropolis Plaza (formerly called the Temple Plaza). Structures 1B-4 and 1B-3 lie on the west side of the plaza, and the lower walls of rooms remain. Between the two is an earlier construction, a free-standing wall with a stone mosaic frieze that faces west (away from the plaza). When discovered, the frieze had depictions of Kinich Ahau, the sun god, and these were left in place for a time. Although the heads of the sun god were later removed, the beaded collars and pectorals worn by the figures are still in place. The frieze is covered with a corrugated plastic roof that transmits enough light to see the

Monument 8 (Stela H), west side, showing the rare mat pattern of the glyphs, Quiriguá. A.D. 751.

Monument 8 (Stela H), north side, Quiriguá. A.D. 751.

remains. The free-standing wall is believed to have been the east wall of a patio that opened to the west.

The south side of the plaza is bounded by Structures 1B-2 (on the west and near plaza level) and 1B-1, which sits on a platform, the lower part of which abuts 1B-2. The lower walls of both structures are standing. There are three exterior doorways in Structure 1B-1, each leading to a small chamber. At the back of each chamber is a step, two feet above floor level, carved on its front edge with hieroglyphs, some of which are well preserved. The steps lead to other small chambers. Originally a band of glyphs formed a medial molding on the exterior of the building; along with the glyphs on the steps, these recorded the date A.D. 810, the latest recorded date at Quiriguá. The platform that supports Structure 1B-1 is fronted by a broad stairway on the north (plaza) side. Set into the stairway are two sloping

Monument 10 (Stela J), east side, Quiriguá. A.D. 756.

Monument 11 (Stela K), west and south sides, Quiriguá. A.D. 805.

areas with a few remains of carving of the heads and arms of figures.

On the north side of the plaza, at the top of a broad stairway, is Structure 1B-5, the largest building at Quiriguá; it is entered by a single doorway on the south that gives access to its seven interconnected chambers. The walls of the structure are standing. Excavations in the Acropolis uncovered remains of corbeled vault stones, but no vaults are in place today. Studies of the Acropolis show that it was used for various functions but primarily for administrative purposes and as elite residences.

In addition to the site core of Quiriguá, three other groups (A, B, and C) are known; they lie from one to three miles [1.6 to 4.8 kilometers] away. In Group A, Early Classic remains have been found, including Monument 26, a stela dating to A.D. 493; it was discovered in 1978. An unsculptured stela was found in Group C, and a carved but eroded one in Group B.

Ceramic studies show that some areas around Quiriguá were occupied in the Late

Monument 11 (Stela K), bottom of the north side, Quiriguá. A.D. 805.

Preclassic period, and there is evidence that Quiriguá was occupied into the Early Postclassic, perhaps by a foreign group. The site's most brilliant period was from A.D. 740 to 810.

During part of its history, Quiriguá was under the hegemony of Copán. In 725, Copán's ruler, 18 Rabbit, installed Cauac Sky as the ruler of Quiriguá. In 738, Cauac Sky defeated and sacrificed 18 Rabbit, and Quiriguá gained its independence from

Copán. This event signaled the beginning of Quiriguá's great period.

Recent History

The ruins of Quiriguá lie on a large tract of land once owned by a Señor Payés, who visited the tract just once, but who saw the ruins. He reported them to his three sons and to Carlos Meiney, a Jamaican Englishman living in Guatemala, who in turn told

Structures 1B-3 (left) and 1B-4 (right) on the west side of the Acropolis plaza, Quiriguá. Under the shelter between the two structures is a stone mosaic frieze that faces away from the plaza. Late Classic period.

John Lloyd Stephens and Frederick Catherwood about them in 1840. The elder Payés had recently died and his sons had inherited the tract of land. Neither the Payés sons nor Meiney had seen the tract, but plans were then under way for two of the sons to visit it. They invited Stephens and Catherwood to join them on the trip. Stephens had duties to attend to in San Salvador, but Catherwood accompanied the Payés brothers to Quiriguá, and during the one day he spent at the site he sketched two of the stelae. Stephens reported Catherwood's trip to Quiriguá in his 1841 book.

Alfred P. Maudslay visited Central America for the first time in 1881, on "a journey which was undertaken merely to escape the rigours of an English winter." Quiriguá was the first ruin he saw, and he immediately decided to take a permanent interest in Central American archaeology. He stayed at Quiriguá only three days on his first visit, but he returned on three other occasions through 1894, when his wife accompanied him. During these trips he felled the large trees, cleared the bush, photographed the monuments, and made molds of the sculptures. He also made drawings of the figures and glyphs and on later trips carefully compared them with the originals. In addition, he surveyed and partially excavated the site core.

Further work was done at the site from 1910 through 1914 under the direction of Edgar Lee Hewitt for the School of American Archaeology of the Archaeological Institute of America. Shortly thereafter, the Carnegie Institution of Washington sup-

Part of the stone mosaic frieze between Structures 1B-3 and 1B-4, Quiriguá. Late Classic period.

ported work off and on from 1915 through 1934. Sylvanus G. Morley, Oliver G. Ricketson, Earl H. Morris, and Gustav Stromsvik were important contributors during that time. The United Fruit Company, which by then owned the land on which Quiriguá was located, in 1910 set aside 75 acres surrounding the site core to be maintained as an archaeological park, leaving the jungle untouched in the midst of the banana plantation.

Quiriguá was one of the first Maya sites to be so thoroughly studied, though little of the architecture was restored. The structures that Morley had cleared and excavated once again became overgrown with jungle vegetation.

In 1975, an intensive excavation and restoration project was begun under the direction of William R. Coe and Robert J. Sharer. This venture was jointly sponsored by the University Museum of the University of Pennsylvania, the National Geographic Society, and the Guatemalan government; it continued through 1979. During this work, the Acropolis was excavated, the monuments were cleaned and preserved, the outlying groups were studied, and Monument 26 was discovered. The restoration of the architecture seen today is one of the results of this project.

Connections

1. Teculután to Quiriguá: 48.7 miles [78.4 kilometers] by paved road (1:02), then 2.1 miles [3.3 kilometers] by good rock road (:07).

2. Guatemala City to Quiriguá: 130.9 miles [210.7 kilometers] by paved road (some poor) (3:24), then 2.1 miles [3.3 kilometers] by good rock road (:07).

Structure 1B-1 at the south end of the Acropolis Plaza, Quiriguá. There is a step carved with hieroglyphs on its front edge in each of the three chambers. A.D. 810. The small Structure 1B-2 is on the right at plaza level.

Getting There

1. From Teculután, take Highway CA 9 heading northeast to the cutoff for Quiriguá. There is a sign at the junction, but it is easily missed; keep an eye out for it. Turn right at the junction and proceed straight ahead through banana groves. As you approach the entrance for the parking area at Quiriguá, you will pass a control gate (which someone may have to lift to allow you through). Shortly afterward you turn right and enter the parking area for the site. From there you follow a foot trail to the Great Plaza.

There are two fairly good hotels on Highway CA 9 near the east end of Teculután: El Atlantico and the Longarone.

They are next to each other on the right (south) side of the highway.

2. From Guatemala City, head northeast on Highway CA 9 to the Quiriguá cutoff and follow the preceding directions.

Buses traveling along Highway CA 9 pass the Quiriguá cutoff frequently, and reportedly there is motorbike shuttle service from the junction to the ruins. It is advised that you make arrangements to be picked up later.

Over the years, amenities for visitors to Quiriguá have increased. There are rest rooms to the left of the foot trail shortly after it leaves the parking area. In a building near the parking area, ice-cold soft drinks and beer are sold, as are packaged snacks. There are tables and benches that you may use to eat a picnic lunch if you have brought one along, and this is recommended.

Quiriguá is open from 8:00 A.M. to 6:00 P.M. daily. Allow 3.5 hours for a visit. Although it is possible to visit Quiriguá on a day trip from Guatemala City, if you spend the recommended time at the site and allow 30 minutes for a picnic lunch, it would take over 11 hours. It would be better to stop at Teculután the night before and get to Quiriguá early the next morning; then return to Teculután or Guatemala City.

SECTION 6

• • • •

HONDURAS

North side of the altar of Stela D, Copán. A.D. 736.

GENERAL INFORMATION FOR SECTION 6, HONDURAS

Honduras covers 43,277 square miles [112,088 square kilometers] and is the second largest country in Central America after Nicaragua. Its population is around 5 million, and a large majority of its people are mestizos (Spanish and Indian). The remainder are Indians of various ethnicities, Europeans, and Garifunas (African and Carib Indians).

The name Honduras means "depths" in Spanish, and there are two differing explanations for the name. One is that it refers to the deep waters offshore found by Columbus; the other says the name alludes to the deep, wavelike valleys and ridges that cover most of the country.

Honduras is bordered on the north by the Caribbean Sea, on the west by Guatemala, on the south by El Salvador and the Gulf of Fonseca on the Pacific, and on the east by Nicaragua. The north and south coastal areas are relatively flat; the rest of the country is mountainous. The Bay Islands, off the north coast, attract visitors interested in scuba diving and snorkeling.

Tegucigalpa (often called simply Tegus) is the capital of Honduras and the country's largest city, with a population of 600,000. The name means "Silver Hill," referring to the city's founding in 1578 as a silver and gold mining center. This pleasant city became the capital of Honduras in 1880.

Tegucigalpa is centrally located in Honduras. It lies to the east of the Choluteca River; on the west side of the river is Comayagüela, which became a part of Tegucigalpa in 1938. The second largest city in Honduras is San Pedro Sula, with a population of more than 300,000. Situated near the north coast of the country, it is the major commercial center of Honduras.

All visitors to Honduras must have a passport. Citizens of Canada, the United States, and some other countries do not need a visa for stays of less than 30 days. For longer stays and for citizens of some countries, a visa is required. Since entry regulations change frequently, you should check with the nearest Honduran consulate for current requirements and get a visa ahead of time if need be.

The unit of currency in Honduras is the lempira (locally called "lems"). The lempira (L in front of the number) is being steadily devalued, so it is impossible to say what the exchange rate will be at a particular time. As a rough guide, the rate was 9.5 lempiras to one U.S. dollar in 1995. Major credit cards are accepted at the moderate and better hotels and at some restaurants.

Places to stay that will be of interest to the reader are Tegucigalpa, San Pedro Sula, and Copán Ruinas (the town near the archaeological site, formerly called San José de Copán). All three places have excellent hotels (some of which are rather expensive), as well as more modest ones. All of the better hotels, of course, have restaurants and bars.

The Hotel Marina in Copán Ruinas was enlarged and greatly improved in 1992. Before that, from time immemorial, it was a humble establishment without hot water and with electricity for only a few hours in the evening. It is now a delightful, first-rate operation. The rooms are large and air conditioned, there is a nice swimming pool, and the grounds are well kept and planted with colorful tropical vegetation. The restaurant serves excellent food.

Two newer hotels (one luxury and one more modest) have opened on Highway 11, east of the entrance to the ruins of Copán, so now there are more choices of places to stay when you visit the site.

Highway CA 5 (formerly Highway 1) and Highway CA 4 (formerly Highway 18) have two lanes, but they are both excellent, wide, smooth roads. Only short sections near Tegucigalpa and San Pedro Sula have four lanes. See "Copán" for additional road information.

There are car rentals in Tegucigalpa and San Pedro Sula; they are at the international airports, at agencies in town, and at some of the major hotels in both cities. You do not

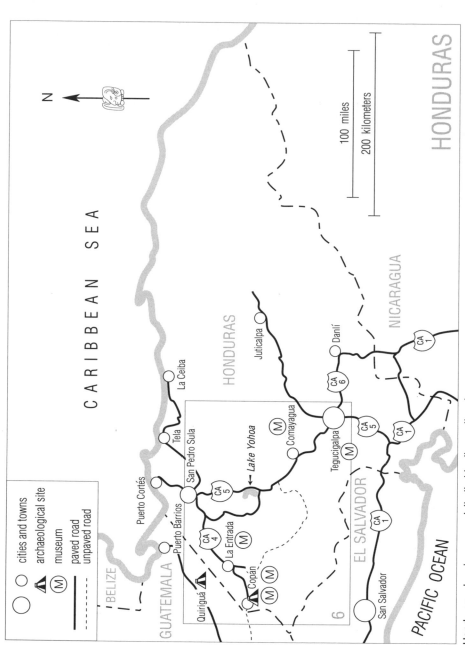

Honduras, showing areas delimited by the sectional map.

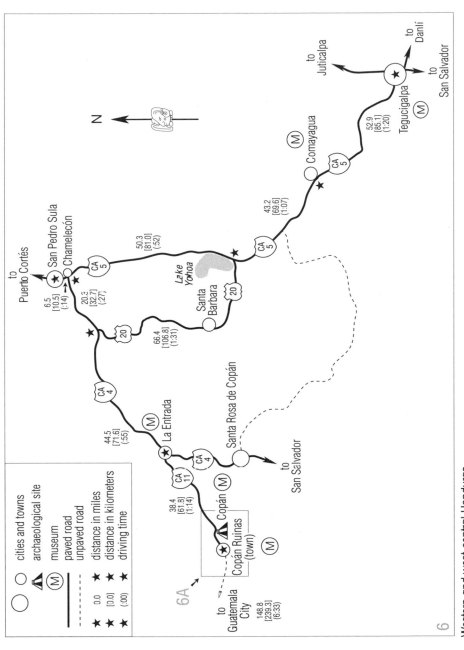

N

cities and towns
archaeological site
(M) museum
paved road
unpaved road
distance in miles 0.0
distance in kilometers [0.0]
driving time (:00)

★ 0.0
★★ [0.0]
★ (:00)

to Puerto Cortés

San Pedro Sula
Chamelecón
6.5 [10.5] (:14)
CA 5
20.3 [32.7] (:27)
20
50.3 [81.0] (:52)
Lake Yohoa
Santa Barbara
66.4 [106.8] (1:31)
20
CA 5
CA 4
44.5 [71.6] (:55)
La Entrada (M)
CA 4
CA 11
Santa Rosa de Copán
to San Salvador
38.4 [61.8] (1:14)
Copán (M)
Copán Ruinas (town)
(M)
6A
to Guatemala City
148.8 [239.3] (6:33)

Comayagua (M)
CA 5
43.2 [69.6] (1:07)
to Juticalpa
Tegucigalpa
(M)
52.9 [85.1] (1:20)
to Danlí
to San Salvador

Western and west-central Honduras

6

need a high-clearance vehicle or four-wheel drive to reach the places covered in this guide. A standard vehicle is perfectly adequate.

A sufficient number of gasoline stations can be found on the routes covered in the text, so gas pump symbols are not used on the maps.

The points of reference for distances and driving times are as follows: (1) in San Pedro Sula, the central park (plaza) in the center of town; (2) in La Entrada, the junction of Highways CA 4 and CA 11 (the road to Copán); (3) in Copán Ruinas (town), the main plaza in town; (4) in Chamelecón, the junction of Highways CA 5 and CA 4; (5) in Comayagua, the junction of Highway CA 5 and the road into town (next to a Texaco gasoline station); and (6) in Tegucigalpa, the bridge over the Choluteca River near the National Stadium.

Buses run along all the roads going to Copán and to all the cities and towns where the archaeological museums are located; service is fairly frequent.

There are a number of travel agencies in Tegucigalpa and San Pedro Sula that can arrange tours to Copán and other points of interest.

One of the main crafts in Honduras is woodcarving, and items of this type (generally carved from mahogany) are available in tourist shops. Other interesting articles are leather goods, baskets, and textiles, found in the same places.

There are a number of places of interest in Honduras that are not within the scope of this book. See "General Advice" for a list of guidebooks that have this information.

★ ★ ★
NATIONAL MUSEUM OF HONDURAS
(Tegucigalpa Museum)

The Honduran Institute of Anthropology and History, created in 1952, is responsible for the conservation and protection of Honduran cultural materials, and it operates the Tegucigalpa Museum.

The museum is in an interesting two-story building constructed in 1938 as a residence for Julio Lozano Díaz, once president of Honduras, and his wife, Laura Vijil de Lozano. Upon her death in 1974, the widowed doña Laura bequeathed the residence (known as the Villa Roy) to be used as the museum. At that time the museum was in another location and was looking for a new home. The museum houses colonial-period items, historical and ethnographical sections, and archaeological displays. Most are well labeled.

The first floor displays include temporary exhibits, personal objects belonging to the Lozanos, and natural science displays.

A stairway leads to the second floor, where exhibits begin with an introduction to the study of humankind. Afterward comes pre-Hispanic technology, including a mano and metate, jewelry (ear flares and necklaces), and musical instruments (conch shell trumpets and ceramic whistles).

In the room devoted to archaeology there are ceramic vessels (some of which are attractive polychromes), maps, and a large, decorative metate. One area is devoted to Copán and displays more polychrome pots, exhibits of cranial deformation, carved jade, a chronological chart, and a mural-size reproduction of Tatiana Proskouriakoff's restoration drawing of Copán. There is also a model of Copán.

The real gem of the collection is also in this area. It is a stone bench from Copán, carved with glyphs on its front edge. It has two vertical supports, each carved with an upturned human face in profile, accompanied by astronomical symbols. The bench is well preserved.

In the room devoted to the colonial period, large pots and bowls are displayed, along with a copy of the nation's act of independence. There are also a coat of mail and photographs of old churches and other buildings.

Stone bench carved with hieroglyphs, and supports carved with astronomical symbols, Copán. Late Classic period. On display in the Tegucigalpa Museum.

The next room is devoted to handsome ethnographic exhibits. These show the typical clothing, tools, and musical instruments of some of the cultural groups who live in Honduras—Misquitos, Sumos, Garifunas, Lencas, and others.

The last room is devoted to the life of Dr. Jesús Aguilar Paz, a famous Honduran doctor, explorer, and teacher. He drew sketch maps of various parts of the country, and these, in addition to the instruments he used, are displayed with other memorabilia. The information provided by his sketch maps was used to produce the first modern published map of Honduras in 1933. A beautiful pre-Columbian jade-and-bone necklace that he acquired during his travels was donated to the museum by his family; it is found in this room.

The museum perches on a steep hill in

Bario Buenavista near Concordia Park, but unless you are familiar with Tegucigalpa, I recommend taking a taxi to the museum and possibly having it wait for you. The city—with its one-way and interrupted streets—is difficult to negotiate on your own.

The museum is open from 8:30 A.M. to 3:30 P.M. on Wednesday through Sunday. It is closed on Monday and Tuesday. As you near the museum on the uphill road, you come to a gate with a guard and then the ticket office, where a few publications are sold. You can drive from there (steeply upward on a cobblestone road) to the museum itself. Allow an hour to see and photograph the collection. Lighting is fair in some areas, but you should still have fast film because flash is not allowed.

★ ★
COMAYAGUA ARCHAEOLOGICAL MUSEUM
(Comayagua Museum)

The Comayagua Museum was inaugurated in 1968 in a building that dates to the nineteenth century. Most of the collection comes from the Department of Comayagua, but two monuments are from Copán. They are similar carved panels, each depicting a richly attired figure. According to the labels—and all of the displays are well labeled—the panels come from Structure 22 and were erected by Yax Pac, the sixteenth ruler in Copán's dynasty. The panels are fairly well preserved.

Salvage archaeology was carried out from 1980 to 1986 in the Department of Comayagua, along two river systems that would become flooded after the completion of El Cajón hydroelectric dam. During reconnaissance of the area, more than 130 pre-Columbian sites were recorded and the larger ones were intensively excavated. The largest was Saltirón Viejo, with almost 400 structures. Photographs of this excavation are on exhibit at the museum, as are pots with offerings that came from the site.

Ceramics from various periods are on display, many of them in mint condition. There are exhibits of lithic technology, an archaeological map of the Department of Comayagua, obsidian cores, bark beaters, and jade pectorals. A platform in one room supports manos and metates and a large stone with four rimmed depressions. A pounding handstone sits in one of the depressions. No doubt the device was used for pounding seeds.

The most interesting object in the museum is a stela from El Cedral, found near one of the rivers where salvage archaeology was carried out. The monument stands more than five feet tall and is carved on its two broad sides. It was found without cultural associations and its date is unknown, but it is different from other carved stelae in Honduras—the designs are not Classic Maya. It is believed that the indigenous cul-

Stela from El Cedral. Date unknown. On display in the Comayagua Museum.

tural group who occupied the river systems in this part of Honduras may have been of Lenca rather than Maya affiliation.

The museum also houses some colonial artifacts: jugs, bottles, painted tiles, and plates. There is also a large bell dated 1899.

Comayagua lies mostly to the northeast of Highway CA 5, which goes from San Pedro Sula to Tegucigalpa, and the museum is not difficult to reach. It is only five minutes from the highway. Turn off the highway at a Texaco gasoline station, first going northeast and then following the street as it curves to the north. You will soon encounter cross streets (their numbers increase as you go). Look for 6th (Sexta) Calle (Street) and turn right. From there go four blocks. The museum is on the left at the far end of the fourth block. Across the street (fifth block) is a small plaza alongside which you can park. While you are at the plaza, take a look at Honduras's first printing press. It was brought to the country in 1829 by General Francisco Morozán and is now displayed on a cement base in the plaza.

The museum is open from 8:30 A.M. to noon and 1:00 to 4:00 P.M. Wednesday through Friday. It opens a half hour later on Saturday and Sunday. It is closed on Monday and Tuesday. Allow 45 minutes to visit the museum. Photography is permitted but flash is not. Use fast film.

★ ★
LA ENTRADA ARCHAEOLOGICAL MUSEUM
(La Entrada Museum)

La Entrada Museum is in the town of the same name, on the west side of Highway CA 4. It houses materials recovered from work done by La Entrada Archaeological Project under the auspices of the Honduran Institute of Anthropology and History and the Technical Mission of Japan.,

Many sites in the area were recorded by the project, and major excavations and restoration were undertaken at El Puente. Most of the museum displays deal with El Puente and Los Higos; both sites are near La Entrada.

At the museum entrance there is a rather crudely carved stone figure from El Puente, a site that has 18 plazas. Farther along you will see maps, charts, and displays of ceramics and lithics. A stone snakehead tenon from Los Higos is on exhibit, as is a photograph of a stela from that site and a diagram of one of the pyramids at El Puente, showing its various construction phases.

One unusual feature is a display of Jap- anese ceramics from various periods, supplied by the Technical Mission of Japan. A nearby chart shows the chronology of the ceramic phases in Japan in relation to the Maya periods.

The museum is open on Tuesday through Sunday from 8:00 A.M. to noon and 1:00 to 4:00 P.M. It is closed on Monday. Photography is permitted but flash is not. The lighting is fair, but you will still need fast film. Allow 30 minutes to view the collection.

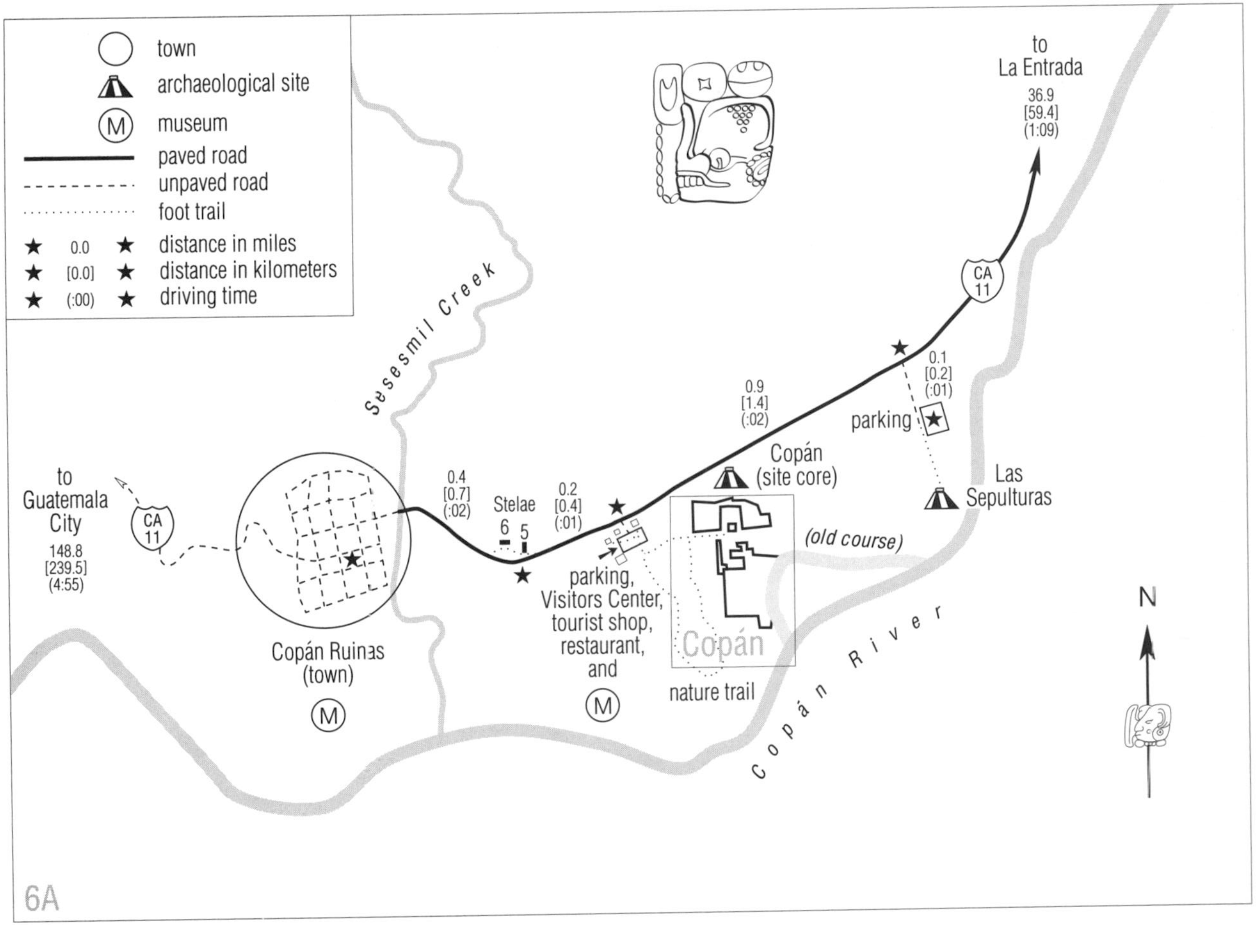

Detail of the Copán area

6A

Legend:
- ○ town
- △ archaeological site
- Ⓜ museum
- ▬▬▬ paved road
- ----- unpaved road
- ········ foot trail

- ★ distance in miles
- ★★ distance in kilometers
- ★★★ driving time

- ★ 0.0
- ★★ [0.0]
- ★★★ (:00)

N

to La Entrada
36.9
[59.4]
(1:09)

CA 11

0.1
[0.2]
(:01)

parking

Las Sepulturas

Copán (site core)

0.9
[1.4]
(:02)

Copán
(old course)

Copán River

nature trail

parking, Visitors Center, tourist shop, restaurant, and

0.2
[0.4]
(:01)

Stelae 6 5

0.4
[0.7]
(:02)

Sesesmil Creek

Copán Ruinas (town)

to Guatemala City
148.8
[239.5]
(4:55)

CA 11

Serpent-head tenon from Los Higos. Late Classic period. On display in La Entrada Museum.

COPÁN

(koh-PAHN)

Derivation:
There are a number of possible derivations; the first is considered most probable. (1) Named for Copán-Calel, chief of the region at the time of the Spanish conquest. (2) Capital of Co. (3) From the Nahuatl word *copantl,* meaning "pontoon" or "bridge."

Original name:
Xukpi, the Chol Maya name for the motmot (a colorful tropical bird), according to Matthew G. Looper.

Location:
Extreme western part of the Department of Copán, Honduras.

Maps: 5 (p. 174), 6 (p. 251), and 6A (p. 256)

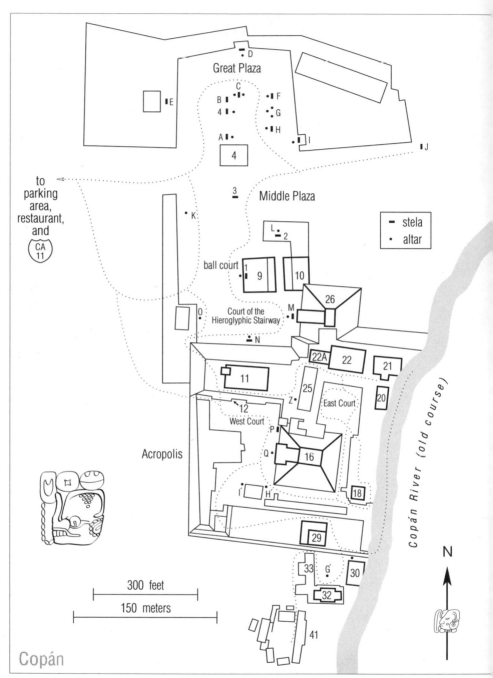

Great Plaza

D

C
B
4
A

F
G
H
I

E

J

4

Middle Plaza

3

to
parking
area,
restaurant,
and
CA
11

K

L
2

ball court

9
1

10

26

Court of the
Hieroglyphic Stairway

O

M

N

— stela
• altar

22A
22
21

11

25

20

Z
East Court

12

West Court

P

Acropolis

Q

16

I
H

18

29

300 feet

150 meters

33
G
30

32

41

Copán River (old course)

N

Copán

Modified after Núñez Chinchilla.

The altar of Stela D, view of the north side, Copán. A.D. 736.

The Site

Copán is one of the most extraordinary sites in Mesoamerica—and it is probably the most photogenic. For the last 20 years the site has been extensively studied by a host of international scholars, representing a variety of disciplines. Restoration of many of Copán's recently excavated structures has ensued, and there is more to see there today than ever before. Three areas are of interest for the visitor: the site core (Main Group), Las Sepulturas (an elite residential area to the east), and Stelae 5 and 6 (to the west of the site core along Highway CA 11, on the way to the town of Copán Ruinas).

There is a visitors' center near the Main Group, where tickets for the site are sold. Nearby is the new site museum, scheduled to open in stages. It will eventually house the carved monuments from the site, which will then be replaced with replicas. From the visitors' center, a trail heads east to a building where you sign a registra-

tion book; just past the building are some carved monuments from the site. The trail continues to the site core and enters it near Structure 4, which borders the south end of the Great Plaza. There are six stelae and several altars in the center of the plaza, and three stelae along the edges. Stela E is on the top of a terrace on the west side of the plaza, Stela D and its incredible altar are at the extreme north end of the plaza, and Stela I is recessed in a niche in a wall at the southeast corner of the plaza. Some of the monuments are protected by shelters, and all of the major monuments are labeled. The grass in all the plazas and courts at Copán is kept neatly cut, and it is easy to get around.

Many of Copán's stelae are carved in very high relief, almost approaching sculpture in the round in some cases. They are carved from a greenish andesite, a material superior to the limestone used for monuments in most of the Maya area. The quality of the carving is superb, and many of the

Stela F, portraying 18 Rabbit, Copán. A.D. 721.

monuments are well preserved. Just roam around the Great Plaza and enjoy. Because the stelae are carved on all four sides, it would be good to allow some morning and some afternoon hours for best photographic results.

The Great Plaza stelae (except for E and I) were erected by 18 Rabbit, a Copán ruler who reigned from A.D. 695 to 738, when he was captured and beheaded by Cauac Sky of Quiriguá. Copán had controlled Quiriguá from around the later half of the fifth century; with the capture and

sacrifice of 18 Rabbit, Quiriguá won its independence.

Some highlights of the monuments are as follows. At the upper corners of the front of Stela B (A.D. 731) are macaw heads, thought by some early writers to be elephant heads; this supported their idea that the Mayas came directly from Asia, an idea that has been totally discredited. Stela D (736) has rare full-figure glyphs on its back (north) side and a double-headed altar in front. The figure on Stela H (730) wears a long beaded skirt and was once thought to

Altar G1, south side, Copán. A.D. 800.

represent a woman; it is now known that the figure represents 18 Rabbit. Standing alone, to the east and outside the Great Plaza, is Stela J (702), with glyphs in the rare mat pattern; this monument was also erected by 18 Rabbit, to commemorate the first Period Ending after his accession to power. Stela E (554) was erected by Waterlily Jaguar; it is the earliest monument associated with the Great Plaza. Stela I (675) was erected by Smoke Imix God K, the father of 18 Rabbit and the preceding ruler of Copán, who reigned from 628 to 695.

South of the Great Plaza is the Middle Plaza, with Stela 3 in the center and the ball court and its monuments on the southeast. Stela 3 (A.D. 652) was erected by Smoke Imix God K, and the same ruler erected two other stelae associated with the ball court: Stela 2 (652), on an L-shaped terrace extension north of the ball court, and Stela 1

(668), on the west side of Structure 9, the building that forms the west side of the ball court. Behind Stela 2 is Altar L, the carving of which is unfinished. The final pretender to Copán's throne, U Cit Tok, is depicted, and the date 822 is recorded. This is the last dated monument at Copán. U Cit Tok was from a different lineage than his predecessor, Yax Pac, and the new dynasty he founded ended with him. In the ball court proper, at the top of both sloping sides, are stylized macaw heads—three on each side. The ball court was reconstructed several times, and carved center markers were installed, though they are no longer in place. A fine marker from the second ball court is in the museum in town.

To the south of the ball court is the Court of the Hieroglyphic Stairway, bounded on the east and south by two of Copán's monumental structures—the building with the Hieroglyphic Stairway (Structure 26)

Stela H, portraying 18 Rabbit, Copán. A.D. 730.

and the Temple of Inscriptions (Structure 11), respectively. The Hieroglyphic Stairway has more than 1,250 glyph blocks and is the longest Maya hieroglyphic text known; indeed, it is the longest text of any kind from pre-Columbian America. The stairway was erected during the reign of Smoke Shell, who acceded to the throne in A.D. 749, and it records events in the history of Copán from at least 553 to 756. The stairway is protected by a canvas awning, but enough light is transmitted for photography.

At the foot of the Hieroglyphic Stairway is Stela M (A.D. 756), erected by Smoke Shell, who also erected Stela N (761) at the base of the huge stairway leading to the Temple of Inscriptions (Structure 11) on the south side of the Court of the Hieroglyphic Stairway. Stela N is noted for being the closest thing to sculpture-in-the-round found at Copán. Both main figures on the stela show deep undercutting, which in places almost separates the figure from its background.

At the southwest corner of the Court of the Hieroglyphic Stairway, a trail leads to a modern stairway that curves around to the platform supporting Structure 11. Access to the structure itself is on the west side. Structure 11 was dedicated in A.D. 773 by Yax

Stela I, portraying Smoke Imix God K, Copán. A.D. 675.

ac, the last great ruler of Copán, and some of the walls of the structure are carved with hieroglyphs. From the south side of the platform of Structure 11, head west (without descending to the West Court) to Platform 25, where there is a large sculptured head with *ik* signs on its cheeks. Nearby is Altar Z (771), with well-preserved glyphs; it too was erected during the reign of Yax Pac.

To the north of Platform 25 is the Popol Na, also called the Council House or Mat House (Structure 22A), dedicated in A.D. 746 by Smoke Monkey. It was partly restored in 1990. There are three plaited mat motifs on the front (south) facade of the structure, one above each of three doorways that were originally supported by wooden lintels. When the structure was excavated in 1988, charred fragments of wood were found on the floor, indicating that the lintels had burned and caused the doorways to collapse. In the case of the west doorway, the mat motif fell with the stones in order, and an intact mat motif was found in place on the east face of the structure, making an accurate reconstruction possible. Other decorations originally incorporated into the Popol Na were human figures seated upon

The ball court, Copán, with Stela 2 (A.D. 652) at the far end, view from the south.

Structure 26 (A.D. 753), Copán, with an awning over the Hieroglyphic Stairway, and Stela N and its altar at right (A.D. 761).

The Hieroglyphic Stairway of Structure 26, Copán. A.D. 753.

glyphs, and separate glyphs as well; these have not been reincorporated.

To the east of the Popol Na is the Temple of Meditation (Structure 22), which sits at the top of a stairway at the north end of the East Court. This structure was erected by 18 Rabbit in A.D. 715 and features some of the most remarkable sculpture at Copán. Its entrance takes the form of a huge monster mouth, the upper parts of which have fallen but the teeth of which are in place at floor level. Just inside this doorway is another that leads to an inner

sanctuary. A step up through the doorway is supported by carved glyphs interspersed with skulls. Crouching supernatural figures on either side of the doorway support a two-headed monster representing the heavens; the monster continues across the top of the doorway. The exterior corners of Structure 22 are decorated with Witz monsters.

To the east of Structure 22 is Structure 21, part of which fell into the Copán River before its course was rechanneled. From Structure 21, walk back to Structure 22 and

Glyph-carved stones in a wall of Structure 11 (Temple of Inscriptions), Copán. Dedicated by Yax Pac in A.D. 773.

descend the stairway to the East Court. You can look down into a sheltered excavation in the northeast corner of the court where there are remains of stone and stucco sculptures. There is also a step carved with two rows of hieroglyphs that record the date A.D. 573. The building, called the Ante Structure, was erected during the reign of Moon Jaguar, who ruled from 553 to 578.

On the west side of the East Court is the Jaguar Stairway. It rises in three levels and has figures of two jaguars—in rather lighthearted poses—flanking the lower level. The circular depressions in the figures were probably once filled with obsidian discs. There are death's-heads carved on either end of the lower stairway. A stair block, centered on a higher level, represents the setting sun (in human form) sinking into the jaws of the earth monster.

At the southwest corner of the East Court, an excavation has been made into Structure 16, and you can look down into it. What you see is the decorated facade of

Three-dimensional sculpture on Platform 25 in the Acropolis, Copán.
Late Classic period. Note *ik* signs on the cheeks.

n earlier structure called Rosalila, about which more later.

From the East Court, head south along corridor that is flanked by the rear of tructure 16 (on the west) and the terrace hat supports Structure 18 (on the east). At the end of the corridor, on the left east), is Structure 18; the easiest access to t is by a modern stairway at its southeast orner. This small structure was erected by ˈax Pac in A.D. 800. The stones in the two airs of doorjambs are carved and form anels; in one of them, Yax Pac is depicted randishing a lance. The vertical part of a ench inside the room is carved with rotesque heads. By 820 Yax Pac had died,

and his survivors dedicated Stela 11 to him, placing it on or inside of Structure 18. The text on the stela states that the old dynasty, founded by Yax K'uk Mo', ended with Yax Pac. This is an unusual monument for Copán; its shape is cylindrical, and Yax Pac is portrayed in profile, the only profile depiction known from Copán. Stela 11 is in the museum in town.

To the north of Structure 18, atop the terrace that supports it, are a number of sculptures. One of the most interesting is a jaguar altar on the east side of the terrace.

From Structure 18, head west along the south side of Structure 16 to the West Court. As you enter the court you come to

Altar Z, Copán. Dedicated by Yax Pac in A.D. 771.

two rectangular altars (H´ and I´), carved with glyphs on their edges. From the southwest corner of the West Court, a trail goes downhill (to the east) to an elite residential group and on to the river cut of the Acropolis. I will describe these areas shortly.

The principal building on the West Court is Structure 16 on the east side. This large pyramidal structure rises in tiers and has a western stair and the remains of a temple on top. Stone-carved skulls decorate part of the stairway; they were placed there when Yax Pac refurbished the building. In 1989, when archaeologists tunneled into the building, they found earlier construction inside; one almost intact structure was named Rosalila. This structure—perhaps

erected during the reign of Butz´Chan (A.D. 578 to 628)—had been carefully preserve before it was buried by later construction The ancient Mayas had applied coarse, thic plaster to the entire building, preserving a the modeled stucco decoration on its su face. In all other cases known at Copán, an in most of the rest of the Maya area as wel earlier structures were partly demolishe and filled—ritually killed—before being cov ered with new construction. There are number of construction phases in Structur 16; clearly Rosalila is the most noteworth Inside Rosalila, excavators uncovered an ex traordinary cache of nine exquisite eccen tric flints and other objects, the most spec tacular ceremonial offering ever found a

The East Court of the Acropolis, Copán, view from the south. Structure 22A (Popol Na) (left) (A.D. 746), Structure 22 (Temple of Meditation) (center) (715), and the remains of Structure 21 (right) (Late Classic period). The shelter at center right protects the Ante Structure (573).

Structure 22A (Popol Na) (A.D. 746), with part of Structure 22 (Temple of Meditation) (715) on the right, Copán.

Structure 22 (Temple of Meditation), Copán. A.D. 715.

Copán. It is believed that eccentric flints were attached to the tops of staffs and brandished by the ruler during ceremonial activities.

In front of Structure 16, at the foot of the stairway, is the famous Altar Q (A.D. 776), carved with 16 seated figures, four on each of its sides, and with a panel of glyphs on the top. The altar has been known since 1834, and there was a great deal of speculation over the years about what it signified. It is now known, thanks to epigraphic advances in the last three decades, that the figures on the altar depict rulers of Copán. On the west side of the altar, the two central figures face each other; the one on the left depicts Yax K'uk Mo', the founder of the Copán royal dynasty, who is handing a baton of office to Yax Pac, the sixteenth ruler in the dynasty. The other figures are the kings who ruled in between these two,

seated in the sequence in which they ruled, each on top of a glyph, generally the ruler's name glyph. Altar Q commemorates the accession of Yax Pac. In a subfloor crypt jus to the east of the altar, Yax Pac placed 15 jaguars, sacrificed as an offering—one fo each of his ancestors. Although Yax K'ul Mo' was the founder of Copán's most famou dynasty, he was not Copán's first ruler Some Late Classic monuments are inscribec with dates referring back to A.D. 159 and 160 and to the name Smoke Codex God K these may be references to the founding o the kingdom.

To the north of Altar Q, and also or the east side of the West Court, is Stela I (A.D. 623) depicting Butz' Chan. The stela was moved to this location from an earlie one, perhaps from in front of Rosalila befor the structure was ritually buried.

The north side of the West Court is

The highly decorated doorway into the inner sanctuary of Structure 22 (Temple of Meditation), Copán. A.D. 715.

bounded by the Reviewing Stand (Structure 12). It is a stairway with depictions of kneeling figures at the tops of the steps on the east and west ends. A serpent writhes out of the mouth of each figure, and the west figure holds an object inscribed with an *ik* sign (as no doubt the east figure held originally). There are glyphs on the steps below each figure. In front of the Reviewing Stand, at the level of the court, are three carved floor slabs.

From the northwest corner of the West Court, a trail leads back to the site entrance.

Several structures have been excavated and partly restored in the elite residential group south of the Acropolis and on a lower level. These structures surround a plaza, and one (Structure 29) is on a higher terrace. Struc-

ture 29 is a square platform atop which are two long rooms arranged in an L shape on the northwest corner. The lower walls of the structure have been restored, and the highly decorated upper facade has been reassembled at ground level nearby for eventual incorporation above the lower walls. A good deal of sculptural decoration (depicting death symbolism) was found associated with the structure, including inverted *ik* symbols and corner death's-heads. The structure was devoted to the worship of deceased ancestors.

At the south end of the plaza is Structure 32, which lies on a platform fronted by a broad stairway that goes to the top of the platform. There are three rooms in a row, separated by narrow passages, and another stair, made of massive stones, leads upward

Detail of the sculpture on Structure 22 (Temple of Meditation), Copán, showing a supernatural figure crouching on a skull and supporting a two-headed monster. A.D. 715.

to the central room. Little remains of the end rooms, but the lower walls of the central room have been restored. Structure 32 once supported sculptural decorations including six seated figures and six waterlily monster masks. In 1892, when the structure was first studied, Altar F´ was found in the debris at the south side of the building. Almost a century later the glyphs on the altar were deciphered; they state that a noble named Chac made an offering in A.D. 775 and acceded to a high office in 798. Altar G´, in the center of the plaza, also mentions Lord Chac.

Structure 30, on the east side of the plaza, is a platform with steps on the west side; its superstructure is gone. When this area was excavated, a previously unknown altar was found in a midden on the north side of the structure. This circular monument has glyphs along the outside edge that are in mint condition. It too records the offering made by Lord Chac, who may have been a younger brother of Yax Pac; it is believed that Lord Chac ruled this section of Copán. The altar has been removed and replaced with a fine cement replica. Excava-

Jaguar sculpture on the left (south) of the Jaguar Stairway, on the west side of the East Court, Copán. Late Classic period.

tions in this area suggest that some of the buildings were deliberately destroyed in the late eighth century by burning the wooden lintels in niches and doorways, which caused the structures to collapse.

From this area a trail heads east and then north, following the now-dry bed of the old course of the Copán River. The river eroded the east side of the Acropolis for many years before it was rechanneled, and what you see today along the river cut is the stratigraphy of the Acropolis with its many layers of construction visible. This impressive sight becomes even more remarkable when you realize that the entire Acropolis, which rises 98 feet [30 meters] above ground level, is the work of human hands. Openings in the east face of the Acropolis seen today are the entrances to (or exits from)

tunnels dug by archaeologists, except for one triangular opening that is a drain from the East Court built by the ancient Mayas. By 1993, two miles of tunnels had been dug into the Acropolis to study buried structures, and the work continues. The surface of the river cut is being stabilized with stones.

Las Sepulturas residential area of Copán is joined to the site core by a *sacbé,* but access today is via Highway CA 11, then by an unpaved cutoff (marked with a sign), and finally by foot trail. There is no direct pathway between the site core and Las Sepulturas; the site core is encircled by a fence.

Of some 40 residential compounds in Las Sepulturas, about half have been investigated. Some structures in Group 9N-8 have

The stair block above the Jaguar Stairway on the west side of the East Court, Copán. Formerly called the Venus Altar. Late Classic period.

been restored, and this is the part visitors see today. The most important building in the group is the House of the Bacabs, also called the Palace of the Scribes (Structure 9N-82), a large elite residence that originally had a vaulted masonry roof. The lower walls of the structure are standing, including two facade sculptures depicting human torsos surrounded by intricate borders that represent the maw of the underworld. The figure on the left (as you face the structure) still holds a sectioned conch-shell ink pot in his hand. The residence was occupied by Mac Chaanal, a royal scribe, and his family. The upper facade of the building is no longer in place, but it originally had facade sculpture as well.

The middle of the third step of the stair that gives access to the structure is carved with glyphs; they are on an axis with the doorway. Inside the structure an elaborately carved stone bench was discovered during excavation. The original, now in the museum in town, has been replaced with a replica. The beautifully carved full-figure glyphs on the bench record the date A.D. 781, the time when the residence was dedicated; Yax Pac, Copán's reigning ruler, participated in the rites. The restored area of Las Sepulturas is kept well cleared, and it is easy to roam around the many substantial residences.

Stelae 5 and 6 are located along a foot path just north of Highway CA 11; across the highway is a wide spot where you can park. Stela 5 stands just a few feet from the highway and is visible from it. Stela 6 (under a shelter) is set back a bit farther. The monu-

Structure 18 with carved doorjamb and bench, Copán. Erected by Yax Pac in A.D. 800.

ments were erected by Smoke Imix God K in A.D. 677 and 682, respectively, and both stelae are accompanied by altars. There is a depiction of Tlaloc on the loincloth apron of Stela 5 (west side) and Mexican Yearsigns and more Tlaloc depictions on Stela 6.

Copán was first occupied by sedentary farmers in the second half of the second millennium B.C. Excavations at Las Sepulturas uncovered a house that may date to the Early Preclassic Rayo ceramic phase (1200 to 900 B.C.). The numerous artifacts discovered with it included ceramic vessels, flint and obsidian tools, grinding stones, and figurines. This house was found below the patio in front of the house of the scribe Mac Chaanal. Burials in Las Sepulturas during the very early Middle Preclassic period contained ceramics in a style related to that of the Olmec. Although Late Preclassic re-

mains have been uncovered in the Copán area, they are not as elaborate as those found in other parts of the Maya area during that time. Why this is so is an unresolved question. Two Late Preclassic potbelly sculptures, of the type found on the Pacific slope and in the highlands of Guatemala, were discovered at Copán, one buried below Stela 4 and the other under Stela 5. The sculpture found under Stela 4 is now on the grass near the back of the stela in the site core.

From around A.D. 400 to 700, population in the area increased greatly, and the carving of the great stone monuments began. Stela 63 is inscribed with the date 435 and the name of Yax K'uk Mo'; it is, however, a retrospective monument erected by his son, Mat Head, around 465. This is the earliest dated monument known from Copán; it was found ritually buried in an

Structure 16, west side, Copán. Late Classic period. The almost intact Rosalila structure was found inside Structure 16.

Altar Q, Copán, depicting 16 rulers in the Copán dynasty. The figure at left center is Yax K'uk Mo', who hands the baton of office to Yax Pac at right center. A.D. 776.

Figure on the east end of the Reviewing Stand, with glyphs on the steps below. Located at the north end of the West Court, Copán. Late Classic period.

earlier building inside Structure 26 in 1989. Copán continued to grow, and at its peak at around 800, a population of more than 20,000 inhabitants occupied an area of 9.3 square miles [24 square kilometers] in which the remains of 3,450 structures have been recorded. In the urban nucleus of 0.2 square mile [0.6 square kilometer] surrounding the Acropolis, more than 1,000 structures have been found.

After A.D. 822, no new monuments were erected, and the central political authority seems to have weakened about this time. People continued to live at Copán, however, perhaps until as late as 1200 in some areas, after which the site was virtually abandoned.

Recent History

The existence of Copán and a description of the site were first reported in a letter written to Philip II, king of Spain, by Diego García de Palacio, dated March 8, 1576. Palacio, a member of the Royal Audiencia of Guatemala, was under orders from Philip to report, among other things, on the antiquities of the New World. After visiting the site and studying its architecture, Palacio correctly assumed that Copán was built by the

Upper level of Structure 29, Copán, assembled at ground level for eventual incorporation above the lower part of the structure. The structure was devoted to ancestor worship. Late Classic period.

same "nation" that had erected the buildings previously discovered in Yucatán and Tabasco by the Spaniards.

Some time around 1820, Jean Frédéric Waldeck—better known for his work at Palenque and Uxmal—spent a month sketching the ruins of Copán.

An important report on the site was that of Colonel Juan Galindo, who headed the first archaeological expedition to Copán for the Guatemalan government in 1834. He published several articles in North American, English, and French periodicals.

A great many more people learned of Copán, however, when John Lloyd Stephens published his popular narrative, *Incidents of Travel in Central America, Chiapas, and Yucatán,* in 1841. Engravings of Frederick Catherwood's admirable drawings published

with the text brought to light the splendor of Copán's sculptures. Stephens also published a map of Copán, but, oddly enough, it shows north and south reversed. He apparently used this map in reconstructing his visit, as his narrative is consistent with it.

During the remainder of the nineteenth century and into the twentieth, many archaeologists and institutions investigated Copán. Among them were the Englishman Alfred P. Maudslay, who published many beautiful photographs and carefully detailed drawings. The Peabody Museum of Harvard University sent several expeditions to Copán, led by Marshall H. Saville, John G. Owens, and George B. Gordon. The site and its monuments were studied by Eduard Seler, Herbert J. Spinden, J. T. Goodman, Sylvanus G. Morley, Sir J. Eric S. Thomp-

Detail of figure adorning the upper level of Structure 29, Copán. Late Classic period.

son, Gustav Stromsvik, Alfred V. Kidder, Aubrey Trik, John M. Longyear III, Tatiana Proskouriakoff, and others. Much of this work was sponsored by the Carnegie Institution of Washington, in cooperation with the Honduran government.

During this time, the hieroglyphs were recorded and studied, the stelae were repaired and uprighted where necessary, some of the architecture was restored, and many tombs were excavated. Perhaps one of the most beneficial endeavors was the Carnegie Institution's rechanneling of the course of the Copán River, which prevented further destruction of the site. Some structures reported by Stephens less than a hundred years before had already disappeared.

In 1952, the Honduran government created the Honduran Institute of Anthropology and History (IHAH), and Jesús Núñez

Chinchilla was named its first director. Copán's archaeological zone was placed under IHAH's responsibility.

Since 1975, work in the Copán area has been continuous. Gordon R. Willey of Harvard University, at the invitation of IHAH, went to Copán to design a long-term program of research and restoration to be sponsored by the Honduran government. In consultation with William R. Coe and Robert J. Sharer, Willey conducted a survey of the site core and the Copán valley and made recommendations; this began the modern, multidisciplinary approach to the study of Copán.

In 1977, Claude F. Baudez, of the French Center of Scientific Research, directed the first phase of the Honduran government's project. In 1980, William T. Sanders and David L. Webster, both of Pennsylvania State University, directed the

The front (north side) of Structure 32, Copán. Late Classic period.

second phase, and in the same year UNESCO declared Copán a World Heritage Site. In 1985, the Copán Mosaic Project, incorporated into the Honduran-government-sponsored Copán Acropolis Archaeological Project, was formed, with William L. Fash, then of Northern Illinois University, as director. The goal of the project was to conserve and rearticulate the tens of thousands of fragments of tenoned facade sculptures that once adorned dozens of masonry structures at Copán. Extensive excavations have been carried out in the Acropolis in a project co-directed by Fash and Ricardo Agurcia Fasquelle of IHAH; Sharer and David Sadat participated in the work, which is continuing.

Beginning in 1990, Lord Chac's residential area was excavated by E. Wyllys Andrews V, of the Middle American Research Institute of Tulane University. C. Rudy Larios is in charge of restoring the recently excavated structures.

Funding for the many projects has come from the Honduran government, the universities and institutions whose scholars are involved, and the United States Agency for International Development.

In addition to the archaeologists' excavations, restorations, and ceramic studies, epigraphers have studied and deciphered many of Copán's voluminous texts. They are Berthold Riese, Peter Mathews, Linda Schele, David Stuart, and Nicolai Grube. Because of the efforts of the many scholars involved in the various projects, more is now known about Copán than about any other Maya site.

The Acropolis River Cut (Archaeological Cut) showing the stratigraphic layers of construction of the Acropolis, Copán. The triangular opening at upper left is a drain from the East Court constructed by the ancient Mayas. The other openings are tunnels excavated by archaeologists in recent years.

Connections

1. Copán Ruinas (town) to Copán: 0.6 mile [1.0 kilometer] by mostly paved road (:03).

2. San Pedro Sula to Copán: 109.1 miles [175.6 kilometers] by paved road (2:47).

3. Tegucigalpa to Copán (via Chamelecón): 249.0 miles [400.7 kilometers] by paved road (5:52).

4. Teculután (Guatemala) to Copán Ruinas (town) 31.3 miles [50.3 kilometers] by paved road (:43), then 35.2 miles [56.6 kilometers] by rock road (1:50).

5. Guatemala City to Copán Ruinas (town): 113.5 miles [182.6 kilometers] by paved road (3:05), then 35.2 miles [56.6 kilometers] by rock road (1:50).

Getting There

The town of Copán, now known as Copán Ruinas, was once called San José de Copán.

Structure 9N-82 (House of the Bacabs), the residence of the scribe Mac Chaanal in Las Sepulturas, Copán. A.D. 781.

Sculptured figure holding a sectioned conch-shell ink pot, on the facade of Structure 9N-82 (House of the Bacabs), in Las Sepulturas, Copán. A.D. 781.

1. From the northwest corner of the town plaza (in front of the Hotel Marina), go two blocks to the east and turn left; then go one block and turn right. After one block you will cross a bridge over the Sesesmil Creek; continue straight ahead to the entrance to the site (on your right and marked with a sign).

2. From San Pedro Sula, head south on Highway CA 5 to Chamelecón, where you will come to a toll gate. Shortly after the gate there is a cutoff to the right marked "Occidente." Take this cutoff (Highway CA 4) and proceed to La Entrada. At La Entrada there is a cutoff to the right (Highway CA 11) for Copán, marked with a small sign. The cutoff is near a Texaco gas station. Though paved, the road from La Entrada to Copán is rather patchy. When approaching Copán from this direction, you will pass the cutoff for Las Sepulturas first, then the entrance for the site core, and finally, the town.

3. From Tegucigalpa, take Highway CA 5 heading northwest toward Chamelecón. After you cross the Chamelecón River bridge, it is 0.3 mile [0.5 kilometer] to the "Occidente" sign, where you turn left; then follow the directions for Connection 2. There is another possibility for part of the route when you go from Tegucigalpa to Copán. At the south end of Lake Yohoa there is a cutoff to the left (Highway 20) that goes through Santa Barbara and on to Highway CA 4. This route is 4.2 miles [6.8 kilometers] shorter than the first. Highway 20 is a good road but not as good or as wide as the other highways; using this route will actually take a few minutes longer in driving time.

4. From Teculután, Guatemala (Map 5), head northwest on Highway CA 9 to Río Hondo and the junction with Highway CA 10. Turn right onto CA 10 and follow it through the outskirts of Chiquimula, then on to Vado Hondo and the cutoff for Copán (marked with a sign). Turn left onto the rock road and proceed to Copán Ruinas; then follow the directions for Connection 1. For the reference point in Teculután, see "General Information" for Section 5, South-

Stela 6, west side, showing depictions of Tlaloc and a Mexican Yearsign, Copán. Erected by Smoke Imix God K in A.D. 682. The stela is located just off the road between the site core and the town of Copán Ruinas.

ern Guatemala. For hotels in Teculután, see "Quiriguá."

5. From Guatemala City, head northwest on Highway CA 9 to Teculután; then follow the directions for Connection 4.

If you go to Copán starting from the Guatemala side, be prepared to spend some time crossing the international border. Copán can be reached by bus from San Pedro Sula, Tegucigalpa, Teculután, or Guatemala City, although some changes of bus are required. Copán can also be reached on tours from these places, except perhaps Teculután.

If you reach Copán Ruinas on your own and would like to have a personal guide for the ruins, ask at the Hotel Marina, across the street from the main plaza in town.

At the visitors' center at the site core, a small guidebook for Copán is generally available. Written by Fash and Agurcia, with illustrations by Barbara Fash, it is titled *History Carved in Stone: A Guide to the Archaeological Park of the Ruins of Copán.* William L. Fash also wrote a 1991 book that is longer and gives more details about the site, its rulers, and the discoveries made during the most recent work. It is titled *Scribes, Warriors and Kings.* Both volumes are recommended. An older work (1972) that can be recommended for its fine photographs and other illustrations (the information in the text is now, of course, somewhat dated) is *Copán: Home of the Mayan Gods,* by Francis Robicsek.

Near the visitors' center is a restaurant, and nearby, a tourist shop with rest rooms. When visiting the site it would be a good idea to carry a canteen of water, considering the amount of time you will be spending there. The ruins are open daily from 8:00 A.M. to 4:00 P.M. Allow a day and a half (or more) to see Copán properly, including Las Sepulturas, the stelae along the highway, the museum in town, and the new site museum.

Copán now receives 50,000 visitors annually, and for the protection of the remains, certain areas are restricted; they are marked with small signs. These are generally rooms of structures that you may look into but not enter.

The back of Altar U, Copán. A.D. 795. On display in the Copán Museum in Copán Ruinas.

★ ★ ★
REGIONAL MUSEUM OF COPÁN
(Copán Museum)

The Copán Museum, inaugurated in 1939, is located in the town of Copán Ruinas on the southwest corner of the main plaza. In both indoor and outdoor sections, it offers some interesting remains from Copán and other nearby sites.

The first room of the museum provides an introduction. The next covers the history of the site and includes displays from the Early Preclassic period through Late Classic times. Some impressive stone monuments are found in the next room. They include carved stelae, the large carved head of an old man from Structure 11, and the intricate Altar U. There is also a carving of a killer bat from Structure 20 and a case with eccentric flints. An explanation of Altar Q—one of the most important monuments at Copán—is given.

The remaining rooms display the beau-

Sculpture of the patron of Maya scribes, found in Structure 9N-82 (House of the Bacabs) in Las Sepulturas, Copán. Late Classic period. On display in the Copán Museum in Copán Ruinas.

tifully preserved and intricately carved bench from the House of the Bacabs in Las Sepulturas group and the three-dimensional carving of a scribe from the same structure. There is also a beautifully carved ball court marker, a model of the site of Copán, a display showing special occupations, and a burial. Nearby is the unusual Stela 11 (A.D. 820), which shows a posthumous depiction of Yax Pac, the sixteenth ruler in Copán's dynasty. The stela is cylindrical and shows the head of Yax Pac in profile. This is the only profile treatment of a figure on a stela known from Copán. The back of the stela is carved with glyphs.

Stela 7 (A.D. 613) is in the outdoor patio section. It portrays the eleventh ruler in Co-

pán's dynasty, Butz´ Chan, on the front and is carved with glyphs on the back and sides. It was originally erected about 100 yards [90 meters] south of where it now stands. There are a few pieces of three-dimensional sculpture in the patio as well.

The Copán Museum is open daily from 8:00 A.M. to 4:00 P.M. Photography is allowed but flash is not. The labeling of the collection is good, the items are attractively displayed, and the lighting is adequate for viewing the objects. In some rooms there is enough ambient light for photography. In others the light level is low; use fast film.

Allow an hour to see and photograph the collection.

SECTION 7

• • • •

EL SALVADOR

Boulder carved with an Olmec figure, Las Victorias. Middle Preclassic period. On display outside the Tazumal Museum.

GENERAL INFORMATION FOR SECTION 7, EL SALVADOR

El Salvador, the smallest and most densely populated of the Central American countries, covers an area of 8,124 square miles [21,041 square kilometers] and is home to somewhat more than 5 million people. The population is largely mestizo (Spanish and Indian), with small percentages of pure Indian and pure European. The country is bounded on the north and east by Honduras, on the south by the Pacific Ocean, and on the west and northwest by Guatemala. El Salvador is the only Central American country without a coast on the Caribbean. San Salvador, the capital, is centrally located; its population is 500,000.

All visitors to El Salvador need a passport; citizens of Canada and the United States also need visas. Citizens of some western European countries do not need visas, but regulations can change at any time. Check with your nearest El Salvadoran consulate for current regulations and get your visa before you leave home (if you need one).

El Salvador's currency is the colón (¢ in front of the number). The exchange rate with the United States dollar is not stable, and it is impossible to say what it will be at a given time. As a guide, the rate was 8.8 colones to one U.S. dollar in 1995. United States dollars are accepted in upscale hotels and restaurants, as are major credit cards.

There are car rental agencies in San Salvador at the international airport, at the agencies' main offices in town, and at the luxury hotels. Standard vehicles are adequate to reach the archaeological sites in El Salvador that are covered in this book. It is possible to get around the country by buses, which run frequently but are generally packed.

All of the sites and museums covered here are within three hours' driving time from San Salvador, making it the best stopover. The city has hotels in various price ranges and the only first-class hotels in the country. There are budget and/or modest hotels at Santa Ana, on the shore of Lake Coatepeque, in Cerro Verde National Park, at La Libertad and west along the coast, in San Miguel, and at a few other places. Tour operators in San Salvador offer a variety of trips. No doubt you could arrange with them to take you to the archaeological sites.

The roads in El Salvador that go to the archaeological sites are mostly paved; they are fairly good and are better marked than those in most of the other countries. The only problem you may encounter is where a road is being resurfaced. Unfinished sections will be bumpy and you will have to drive slowly. It is impossible to say where you might meet with this problem since the situation is continually changing. Your car rental agent will be able to give you current information. There are a few short stretches of unpaved roads, and these are mentioned in "Connections" and "Getting There" for the individual sites.

The point of reference used in the text and on the maps for distances and driving times is in San Salvador; it is the Plaza of the Americas, with its statue of Christ standing atop the world on the top of a tall column (Monument to the Savior of the World). This is at the junction of Avenida (Avenue) Franklin Delano Roosevelt and Calle (Street) Santa Tecla (which is also Highway CA 1, the Panamerican Highway).

An adequate number of gasoline stations can be found in El Salvador, both in the capital and along the highways, so gas pump symbols are not used on the maps.

Native handicrafts available in El Salvador include hammocks, basketry, textiles, painted wooden and tin objects, and ceramics. Two good places to shop are Mercado Ex-Cuartel (an artisan market occupying a whole square near the center of San Salvador) and the National Artisans Market on Highway CA 1 (Calle Santa Tecla), southwest of the center of town. This is just before the San Salvador Museum. Both sell handicrafts from around the country.

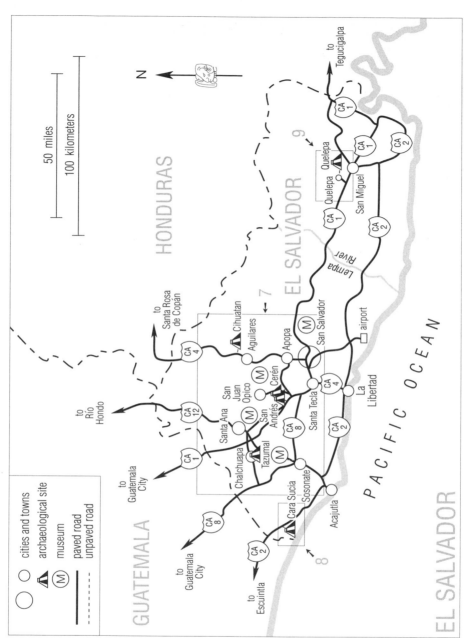

El Salvador, showing areas delimited by the sectional maps.

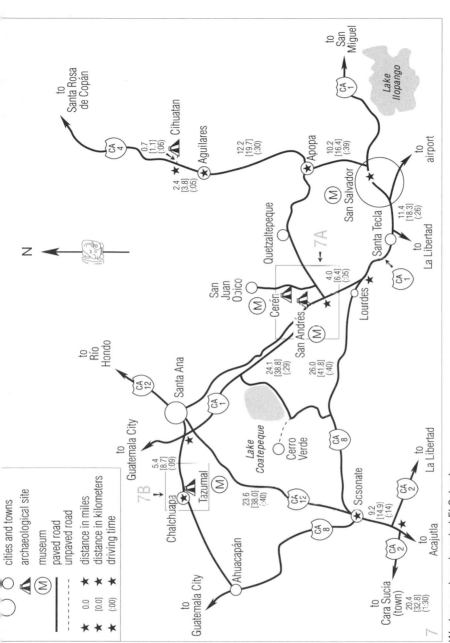

Map Legend

- ◯ cities and towns
- ▲ archaeological site
- Ⓜ museum
- —— paved road
- ----- unpaved road

distance in miles	0.0	★
distance in kilometers	[0.0]	★★
driving time	(.00)	★★★

N ←

to Santa Rosa de Copán

CA 4

0.7 [1.1] (.06)

2.4 [3.8] (.05)

Cihuatan ▲

Aguilares

12.2 [19.7] (.30)

10.2 [16.4] (.39)

Apopa

to San Miguel

CA 1

Lake Ilopango

San Salvador Ⓜ

Santa Tecla

11.4 [18.3] (.26)

to airport

to La Libertad

7A

Quetzaltepeque

San Juan Opico

Cerén ▲ Ⓜ

San Andrés ▲ Ⓜ

4.0 [6.4] (.05)

Lourdes

CA 1

24.1 [38.8] (.29)

26.0 [41.8] (.40)

to Río Hondo

CA 12

Santa Ana

CA 1

Lake Coatepeque

Cerro Verde

CA 8

to Guatemala City

5.4 [8.7] (.09)

7B

Chalchuapa ▲

Tazumal ▲ Ⓜ

23.6 [38.0] (.40)

CA 12

Scsonate

9.2 [14.9] (.14)

Ahuacapán

CA 8

CA 2

to Acajutla

CA 2

to La Libertad

to Cara Sucia (town)

20.4 [32.8] (1:30)

to Guatemala City

7

Western and west-central El Salvador

The many other points of interest in El Salvador, in addition to the archaeological sites and museums, are covered in the general guides for Central America.

You can reach (or almost reach) all of the sites included here without a guide. Where you need a guide for the final leg of a trip, it is mentioned in the text for that site.

★ ★ ★
NATIONAL MUSEUM DAVID J. GUZMÁN
(San Salvador Museum)

The San Salvador Museum has displays outside the entrance under a covered walkway, inside in rooms surrounding a covered patio, and in the patio as well. The outside displays are stone carvings on pedestals. They are unlabeled but include stylized jaguar heads from western El Salvador and petroglyphs. The most impressive carving is a large jaguar altar from Quelepa that dates to the Late Preclassic period; it lies on a platform at the end of the walkway (to the left as you face the museum entrance).

Inside the museum are large ceramic urns from Cihuatan, a large, hollow ceramic statue of Xipe Totec from the Chalchuapa zone, and an attractive collection of carved jade jewelry and plaques. A chart shows the Pipil migration into Central America. There are some interesting painted ceramic vessels, another that is beautifully carved, and mold-made figurines. A restoration drawing of Cihuatan accompanies photographs of the site and a diagram of its ball court. Another display shows the salvage archaeology carried out at Madre Selva.

In the patio are some large stone carvings, including a Postclassic stela from Tazumal, at one time called the "Virgin of Tazu-

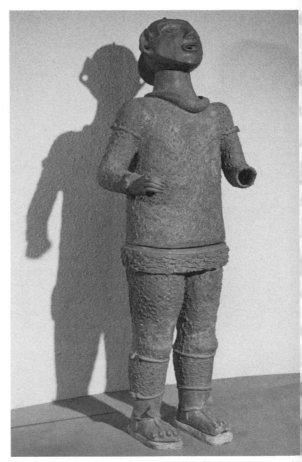

Ceramic statue of Xipe Totec from the Chalchuapa zone in western El Salvador. Postclassic period. On display in the San Salvador Museum.

mal." It depicts a standing figure in frontal view and has glyphs (in a non–Classic Maya style) carved on the edges. Nearby are an Early Postclassic Chac Mool from Casa Blanca and an anthropomorphic jaguar from the same site. You can enter the patio from several of the surrounding rooms.

The museum is fairly well lighted and the interior exhibits are mostly labeled. There is also an area for temporary exhibits.

The museum is open from 9:00 A.M. to noon and from 2:00 to 5:00 P.M. on Tuesday through Sunday. It is closed on Monday. Photography is permitted but flash is not. Allow an hour to see this fine collection.

To reach the museum, take Calle Santa Tecla heading southwest for 1.4 miles [2.3 kilometers] to Avenida Revolución and turn right. The museum is on the left a block ahead; make a U-turn to loop around to the entrance.

Stela from Tazumal, Postclassic period. On display in the San Salvador Museum.

★
CIHUATAN
(see-wah-TAHN)

Derivation:
From "Cihuatlan," Nahuat for "Place of Women."
Location:
Northern part of the Department of San Salvador, El Salvador.
Map: 7 (p. 291)

The Site

The civic and elite residential core of Cihuatan covers about 100 acres [0.4 square kilometers]. It is surrounded by nonelite residences, and the whole site covers almost 1,000 acres [4.0 square kilometers]. Visitors today see only part of the core area, but that is the most interesting part of the site.

As you park and follow the trail to the site, you walk past the partly excavated but unrestored remains of the West Ball Court and a couple of small rubble mounds. The trail continues to Structure P-7 (formerly Structure 1), a pyramid that rises nearly 60 feet [18 meters]. You can see remains of its three original stairways on the north, south, and west sides. Mounds are visible in the fields to the east and southeast of the pyramid. Of more interest are the structures to the north, which are cleared and partly restored.

About 300 feet [90 meters] north of the pyramid is a platform called the Templo de los Idolos, which has short stairways on the north and south sides of the platform. The north stairway is well preserved and has *alfardas* with vertical upper zones. Abutting this, to the north, is the partly restored North Ball Court. From the north end of the ball court you can get good photographs of it, with the Templo de los Idolos and Structure P-7 in the background. There are a couple of cleared platforms to the west of the North Ball Court.

According to William R. Fowler, Jr., it is most likely that Cihuatan was first occupied by Nahua-speaking Pipil from central Mexico or the Gulf Coast region. They invaded central El Salvador at the end of the Late Classic period and developed their settlements—including Cihuatan, the primary regional center—in the Early Postclassic. Abundant Mexican traits have been found at Cihuatan. In the architecture they include *talud-tablero* construction on building facades, fired clay merlons used as roof decorations, and enclosed I-shaped ball courts, among others. Some mold-made Mazapan (Early Postclassic horizon) figurines recovered at Cihuatan are nearly identical to those from Tula in central Mexico. The Mexican deities Tlaloc and Xipe Totec are depicted on Cihuatan's ceramics, and the site's lithic industry is comparable to that of central Mexico.

Cihuatan was burned and destroyed—and many of its ceramics deliberately smashed—at the end of the Early Postclassic period (around A.D. 1200 or 1250), perhaps by another branch of the Pipil.

Recent History

In 1925, Samuel Lothrop was the first archaeologist to visit Cihuatan, although the existence of the site had been known to outsiders since 1879, when it was briefly mentioned by S. Habel. The earliest archaeological work at Cihuatan was undertaken by Antonio E. Sol in 1925 for the Salvadoran government. Sol issued reports on his work in 1929, and the site was partially mapped by Augusto Baratta. In 1944, John M. Longyear III published a compilation of Sol's data in English and included Baratta's site plan. Stanley H. Boggs continued the work sporadically from 1954 through the 1970s. Other work at Cihuatan was undertaken by Fowler, Karen O. Bruhns, and Jane H. Kelly.

In 1989, Fowler's book *The Cultural*

The ball court (foreground), the Templo de los Ídolos platform (midground), and the pyramid Structure P-7 (background), Cihuatan. Early Postclassic period.

Evolution of Ancient Nahua Civilizations: The Pipil-Nicarao of Central America was published by the University of Oklahoma Press. This impressive compendium has extensive information on Cihuatan.

Connection

San Salvador to Cihuatan: 24.8 miles [39.9 kilometers] by paved road (1:14) (see the following note), then 0.7 mile [1.1 kilometers] by dirt road (:06).

Getting There

From San Salvador take Highway CA 4 (Carretera Troncal del Norte) heading north to the cutoff for Cihuatan, north of Aguilares. The cutoff is on the right but is not marked with a sign facing the highway. Look for cement posts and an iron fence. This is the entrance gate and *it* has a sign. Go through the gate and continue to the end of the dirt road, where you can park. From there follow the trail to the site.

Note: When we last visited Cihuatan, part of Highway CA 4 was undergoing resurfacing. This caused delays and necessitated slow driving over some unfinished sections. When this work is finished, the driving time will be less than that indicated here.

There is no food or drink at Cihuatan; take an ice chest and cold drinks. Allow an hour to visit the site.

Buses run on Highway CA 4 and can drop you off at the cutoff for the site. You could also taxi to the site from San Salvador, but that might be expensive.

CERÉN

*(seh-*REHN*)*

Derivation:
The name of the Spanish family that colonized the area in the eighteenth century.

Location:
Central part of the Department of La Libertad, El Salvador.

Maps: 7 (p. 291) and 7A (p. 297)

The Site

Cerén, in the Zapotitán valley of central El Salvador, is a most unusual site. It features no tall temple-pyramids, lavish, multiroomed palaces, or impressive ball courts. What you see are the remains of residences and ancillary domestic and civic buildings of a small, Classic Maya agrarian community. The structures, as well as the tools, utensils, and foodstuffs they contained, were found remarkably well preserved because of ash that fell when the nearby Laguna Caldera erupted between A.D. 585 and 600. The volcano is less than a mile [1.6 kilometers] north of Cerén.

There are three excavated areas, under protective roofs, that you can look down into. Wire mesh surrounds each area, but the openings are big enough to put a camera lens through.

According to Payson D. Sheets, who is excavating the site, the village architecture at Cerén was quite sophisticated. Some structures had earthen walls reinforced with poles, corner columns, and lintels. Other buildings had adobe brick walls, and some had doors made of vertical poles. Cerén was buried under more than 15 feet of ash from Laguna Caldera's eruption; a great deal of the ash was removed during excavation, but some remains, and various layers are quite visible.

Also buried and preserved by the ash were household gardens, where remains of a variety of agricultural products were discovered. In addition to the foodstuffs, there were medicinal plants and maguey, grown for its strong fibers. The crops had been planted in neat rows atop small earthen ridges, one species per row.

In A.D. 175, when the volcano Ilopango erupted, a large part of central El Salvador was devastated, and adjacent areas, including the Zapotitán Valley, were covered with a three-foot-thick layer of ash, forcing the abandonment of the region. The people who settled Cerén probably moved into the area during the fifth century A.D., when it was once again habitable. They built their houses on top of the partly weathered ash from Ilopango's eruption.

Recent History

Cerén was discovered in 1976 when a bulldozer operator, leveling land for a platform to support grain silos, cut the corner of a building buried in ash. Authorities were notified and inspected the building, which was well constructed and well preserved. Believing the building to be only a century old, they allowed the bulldozing to continue and a number of structures were destroyed.

In 1978, Sheets and some of his students from the University of Colorado were conducting an archaeological survey of the Zapotitán Valley and were told about the discovery at Cerén by local people. A brief excavation uncovered only prehistoric artifacts. Sheets then got permission to undertake a full-scale excavation, which began in 1978. Later, the work was interrupted by the war in El Salvador, but it resumed after the war ended.

By 1994, after five field seasons, Sheets reported that 11 buildings had been uncovered at Cerén and that the existence of two dozen or so more was known. Work at the site continues.

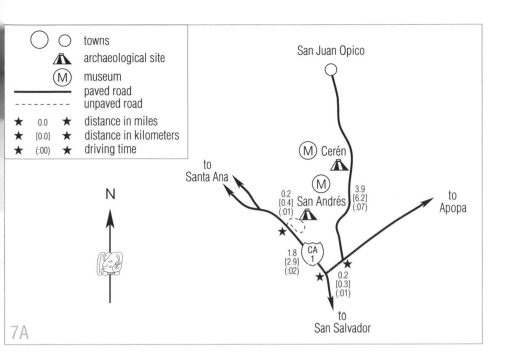

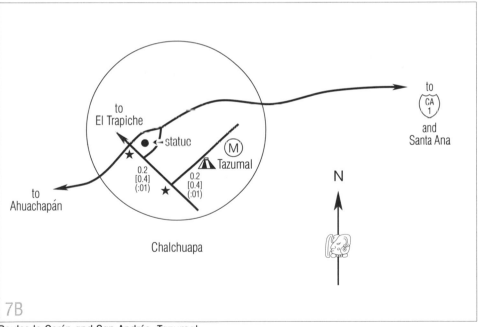

Routes to Cerén and San Andrés, Tazumal

Remains of a house covered with ash, Cerén. Early Classic period.

Storage area of a house buried in ash, Cerén. Early Classic period.

Connection

an Salvador to Cerén: 19.5 miles [31.2 kilometers] by paved road (:39).

Getting There

'rom San Salvador, take Highway CA 1 eading west and then northwest for 15.4 niles [24.8 kilometers]. This will bring you o a cutoff on the right marked with a sign or San Juan Opico. Take this cutoff, and hortly afterward take another cutoff to the left (marked the same way). The entrance to Cerén is 3.9 miles [6.2 kilometers] past the second cutoff, on the left (west) side of the road. There are a couple of signs for Cerén along this last stretch, one shortly before the entrance to the site. Cerén can also be reached by bus or taxi from San Salvador.

The site is open from 9:00 A.M. to 5:00 P.M. on Tuesday through Sunday. It is closed on Monday. Allow 45 minutes for a visit. There is an open-sided pavilion that sells cold drinks and snacks.

★ ★
CERÉN MUSEUM

'he collection of the Cerén Museum is housed in a modern metal uilding at the entrance to the site. 'he exhibits are well lighted and vell labeled. There are attractive isplays of ceramics; the smaller ieces are in glass cases, while ome of the extraordinary larger nes are on platforms. There is a cale model of the site showing the rea excavated up to 1991.

Large color photographs of ne area and the excavations are isplayed, including one of a maney garden preserved by ash. Caronized remains from the garden— acao seeds, chilies, and beans— re in a glass case; there are also examples of carbonized wood and ber. In another case are a few jade eads and a small bone figure of a nan wearing a tall hat.

An especially interesting exibit is the reconstruction of a itchen; it contains all the kitchen nplements that were found in the riginal.

The Cerén Museum is open rom 9:00 A.M. to noon and from :00 to 5:00 P.M. on Tuesday hrough Sunday. It is closed on Monday. llow 20 minutes to view this interesting ollection.

Large ceramic urn, Cerén. Early Classic period. On display in the Cerén Museum.

★ ★
SAN ANDRÉS
(sahn ahn-DREHS)

Derivation:
  Spanish for Saint Andrew.
  Earlier the site was called
  Campana-San Andrés; *campana*
  is Spanish for "bell."
Location:
  Central part of the Department
  of La Libertad, El Salvador.
Maps: 7 (p. 291) and 7A (p. 297)

The Site

San Andrés lies in the broad valley of the
Sucio River, which has many mounds and
apparently was thickly occupied in pre-
Columbian times. San Andrés is the most
interesting group in the area and the only
one that has been systematically excavated.
Its major structures are on the east and
south sides of a plaza that rests atop a large
platform. Some restoration has been done
in this area. Near the southeast corner of
the platform, and on a lower level, are the
remains of another structure; it is composed of terraces of squared stone blocks,
and it has a western stair. Visit this structure first, then climb the platform for a look
at the others.

The major pyramid rises in several
tiers and has a stair on the north side. Construction is of adobe brick covered with
lime plaster—similar to that used at Tazumal and Kaminaljuyú. There were four construction phases on this and other adobe
structures, some of which are visible today.
Climbing the pyramid is no longer allowed.
Abutting the east side of the pyramid are
the remains of the lower walls of a couple of
rooms.

Several structures lie on the east side of
the platform plaza, with stairs facing west.

The stairway approaching the souther
most structure in this row has *alfardas,* ap
parently from at least two constructio
phases. The stepped pyramidal base of th
structure has been partially restored. Clim
this for good photos of the main pyramid
Proceed north for a look at the remains o
the other structures in this row and a below
ground excavation that juts into the plaz
Continue to the north, to the edge of th
platform. On the northeast corner is a lon
projection running east-west, and in th
fields below the platform are several mound
covered with vegetation.

The architectural and ceramic remain
indicate that San Andrés was occupied dur
ing the Classic period and into the Postclas
sic. There is evidence of influence from th
Guatemala highlands, as well as from Co
pán, where the plaza-acropolis arrangemen
of the structures is similar. Ceramics o
Copán type are also found at San Andrés.

Recent History

John M. Dimick excavated San Andrés i
1940 and 1941, and his findings were pub
lished in the latter year by the Carnegie In
stitution of Washington.

In the early 1990s, a new excavatio
was undertaken on the east side of th
plaza; it is visible beneath the shelter.

Connection

San Salvador to San Andrés: 17.2 mile
[27.7 kilometers] by paved road (:33), the
0.2 mile [0.4 kilometer] by dirt road.

Getting There

From San Salvador, head west and the
northwest on Highway CA 1 to the cuto
for San Andrés (marked with a sign). Th
cutoff is shortly after the kilometer 3
marker. Turn right at the sign and follo

The major pyramid at San Andrés, at the south end of the plaza. Classic-Postclassic period.

The southernmost structure on the east side of the plaza, San Andrés. Classic-Postclassic period.

the dirt road to the parking area. When you leave, take the extension of this road and loop around back to the highway. San Andrés can also be reached by bus or taxi from San Salvador.

The site is open from 9:00 A.M. to 5:00 P.M. on Tuesday through Sunday. It is closed on Monday. Allow 45 minutes for a visit. A vendor sells cold drinks and snacks at the site.

SAN ANDRÉS MUSEUM

There are two rooms in the small San Andrés Museum. In the first is a plan of the site, and in the center of the second is a reconstruction model of the main part of San Andrés. Along the walls of this room are drawings of objects found at the site and a few stone artifacts excavated there.

The museum is open from 9:00 A.M. to noon and from 2:00 to 5:00 P.M. on Tuesday through Sunday. It is closed on Monday. Allow five minutes for a visit.

Structure 1, the front (west side), Tazumal. Classic period.

★ ★ ★
TAZUMAL
(tah-soo-MAHL)

Derivation:
  Reportedly, "Place of Sacrifice."
Location:
  Western part of the Department of Santa Ana, El Salvador.
Maps: 7 (p. 291) and 7B (p. 297)

The Site

Tazumal is the most extensively restored and best publicized site in El Salvador. It is also one of the most interesting for visitors. Most of the construction at Tazumal is of adobe, or stone set in adobe, with a facing of lime plaster, and is similar to construction at Kaminaljuyú in the Guatemala highlands and to San Andrés in central El Salvador.

When Tazumal's structures were restored, they were coated with cement.

The most important and interesting building at Tazumal is Structure 1, a large stepped pyramid rising in numerous tiers with vertical walls. Structure 1 has a broad stairway on its west side, and a temple with square columns once crowned its top. An unusual feature is a small, one-room, templelike structure with a flat roof, found on the west side, partway up the pyramid. Its simple decorations are attractive. Structure 1 was rebuilt and added to on many occasions. The afternoon is the best time to photograph the building.

Tazumal is part of a large archaeological zone that occupies the edge of the city of Chalchuapa and is, therefore, called the Chalchuapa zone. Although close together, the individual groups have been given separate names and are treated as separate sites

Remains on the east side of Structure 1, Tazumal. Classic period.

Structure 2, the front (west side), Tazumal. Probably Postclassic period.

in most of the literature. Most, including Tazumal, had beginnings in the Preclassic period.

During the Preclassic period, western El Salvador had trade links with Kaminaljuyú, and this is reflected in the ceramics of the area. During the Classic period, Tazumal was influenced by the architectural style of Kaminaljuyú but looked to Copán for ceremonial pottery when trade with Kaminaljuyú was cut off. There was also a Postclassic occupation of Tazumal, and Mexican (Pipil) influence at this time is evident. The statue of Xipe Totec at the San Salvador Museum dates to this period. It was found 0.5 mile [0.8 kilometer] east of the Tazumal group.

Although Structure 1 was built during the Early and Late Classic periods, other structures at Tazumal are Postclassic. Tazumal was occupied until—or almost until—the time of the Spanish conquest.

Climb Structure 1 for good views of the rest of the site. Other architectural remains include Structure 2, a restored stepped pyramid abutting Structure 1 on the west; a ballcourt-like construction on the south of Structure 1; partially restored remains of several structures on the north side of Structure 1; a below-ground excavation northeast of Structure 1, with evidence of steps; and an overgrown and unexcavated ball court in the modern cemetery across the street from the main part of the site. All these structures are easily visible from the top of Structure 1 and can also be visited at ground level (except for the ball court in the cemetery).

Recent History

Tazumal was excavated by Stanley H. Boggs in 1942, although the site had been known to pot hunters for many years. Under the technical supervision of Boggs, the San Salvador Museum continued investigations in 1943. Additional work at the site was undertaken by William R. Coe, and from 1966 through 1970 by Robert J. Sharer.

Connection

San Salvador to Tazumal: 45.3 miles [72.9 kilometers] by paved road (1:11).

Getting There

From San Salvador, take Highway CA 1 heading west and then northwest for 39.5 miles [63.6 kilometers] to the cutoff for Chalchuapa; almost all of this is four lanes. The cutoff for Chalchuapa is marked for Ahuachapán, *not* Chalchuapa. (Before you reach this cutoff you will pass two cutoffs on the left for Sosonate. Pass these by. The cutoff for Ahuachapán that you want is 2.0 miles [3.2 kilometers] *past* the second cutoff for Sosonate.) Turn left at the cutoff for Ahuachapán and continue to Chalchuapa, 5.4 miles [8.7 kilometers]. As you enter the town you will come to a small park with a statue, where the road bears to the right. Turn left immediately past the park and you will see a sign indicating that Tazumal is straight ahead. Go straight for 0.2 mile [0.4 kilometers] to another sign for Tazumal; turn left at this sign as indicated, and proceed to the site, where you can park on the street, outside the fence that surrounds the site.

There is no food or drink at Tazumal, but there are restaurants in Chalchuapa. Allow 1.5 hours to visit Tazumal.

Chalchuapa can be reached by bus from San Salvador.

★ ★ ★
TAZUMAL MUSEUM

The Tazumal Museum comprises both indoor and outdoor sections. The most outstanding piece outside is a large, irregular boulder carved in bas-relief with four Olmec-style figures. It comes from the nearby site of Las Victorias and dates to the Middle Preclassic period. According to Ignacio Bernal (in *The Olmec World*), "curiously—in view of its great distance from the Metropolitan [Olmec] zone—the style is one of the most characteristically Olmec in the entire Pacific watershed." The principal figure on the boulder gets the best light in the afternoon. Other stone carvings are nearby. None of the outdoor displays is labeled; many of those on the inside are labeled in Spanish and English.

Inside the museum is a large photograph of the statue of Xipe Totec that was found in the Chalchuapa zone and is now on display in the San Salvador Museum. There are models of some of Tazumal's structures, cases with attractive Classic-period ceramics, a couple of nice *hachas,* a plain yoke, and Late Classic heads of figurines. One interesting though mutilated sculpture is Monument 1 from El Trapiche; it dates to the Late Preclassic period and has

Carved boulder portraying an Olmec figure, Las Victorias. Middle Preclassic period. On display outside the Tazumal Museum.

the remains of a hieroglyphic text. A drawing of the monument placed above it shows the remaining details more clearly than the monument itself does.

Other displays include photographs of Tazumal, diagrams of the process of restoration, and elaborate *incensarios*. Another area is used for temporary exhibits.

The Tazumal Museum is well worth seeing while you are at the site; allow 20 minutes for a visit. The museum is open from 9:00 A.M. to 5:00 P.M. on Tuesday through Sunday. It is closed on Monday. There are rest rooms in the museum. Photography is permitted but flash is not.

CARA SUCIA
(KAH-rah SOO-seeah)

Derivation:
  Spanish for "Dirty Face."
Location:
  Southwestern part of the Department of Ahuachapán, El Salvador.
Map: 8 (p. 308)

The Site

Although Cara Sucia is one of the most important sites in western El Salvador, it offers little of visual interest for visitors at the moment. The site is composed of grass-covered mounds—some of impressive size—in a pasture. A trail leads to one of the larger mounds, and you can climb it for views of the others.

Cara Sucia was occupied in Preclassic times and received cultural influence from the Cotzumalhuapa area of southern Guatemala in the Late Classic period. This is evident in sculpture, architecture, ceramics, and figurines. The site was abandoned around A.D. 900; it appears that the Pipil may have played a role in this event.

Recent History

Cara Sucia has been known for some time, and a jaguar sculpture from the site is in the San Salvador Museum. In 1976, Stanley H. Boggs published an article about the sculp-

tures from the site along with other information.

Paul Amaroli, who is currently conducting studies at Cara Sucia, believes that the Cotzumalhuapan traits found at Cara Sucia indicate an actual takeover of the site and region by Cotzumalhuapans.

Connection

San Salvador to Cara Sucia: 67.0 miles [107.8 kilometers] by paved road (but see "Getting There") (2:50), then 0.9 mile [1.5 kilometers] by dirt road (:08).

Getting There

From San Salvador, head west on Highway CA 1 for 11.4 miles [18.3 kilometers] to the junction with Highway CA 8, marked with a sign for Lourdes and Sosonate. Bear to the left at this junction and follow Highway CA 8 to its junction with Highway CA 12. Highway CA 8 curves gently into CA 12, and you are hardly aware that you are changing highways; in addition, there is no sign indicating that you are. Shortly after this gentle curve, you will cross a railroad track at the north end of Sosonate. This is 26.0 miles [41.8 kilometers] from where you joined Highway CA 8 (near Lourdes). From the railroad track, go 9.2 miles [14.9 kilometers] to the west junction with Highway CA 2. At this junction, turn right (west) and proceed to the town of Cara Sucia, 20.4 miles [32.8 kilometers]. The cutoff from the town to the site is unmarked, but it is 0.1

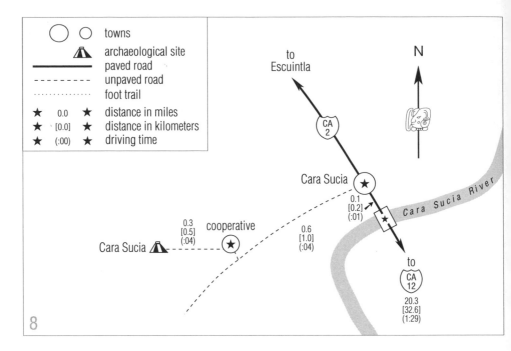

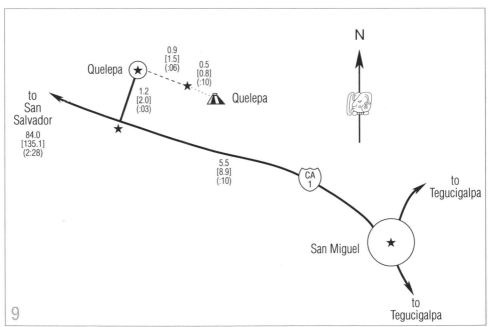

Routes to Cara Sucia and Quelepa

Large mound (center) and a smaller mound (right), Cara Sucia.

mile [0.2 kilometer] past the bridge over the Cara Sucia River. Turn left at the cutoff and go 0.6 mile [1.0 kilometer] to a cooperative that is visible to the right of the road. Ask there for someone to show you the way to the site, or ask them to point it out. From the cooperative, it is 0.3 mile [0.5 kilometer] to a gate that enters a pasture; turn right, go through the gate, and park under some shade trees nearby. The mounds are just beyond and are plainly visible. Allow 30 minutes to look around.

When we visited Cara Sucia, Highway CA 2 was undergoing resurfacing—meaning that the paved highway had been completely torn up. It was slow going for this part of the trip. When this work is finished, you will be able to drive this section faster than is indicated here. Also at that time, there was no sign at the junction of Highways CA 12 and CA 2 indicating a cutoff for Cara Sucia.

There is no food or drink at the site, but cold drinks are available in the town, along the highway. Since the entire trip takes more than six hours, it is better to have food and drink with you.

QUELEPA
(keh-LEH-pah)

Derivation:
Lenca for "Stone Jaguar."
Location:
Central part of the Department of San Miguel, El Salvador.
Map: 9 (p. 308)

The Site

Quelepa is reported to be the most important site in eastern El Salvador. It shares with Los Llanitos—a site 13 miles [20.9 kilometers] south—the distinction of being the easternmost ceremonial site with oriented mounds. Approximately 40 structures are known at Quelepa, and they occupy an area of about 0.2 square mile [0.5 square kilometer]. They are located along the north side of the San Esteban River. A small stream divides the site into the East and West groups, and the latter is the one visitors see today.

The most interesting area of the West Group is an arrangement of mounds, mostly atop a terrace, facing a plaza in the southeastern part of the group. They are eroded, and those that were excavated have been recovered for protection, so no architectural features are currently discernible.

One of the structures excavated in this area proved to be a three-tiered platform with a projecting stairway. The platform apparently supported a building of perishable materials. This structure dates to the Late Classic period, as probably do the other mounds in this group.

From this group, additional mounds—covered with cultivated henequen—are visible to the northeast.

Jaguar altar from Quelepa. Late Preclassic period. On display outside the San Salvador Museum.

Quelepa is believed to have been occupied from around 500 B.C., and according to E. Wyllys Andrews V, "the first inhabitants clearly arrived before 300 B.C." The large and impressive jaguar altar from Quelepa—found in the West Group and now in the San Salvador Museum—dates to this early period and shows certain stylistic ties to monuments from Izapa and Kaminaljuyú. In the Early Classic period, at least two important structures were built in the East Group. During the Late Classic period, architectural activity shifted to the southeastern corner of the West Group. The site was abandoned for unknown reasons around A.D. 1000.

During its long history, Quelepa had contact with and received influences from various areas. In the earliest ceramic levels discovered, there is evidence of trade with highland Guatemala. For the Early Classic period, the ceramics of Quelepa are similar to those from southern Honduras and the Chalchuapa zone of western El Salvador.

For the Late Classic period, there is strong evidence of contact with the culture of Classic Veracruz. One cache of carved stone objects found at Quelepa included yokes, *palmas,* and an *hacha*—objects related to the ritual ball game and more commonly found in the Veracruz area. According to Andrews, "this cache marks the first time all three of these distinctive sculptured forms have been found together." It is perhaps worthy of note that the cache was found 100 yards [90 meters] south of the unexcavated ball court at Quelepa.

There is also evidence of influence from Veracruz in some of the ceramics at Quelepa, including wheeled figurines. These figurines and *palmas* are exceedingly rare in the interlying areas of Chiapas, the Guatemala highlands, and western El Salvador.

Andrews believes that a group strongly influenced by the culture of Classic Veracruz moved into eastern El Salvador around A.D. 600. He holds this view because, in addition to the portable objects—which alone might have indicated trade—new architectural styles and construction methods were introduced at this time.

Recent History

Although Quelepa has long been known in the general area as a major site, the first report of it seems to have been that of Doctor Atilio Peccorini in 1913. In 1926, Peccorini issued another report, and Samuel Lothrop reported on his brief visit to the site. Three years later, Antonio E. Sol visited the site and also issued a report. The first excavations at Quelepa were those of Pedro Armillas in 1949, but his work was not completed or published.

The most extensive work at Quelepa was that undertaken by Andrews. In 1967—sponsored by the Middle American Research Institute (MARI) of Tulane University—he made a reconnaissance trip to El Salvador and undertook preliminary investigations at Quelepa. He returned in 1968–1969, funded by a Fulbright-Hays Fellowship, to carry out more thorough excavations. This work was the basis of his doctoral dissertation, a later version of which was published by MARI in 1976.

Connection

San Salvador to Quelepa: 82.5 miles [137.1 kilometers] by paved road (2:31), 0.9 mile [1.5 kilometers] by dirt road (:03), then about 0.5 mile [0.8 kilometer] on foot (:10). Total: 86.6 miles [139.4 kilometers] (2:44).

Getting There

From San Salvador, head east on Highway CA 1 to the cutoff for the town of Quelepa (marked with a sign). Turn left and proceed to the town. There you should ask around for someone to accompany you to the site, since it is on private property and you will have to go through a gate along the way. You will also need to have someone point out the way on foot and show you around the site.

The town of Quelepa can be reached by bus from San Salvador, but it would no doubt take quite a bit longer than driving your own vehicle. Allow an hour to visit the site once you get there.

There is no food or drink at the site, but cold drinks are available in town. It is better to have food and drink with you.

GLOSSARY

ahau (ahaw): A Maya word for "lord" and the name of the last day in the Maya 20-day month. Its glyphic form represents a stylized face.

alfarda: In architecture, a raised, sloping side section that borders a stairway; balustrade.

apron molding: In architecture, a sloped facing that overhangs an inset, vertical section; it is found on the bases of pyramidal structures. Prevalent in the southern Maya lowlands.

bar-and-dot numerals: A system of enumeration where a bar represents five and a dot represents one. Used by the ancient Mayas and some other Mesoamerican peoples.

Cakchiquel: A Maya group that occupied part of the Guatemala highlands. They entered this area around A.D. 1100 from Tabasco through Chiapas. They were allied with but subordinate to the Quiché until they established their own capital at Iximché around 1470.

Cauac monster: *See* Witz monster.

Chac Mool: The statue of a figure in a recumbent pose, holding a receptacle on its abdomen. Found at Chichén Itzá, Tula, and other sites in Mexico, at Quiriguá, Guatemala, at Casa Blanca, El Salvador, and farther south in Central America.

codex (plural, *codices*): Painted books of pre-Columbian or, in some cases, post-Columbian date. They are made of deerskin or bark paper and are folded like a screen.

CONAP: Initials for the name of the national park service that controls the access gate at Lake Yaxhá, Petén, Guatemala.

consolidated, consolidation: In architecture, a structure that has been stabilized and repaired to prevent further deterioration, without being fully restored.

corbeled vault: The prevalent type of roofing used in Classic Maya structures.

The vault is built up from the tops of vertical walls, and each layer of stone or brick juts past the one below. When the sides of the vault approach each other closely enough, a capstone is added to bridge the remaining gap.

eccentric flints: Knapped flint (and sometimes obsidian) worked into various unusual shapes, sometimes into human profiles. They are found in offertory caches in the Maya lowlands, and may have been attached to wooden staffs for use on ceremonial occasions.

Emblem Glyph: A glyph (generally in three parts) whose main sign refers either to a dynastic name or to a place name.

finca: A Spanish word for a farm or ranch.

glyphs (also *hieroglyphs*): The form of ancient Maya writing, which includes both pictographic and ideographic elements; some glyphs have phonetic value.

Goodman-Martínez-Thompson correlation (also *GMT correlation*): A correlation between the Maya and Christian calendars proposed by Goodman, Martínez, and Thompson. This correlation equates the Maya Long-Count date of 11.16.0.0.0 to A.D. 1539. This correlation is generally, though not universally, accepted.

hacha (Spanish for "ax"): A thin stone object in the shape of an ax, often carved. Associated with the ritual ball game. Prevalent in the culture of Classic Veracruz, and also found in areas influenced by or occupied by people of this culture.

hieroglyphs: *See* glyphs.

Huehueteotl (also *Xiuhtecuhtli*): The old fire god, a deity of central Mexico.

ik: A T-shaped symbol indicating wind or breath, hence, life. When inverted, it signifies the reverse, death.

incensario: An incense burner, censer. They are generally made of fired clay and are often elaborately decorated.

Initial Series (also *Long Count date*): A method of recording dates in the Maya calendar. It represents the total number of days that have elapsed from a mythical starting point, calculated at 3114 B.C. according to the GMT correlation.

Itzamná: The supreme Maya deity; the heavenly monster-god and creator-god.

Izapan style: A style of carving produced at Izapa, Mexico, in the Late Preclassic period. Some traits are U elements, long-nosed gods, a baroque style, and narrative scenes. Monuments in this style are also found at sites along the Pacific slope of Guatemala, in the highlands and the Petén of Guatemala, and elsewhere.

Lenca: A pre-Columbian Indian group that occupied eastern El Salvador and parts of Honduras.

Mam: A Maya group that inhabited the western part of the Guatemala highlands and the Pacific slope of Guatemala and Chiapas, Mexico.

mano: *See* metate.

Mesoamerica: The areas of Mexico and Central America in which high civilizations arose in pre-Columbian times. The region includes parts of western and eastern Mexico; all of central and southern Mexico and the Yucatán Peninsula; all of Belize, Guatemala, and El Salvador; western Honduras; and part of the Pacific Coast areas of Nicaragua and Costa Rica.

metate: A trough-shaped stone used for grinding foodstuffs, generally corn (maize), and accompanied by a cylindrical handstone (mano).

Mexican Yearsign (also *Teotihuacán Yearsign, Mixtec Yearsign,* and *imbricated trapeziform*): A motif of overlapping geometrical elements, probably originating in Mexico, that is associated with warriors. Its shape is similar to a sign that marks year dates in the Aztec codices.

Mixteca-Puebla style (painting): A Postclassic painting style that was a synthesis of the styles of Teotihuacán, Xochicalco, and Veracruz. It was used on polychrome pottery and in codices.

Nahua: A group of people who spoke a Uto Aztecan language; also the language itself.

palace-type structures: *See* range-type structures.

Pipil: A group who spoke an early form of Nahua and who migrated to Central America at various times in the Postclassic period.

Pokomam: A Maya group that inhabited part of the Guatemala highlands around Lake Amatitlán and the part of El Salvador west of the Lempa River.

Quiché: The dominant Maya group of the Guatemala highlands whose capital was built at Utatlán in the Late Postclassic period. They came to the area from Chiapas and the Tabasco Gulf Coast areas in the Early Postclassic period.

range-type structures (also *palace-type structures*): Multichambered structures built on low platforms rather than on tall pyramidal bases. They were probably mostly residential or used for administrative purposes rather than for religious ceremonies.

roof comb: In architecture, a stone superstructure built on the roof of a structure to give additional height and grandeur. The combs are sometimes perforated and are generally decorated.

sacbé: (plural in Maya, *sacbeob*): Literally, "White Road." An ancient Maya road or causeway made of rough-stone blocks topped with crushed stone and then plastered.

stela (plural, *stelae*): A freestanding monolithic stone monument, either plain or carved on one or more sides. Especially prevalent in the Maya area; often accompanied by a drum-shaped altar.

talud-tablero: In architecture, A sloping lower section, or *talus (talud)*, topped by a vertical, rectangular, recessed panel (*tablero*).

Tlaloc: The rain god of central Mexico. He also has an aspect as a war or warrior god.

Witz monster: A zoomorphic creature that is a symbol of a living mountain. The creature is shown with eyelids and *cauac* signs (clusters of discs or circles arranged in triangles).

Xipe Totec: The god of spring of central Mexico. He is generally depicted wearing the skin of a flayed victim.

Xiuhcóatl: The fire serpent, a deity of central Mexico.

yoke: Yoke-shaped stones, sometimes elaborately carved. Related to the ritual ball game. Prevalent in the culture of Classic Veracruz, but also found in other areas influenced or occupied by people of this culture.

zapote (also *sapote* and *sapodilla*): An extremely hard wood found in the lowland Maya area, often used for lintels in pre-Columbian buildings.

ziricote: An attractive brown tropical wood with black streaking.

SELECTED READINGS

Adams, Richard E. W.
   1977   *Prehistoric Mesoamerica.* Boston: Little, Brown. Rev. ed. Norman: University of Oklahoma Press, 1991.
Agurcia Fasquelle, Ricardo, and William L. Fash, Jr.
   1989   Copán: A Royal Tomb Discovered. *National Geographic,* vol. 176, no. 4. Washington, D.C.
   1991   Maya Artistry Unearthed. *National Geographic,* vol. 180, no. 3. Washington, D.C.
Andrews, E. Wyllys, V
   1976   *The Archaeology of Quelepa, El Salvador.* Middle American Research Institute, Publication 42. New Orleans: Tulane University.
Baudez, Claude-François
   1994   *Maya Sculpture of Copán: The Iconography.* Norman: University of Oklahoma Press.
Bernal, Ignacio
   1969   *The Olmec World.* Berkeley: University of California Press.
Bove, Frederick, and Lynette Heller, eds.
   1989   *New Frontiers in the Archaeology of the Pacific Coast of Southern Mesoamerica.* Anthropological Research Papers, no. 39. Tempe, Arizona: Arizona State University.
Bruhns, Karen O.
   1980   *Cihuatan: An Early Postclassic Town of El Salvador.* University of Missouri Monographs in Anthropology, no. 5. Columbia: University of Missouri.
Bullard, William R., Jr., ed.
   1970   *Monographs and Papers in Maya Archaeology.* Papers of the Peabody Museum, vol. 61. Cambridge, Massachusetts: Harvard University.
Carmack, Robert M.
   1981   *The Quiché-Mayas of Utatlán: The Evolution of a Highland Guatemala Kingdom.* Norman: University of Oklahoma Press.
Chase, Arlen F., and Diane Z. Chase
   1987   *Investigations at the Classic Maya City of Caracol, Belize: 1985–1987.* Pre-Columbian Art Research Institute, Monograph 3. San Francisco: Pre-Columbian Art Research Institute.
   1996   *Investigations at Caracol, Belize; 1988–1993.* Pre-Columbian Art Research Institute, Monograph 8. San Francisco: Pre-Columbian Art Research Institute.
Chase, Diane Z., and Arlen F. Chase
   1988   *A Postclassic Perspective: Excavations at the Maya Site of Santa Rita Corozal, Belize.* Pre-Columbian Art Research Institute, Monograph 4. San Francisco: Pre-Columbian Art Research Institute.
Chase, Diane Z., and Arlen F. Chase, eds.
   1992   *Mesoamerican Elites: An Archaeological Assessment.* Norman: University of Oklahoma Press.
   1994   *Studies in the Archaeology of Caracol, Belize.* Pre-Columbian Art Research Institute, Monograph 7. San Francisco: Pre-Columbian Art Research Institute.
Clancy, Flora S., and Peter D. Harrison, eds.
   1990   *Visions and Revisions in Maya Studies.* Albuquerque: University of New Mexico Press.
Coe, Michael D.
   1988   *The Maya.* 4th ed. London: Thames and Hudson.
Coe, William R.
   1969   *Tikal: A Handbook of the Ancient Maya Ruins.* Philadelphia: The University Museum, University of Pennsylvania. 2nd ed. 1988.

Culbert, T. Patrick, ed.
  1991   *Classic Maya Political History: Hieroglyphs and Archaeological Evidence.* Cambridge:
          Cambridge University Press.
Danien, Elin C., and Robert J. Sharer, eds.
  1992   *New Theories on the Ancient Maya.* University Museum Monograph 77. Philadel-
          phia: University of Pennsylvania.
Demarest, Arthur A.
  1986   *The Archaeology of Santa Leticia and the Rise of Maya Civilization.* Middle Ameri-
          can Research Institute, Publication 52. New Orleans: Tulane University.
  1993   Violent Saga of a Maya Kingdom. *National Geographic,* vol. 183, no. 2. Washington,
          D.C.
Fash, William L., Jr.
  1991   *Scribes, Warriors and Kings: The City of Copán and the Ancient Maya.* London:
          Thames and Hudson.
Fowler, William R., Jr.
  1989   *The Cultural Evolution of Ancient Nahua Civilizations: The Pipil-Nicarao of Central
          America.* Norman: University of Oklahoma Press.
Garret, Wilbur E.
  1989   La Ruta Maya. *National Geographic,* vol. 176, no. 4. Washington, D.C.
Graham, Ian
  1967   *Archaeological Explorations in El Peten, Guatemala.* Middle American Research In-
          stitute, Publication 40. New Orleans: Tulane University.
Greene Robertson, Merle
  1972   *Maya Sculpture.* Berkeley, California: Lederer, Street and Zeus.
Hammond, Norman
  1975   *Lubaantun: A Classic Maya Realm.* Peabody Museum Monographs, no. 2. Cam-
          bridge, Massachusetts: Harvard University.
Houston, Stephen D.
  1985   *The Dynastic Sequence of Dos Pilas, Guatemala.* Pre-Columbian Art Research Insti-
          tute, Monograph 1. San Francisco: Pre-Columbian Art Research Institute.
  1993   *Hieroglyphs and History at Dos Pilas: Dynastic Politics of the Classic Maya.* Austin:
          University of Texas Press.
Kelley, Jane H.
  1988   *Cihuatan, El Salvador: A Study in Intersite Variation.* Vanderbilt University Publi-
          cations in Anthropology, no. 35. Nashville: Vanderbilt University.
Kelly, Joyce
  1982   *The Complete Visitor's Guide to Mesoamerican Ruins.* Norman: University of Okla-
          homa Press.
Maler, Teobert
  1901–   *Researches in the Central Portion of the Usumatsintla Valley.* Memoirs of the Peabody
  1903   Museum, II, no. 1. Cambridge, Massachusetts: Harvard University.
  1908   *Researches of the Upper Usumatsintla and Adjacent Region.* Memoirs of the Peabody
          Museum, IV, no. 1. Cambridge, Mass: Harvard University.
  1908   *Explorations in the Department of Peten, Guatemala and Adjacent Region.* Memoirs
          of the Peabody Museum, IV, no. 2.
Maudslay, Alfred P.
  1889–   *Archaeology.* Biologia Centrali Americana. 5 vols. London. Facsimile ed. New York:
  1903   Milpatron Publishing, 1974.
Michel, Genevieve
  1989   *The Rulers of Tikal: A Historical Reconstruction and Field Guide to the Stelae.* Guate-
          mala City: Publicaciones Vista.

Morley, Sylvanus G.
  1946   *The Ancient Maya.* 2d ed., revised by George Brainerd, 1956. 4th ed., revised by Robert J. Sharer. Stanford, California: Stanford University Press.
Orrego Corzo, Miguel
  1990   *Investigaciones arqueologicas en Abaj Takalik, El Asintal, Retalhuleu, año 1988,* reporte no. 1. Guatemala City: Instituto de Antropología e Historia de Guatemala.
Parsons, Lee A.
  1969   *Bilbao, Guatemala: An Archaeological Study of the Pacific Coast Cotzumalhuapa Region,* vol. 2, Publications in Anthropology, 12. Milwaukee, Wisconsin: Milwaukee Public Museum.
  1981   Post-Olmec Stone Sculpture: The Olmec-Izapan Transition on the Southern Pacific Coast and Highlands. In *The Olmec and Their Neighbors,* edited by Elizabeth P. Benson. Washington, D.C.: Dumbarton Oaks.
Porter Weaver, Muriel
  1972   *The Aztecs, Mayas, and Their Predecessors.* New York. 3d ed., San Diego, California: Academic Press, 1993.
Proskouriakoff, Tatiana
  1946   *An Album of Maya Architecture.* Washington, D.C.: Carnegie Institution of Washington. Reprint. Norman: University of Oklahoma Press, 1963.
Quirarte, Jacinto
  1973   *Izapan-Style Art: A Study of Its Form and Meaning.* Washington, D.C.: Dumbarton Oaks.
Robertson, Merle Greene. *See* Greene Robertson, Merle.
Sabloff, Jeremy A., and E. Wyllys Andrews V, eds.
  1986   *Late Lowland Maya Civilization: Classic to Postclassic.* Albuquerque: University of New Mexico Press.
Sanders, William T., and Joseph W. Michels, eds.
  1977   *Teotihuacan and Kaminaljuyu: A Study in Prehistoric Culture Contact.* University Park, Pennsylvania: Pennsylvania State University Press.
Schele, Linda, and David A. Freidel
  1990   *A Forest of Kings: The Untold Story of the Ancient Maya.* New York: William Morrow.
Sharer, Robert J., ed.
  1978   *The Prehistory of Chalchuapa, El Salvador.* 3 vols. Philadelphia: University of Pennsylvania Press.
Sheets, Payson D.
  1979   Maya Recovery from Volcanic Disasters. Ilopango and Cerén. *Archaeology,* vol. 77, no. 3. New York.
  1981   Volcanoes and the Maya. *Natural History,* vol. 90, no. 8. New York.
  1994   Tropical Time Capsule. *Archaeology,* vol. 47, no. 4. New York.
Smith, A. Ledyard
  1982   *Excavations at Seibal, Department of Petén, Guatemala, no. 1, Major Architecture and Caches.* Memoirs of the Peabody Museum, 15. Cambridge, Massachusetts: Harvard University.
Stephens, John Lloyd
  1841   *Incidents of Travel in Central America, Chiapas, and Yucatan.* 2 vols. London. New York, 1854. Reprint. New York: Dover Publications, 1969.
Stuart, George E.
  1989   City of Kings and Commoners. *National Geographic,* vol. 176, no. 4. Washington, D.C.
Stuart, Gene S., and George E. Stuart
  1993   *Lost Kingdoms of the Maya.* Washington, D.C.: National Geographic Society.
Weaver, Muriel Porter. *See* Porter Weaver, Muriel

INDEX

Abaj Takalik, Guatemala, 175–76, 210–16
Abaj Takalik Museum, 216
Abrams, Ira R., 30
Aguateca, Guatemala, 168–70
Aguilar Paz, Jesús, 253
Agurcia Fasquelle, Ricardo, 280, 284
Altun Ha, Belize, 23, 45–51
Alvarado, Gonzalo de, 207
Alvarado, Pedro de, 189, 195, 200
Amaroli, Paul, 307
Anderson, A. H., 32, 50, 64, 70, 82
Andrews, E. Wyllys, V, 280, 311
Antigua, Guatemala, 173
Armillas, Pedro, 311
Arroya de Piedra, Guatemala, 167
Arthes, Federico, 159
Auto insurance, 13
Auto rentals. *See* Car rentals
Aveni, Anthony, 152
Awe, Jaime J., 64, 92

Baratta, Augusto, 294
Bastain, Adolph, 221
Baudez, Claude F., 279
Beetz, Carl, 82
Belize, 19, 23, 55, 87
Belize City, Belize, 19, 23, 55, 57
Belize Museum, 57
Belmopan, Belize, 19, 55, 58
Belmopan Vault, 58, 60
Benque Viejo, Belize, 55, 65
Berendt, Carl H., 221
Bernoulli, Gustav, 140
Bilbao, Guatemala, 217–23
Blom, Frans, 118, 122, 152
Boggs, Stanley H., 294, 305, 307
Bove, Frederick, 222
Bruhl, Gustav, 215
Bruhns, Karen O., 294
Brunhouse, Richard, 98
Bullard, William R., Jr., 42, 50, 60, 123

Cahal Pech, Belize, 61–64
Cahal Pech Museum, 65
Cameras, photographic equipment, 11
Campana-San Andrés, El Salvador, 300
Campbell, Mark D., 64
Caracol, Belize, 57, 75–84
Cara Sucia, El Salvador, 307–309

Carmack, Robert M., 202
Car rentals, 8; in Belize, 19; in El Salvador, 289; in Guatemala, 113, 173; in Honduras, 249
Casa Blanca, El Salvador, 293
Castillo, Bernal Díaz del, 195
Castillo, Jorge and Ella, 181
Catherwood, Frederick, 195, 201, 207, 243, 278
Cayo (San Ignacio), Belize, 55
Cerén, El Salvador, 296–99
Cerén Museum, 299
Cerro Maya, Belize, 28
Cerros, Belize, 28–31
Cerro Verde National Park, El Salvador, 289
Chalchuapa zone, El Salvador, 292, 303, 306
Chamelecon, Honduras, 252
Chase, Arlen F., 26–27, 83
Chase, Diane Z., 26–27, 32, 83
Cheek, Charles D., 185
Chichicastenango, Guatemala, 173
Chichicastenango Museum, 198
Cihuatan, El Salvador, 292, 294–95
Cliff, Maynard B., 29
Clothing, 10
Coe, William R., 129, 140, 244, 279, 305
Comayagua, Honduras, 252
Comayagua Museum, 254–55
Comayagüela, Honduras, 249
Consejo Shores, Belize, 23
Cook, H. J., 32
Cooper Clark, J., 98
Copán, Honduras, 8, 252, 254, 257–86
Copán Museum, 285–86
Copán Ruinas (town), Honduras, 249, 252
Copán Site Museum, 259
Corozal, Belize, 23, 26, 28
Cotzumalhuapan culture, style, 177, 217, 220
Cotzumalhuapa region, Guatemala, 177, 307
Crane, Cathy, 30
Cuello, Belize, 33–35

Dangriga, Belize, 55
Demarest, Arthur A., 165, 170
Departure tax, 8
Dimick, John M., 207, 300
Dos Pilas, Guatemala, 162–67

Douglas, Belize, 31–32
El Baúl, Guatemala, 224–28
El Cedral, Honduras, 254
El Cruce, Guatemala, 111, 113
El Puente, Honduras, 255
El Remate, Guatemala, 111, 113
El Salvador, 289–92
El Trapiche, El Salvador, 306
Entry requirements: for Belize, 19; for El Salvador, 289; for Guatemala, 107; for Honduras, 249

Fash, Barbara, 284
Fash, William L., 280, 284
Fialko, Vilma, 140
Finca El Baúl, Guatemala, 226–28
Finca Las Ilusiones, Guatemala, 229–30
Finca Pantaleón, Guatemala, 231
Floral Park, Belize, 60
Flores, Guatemala, 111, 113, 173
Flores, José and Lisandro, 164
Food supplies, 11
Fowler, William R., Jr., 222, 294
Freidel, David, 29–30, 129
Fuentes y Guzmán, Francisco Antonio, 190, 195

Galindo, Juan, 122, 278
Gann, Thomas, 27, 30, 32, 42, 69–70, 97
Gasoline stations, 19, 114
Gifford, James C., 60, 152
Glass, J. B., 60
Godoy, Carlos, 42–43
Goodman, J. T., 278
Goodman-Martínez-Thompson correlation, 6
Gordon, George B., 278
Graham, Elizabeth, 51, 70–71
Graham, Ian, 118, 152, 159, 165, 169–70
Graham, John A., 159, 213, 215
Greene, Ernestene L., 27, 32
Greene Robertson, Merle, 118, 165, 170
Grube, Nicolai, 280
Guatemala, 107, 111, 173
Guatemala City, Guatemala, 107, 173, 179
Guatemala City Museum, 175–78
Guidebooks, 8–9, 19
Guillemín, Jorge F., 190, 196–97, 202

Habel, Siméon, 221, 294
Hammond, Norman, 32, 34, 92, 98–99, 103

Hatch, Marion P., 217, 224
Healy, Paul F., 74, 83
Heizer, Robert F., 215
Heller, Lynette, 222
Hellmuth, Nicholas M., 118, 123, 128
Hewitt, Edgar Lee, 243
Hokeb Ha, Belize, 58
Honduras, 249–52
Houston, Stephen D., 165
Hoz, Juan José and Gabriela de la, 113
Huehuetenango, Guatemala, 173

Indian Church, Belize, 35, 41
Inomata, Takeshi, 170
Itzab, Estevan, 32
Ivanoff, Pierre, 165
Ixil region, Guatemala, 180
Iximché, Guatemala, 192–98
Iximché Museum, 197–98
Ixlu, Guatemala, 111
Ixtutz, Guatemala, 177

Jackson, L. J., 92
Jennings, Jesse D., 185
Joyce, Thomas A., 97

Kaminaljuyú, Guatemala, 175, 178, 180–81, 183–85
Kelly, Jane H., 294
Kennedy, Tim, 58
Kidder, Alfred V., 152, 185, 279
K'umarcaaj, Guatemala, 200

La Amelia, Guatemala, 161, 177
La Democracia Museum, 234–35
La Democracia Plaza, Guatemala, 232–34
La Entrada, Honduras, 252
La Entrada Museum, 255
Lake Coatepeque, El Salvador, 289
Lake Yaxhá, Guatemala, 111, 113
La Libertad, El Salvador, 289
Lamanai, Belize, 35–44
Lamanai Museum, 44
Laporte, Juan Pedro, 140
Lara, Eusebio, 139
Larios, C. Rudy, 119, 140, 280
Las Ilusiones, Guatemala, 178
Las Sepulturas (Copán), Honduras, 273–74, 283, 286
Las Victorias, El Salvador, 306
Lee, Thomas, 42
Lehmann, Henri, 189

Lehmann, Walter, 215
Leventhal, Richard, 71, 92, 103
Lincoln, William, 118
Longyear, John M., III, 279, 294
Looper, Matthew G., 257
Los Higos, Honduras, 255
Los Llanitos, El Salvador, 310
Lothrop, Samuel K., 201, 311
Lubaantun, Belize, 93–99
Lundell, Cyrus, 122

Mackie, Euan, 70
McKillop, Heather, 92
MacLeod, Barbara, 58
Maler, Teobert, 70, 118, 121–22, 129, 140, 159
Maps, of Belize, Guatemala, Honduras, and El Salvador, 8, 19
Mathews, Peter, 165, 280
Maudslay, Alfred P., 140, 184, 196, 201, 243, 278
Méndez, Modesto, 139
Merwin, Raymond E., 97, 128, 140
Michels, Joseph W., 185
Miles, Suzanna W., 215
Mitchell-Hedges, Frederick A., 97–98
Mixco Viejo, Guatemala, 186–91
Monte Alto, Guatemala, 232–34
Morley, Sylvanus G., 111, 118, 122, 140, 143, 151, 159, 244, 278
Morris, Earl H., 244
Mount Maloney, Belize, 65

Nakum, Guatemala, 124–29
Naranjo, Guatemala, 177
Nebaj, Guatemala, 170
Nim Li Punit, Belize, 90–93
Nohmul, Belize, 31–33
Núñez Chinchilla, Jesús, 279

Orange Walk, Belize, 23
Orrega Corzo, Miguel, 119, 128, 140, 210, 215
Owens, John G., 278

Pacbitun, Belize, 72–75, 84
Palacio, Diego García de, 277
Palacio, Joseph O., 30, 34, 51, 58, 70, 92
Palo Verde, Guatemala, 177
Panajachel, Guatemala, 173
Parsons, Lee A., 215, 217, 220, 222, 229, 233

Pascual Abaj (idol), 198
Patinamit, Guatemala, 192, 195
Peccorini, Atilio, 311
Pendergast, David M., 39, 42, 50–51, 71
Périgny, Maurice de, 127
Petén (Department), Guatemala, 8, 113, 173
Piedras Negras, Guatemala, 177
Popol Vuh Museum, 179–82
Pring, Duncan C., 27, 34
Proskouriakoff, Tatiana, 279
Punta de Chimino, Guatemala, 111
Punta Gorda, Belize, 55, 87
Pusilha, Belize, 98

Quelepa, El Salvador, 292, 310–11
Quintana, Oscar, 119, 128
Quiriguá, Guatemala, 235–46

Rainy season, 14
Ratings, site, 14–16
Retahuleu, Guatemala, 173
Richmond Brown, Lady, 97
Ricketson, Edith B., 152
Ricketson, Oliver B., 152
Riese, Berthold, 280
Río Azul, Guatemala, 178
Río Grande, Belize, 93, 97
Rivera y Maestre, Miguel, 201
Robertson, Robin, 29
Rossbach, Ildefonso, 198

Sabloff, Jeremy A., 158–59
Sadat, David, 280
Salazar, Nancy and Jorge, 111
San Andrés, El Salvador, 300–302
San Andrés Museum, 302
San Antonio (Toledo District), Belize, 55, 87
Sanders, William T., 185, 279
San Miguel, El Salvador, 289
San Pedro Sula, Honduras, 249, 252
San Salvador, El Salvador, 289
San Salvador Museum, 292
Santa Ana, El Salvador, 289
Santa Lucía Cotzumalguapa, Guatemala, 173
Santa Rita, Belize, 26–28
Sapper, Karl, 190, 215
Sastanquiqui, Guatemala, 154
Satterthwaite, Linton, 63, 70, 82
Saville, Marshall H., 278
Sayaxché, Guatemala, 111, 113